D1622115

AMERICAN CATHOLICS AND CIVIC ENGAGEMENT: A DISTINCTIVE VOICE

AMERICAN CATHOLICS IN THE PUBLIC SQUARE
Edited by Margaret O'Brien Steinfels

The American Catholics in the Public Square series is a joint effort between Sheed & Ward and the Commonweal Foundation with special funding from the Pew Charitable Trusts. The result of a three-year study sponsored by Pew aimed at understanding the contributions to U.S. civic life of the Catholic, Jewish, mainline and evangelical Protestant, African-American, Latino, and Muslim communities in the United States, the two volumes in this series gather selected essays from the Commonweal Colloquia and the joint meetings organized by the Commonweal Foundation and The Faith and Reason Institute, a conservative think tank in Washington. Participants in the Commonweal colloquia and the joint meetings—leading Catholic scholars, journalists, lawyers, business and labor leaders, novelists and poets, church administrators and lobbyists, activists, policy makers and politicians—produced approximately forty-five essays presented at ten meetings that brought together over two hundred and fifty participants. The two volumes in the American Catholics in the Public Square Series address many of the most critical issues now facing the Catholic Church in the United States by drawing from the four goals of the colloquia—to identify, assess, and critique the distinctive elements in Catholicism's approach to civic life; to generate concrete analyses and recommendations for strengthening Catholic civic engagement; to encompass a broad spectrum of political and social views of Catholics to encourage dialogue between Catholic leaders, religious and secular media, and political thinkers; to reexamine the long-standing Catholic belief in the obligation to promote the common good and to clarify how Catholics may work better with those holding other religious or philosophical convictions toward revitalizing both the religious environment and civic participation in the American republic.

Volumes in the American Catholics in the Public Square Series

American Catholics and Civic Engagement: A Distinctive Voice
American Catholics, American Culture: Tradition and Resistance

AMERICAN CATHOLICS AND CIVIC ENGAGEMENT: A DISTINCTIVE VOICE

Volume 1

American Catholics in the Public Square

Edited by
MARGARET O'BRIEN STEINFELS

A SHEED & WARD BOOK
ROWMAN & LITTLEFIELD PUBLISHERS, INC.
Lanham • Boulder • New York • Toronto • Oxford

A SHEED & WARD BOOK

ROWMAN & LITTLEFIELD PUBLISHERS, INC.

Published in the United States of America
by Rowman & Littlefield Publishers, Inc.
A wholly owned subsidiary of The Rowman & Littlefield Publishing Group, Inc.
4501 Forbes Boulevard, Suite 200, Lanham, Maryland 20706
www.rowmanlittlefield.com

PO Box 317
Oxford
OX2 9RU, UK

British Library Cataloguing in Publication Information Available

Library of Congress Cataloging-in-Publication Data

American Catholics and civic engagement : a distinctive voice / edited
by Margaret O'Brien Steinfels.
    p.   cm.— (American Catholics in the public square series ; v. 1)
"A Sheed & Ward book."
Includes bibliographical references and index.
ISBN 0–7425–3158–9 (alk. paper)—ISBN 0–7425–3159–7 (pbk. : alk.
paper)
    1. Christianity and politics—Catholic Church—Congresses. 2.
Sociology, Christian (Catholic)—United States—Congresses. 3.
Christianity and politics—United States—Congresses. 4. Catholic
Church—Doctrines—Congresses. I. Steinfels, Margaret O'Brien, 1941–
II. Series.
BX1407.P63 A46 2004
261.8'088'r22—dc21   2003013285

Printed in the United States of America

♾ ™ The paper used in this publication meets the minimum requirements of American
National Standard for Information Sciences—Permanence of Paper for Printed Library
Materials, ANSI/NISO Z39.48–1992.

CONTENTS

v

PREFACE

American Catholics in the Public Square was a three-year project (2000–2003) supported by a grant from the Pew Charitable Trusts. It was part of a Pew-funded family of studies aimed at understanding the contributions to U.S. civic life of the Catholic, Jewish, mainline and evangelical Protestant, African-American, Latino, and Muslim communities in the United States.

The Catholic study was undertaken jointly by the Commonweal Foundation, which publishes *Commonweal* magazine, and The Faith and Reason Institute, a conservative think tank in Washington, D.C. The two partners in this enterprise conducted much of it in parallel but separate tracks addressing various aspects of Catholic social thought, of the church's institutional activities, and of individual Catholics' presence in politics and civil society. The Latino project was organized independently and includes both Catholic and evangelical partners. The two volumes in this series gather selected essays from the Commonweal Colloquia and the joint meetings organized by the Commonweal Foundation and The Faith and Reason Institute. The publications of the Faith and Reason Institute are available from its Washington office.

American Catholics in the Public Square was designed to examine and explore Catholic participation in the nation's civic life. Its four major goals were:

1. To identify the distinctive elements in Catholicism's approach to civic life; to explore the strengths and weaknesses of this tradition in the American context; to discover how (and how successfully) this tradition is being transmitted; to identify obstacles within the Catholic Church itself and the Catholic community to a more robust and distinctive Catholic presence in the public square; and to analyze both receptivity and resistances in the larger American culture to the Catholic presence.

2. To generate concrete analyses and recommendations for strengthening Catholic civic engagement—not in an attempt to devise a platform or simple formulas, but simply as a way to gather a range of ideas about current practices and imaginative possibilities that Catholic leaders in various spheres can evaluate, adapt, adopt, or discard as they see fit.

3. To encompass a broad spectrum of political and social views of Catholics so as to encourage dialogue between sectors of a large and diverse church who often do not come into significant contact with one another and to open up lines of inquiry that will capture the attention of Catholic leaders, religious and secular media, and political thinkers in a way that could extend the discussion well beyond this project.

4. To reexamine the long-standing Catholic belief in the obligation to promote the common good and to clarify how Catholics may work better with those holding other religious or philosophical convictions toward revitalizing both the religious environment and civic participation in the American republic.

Participants in the Commonweal colloquia and the joint meetings—leading Catholic scholars, journalists, lawyers, business and labor leaders, novelists and poets, church administrators and lobbyists, activists, policy makers and politicians—produced approximately forty-five essays presented at ten meetings that brought together over two hundred and fifty participants. Each meeting included three to five presentations, two appointed respondents for each, and extended discussions with invited participants. The project's findings address many of the most critical and neuralgic issues now facing the Catholic Church in the United States. Public attention to the church's handling of sexual abuse cases will undoubtedly have an impact on both the church's role in public life and that of individual Catholics visibly trying to relate their civic responsibilities to their faith.

Those essays and responses not published in these volumes are available at www.catholicsinpublicsquare.org.

ACKNOWLEDGMENTS

American Catholics in the Public Square would not have succeeded without the spirit of solidarity, cooperation, and sense of the common good so often spoke about in these pages and at our meetings. The *Commonweal* staff, which puts out the magazine every two weeks, pitched in on all phases of the project, beginning, middle, and end. Special thanks go to Paul Baumann and Grant Gallicho who attended every meeting, even the difficult ones. Successive business managers, first, Gregory Wilpert helped construct the budget and, then, Paul Kane kept us on budget and in the black. Tiina Aleman, production editor and Web mistress, created the project's Web site and made the copy for this book as digitized as possible—and she put out the magazine, too! John Garvey generously assisted with the copyediting of the books. Scott Appleby of the University of Notre Dame served as consultant, advisor, presenter, and reader par excellence.

Many of the meeting participants took a keen interest in the project, some even coming to more than one meeting: Tom Baker, Mary Segers, Mark Massa, John Coleman, Philip Murnion, Barbara Whitehead, Paul Moses, Richard Doerflinger, John McGreevy, and Ned Dolejsi were especially generous with their time and their knowledge. The joint meetings, which were an integral part of the project, were organized by Peter Steinfels on behalf of *Commonweal* and Robert Royal of the Faith and Reason Institute; they were an eye-opener to all of the participants. Luis Lugo of the Pew Charitable Trusts first proposed the project and with his colleague Kimon Sargent has maintained a steady interest in its progress.

Finally the deepest gratitude goes to Regina Garvey, the project's administrator, whose intelligence, diligence, serenity, hospitality, and good humor kept us all on track and convinced that the project could be managed and brought to a successful end.

INTRODUCTION

HISTORICAL BACKGROUND

Catholics have been present in America since before the War for Indepen-dence. From Lord Baltimore's experiments in Maryland to the arrival of groups of immigrants in Pennsylvania, New York, and the New England states, Catholics faced a specific problem: how to maintain their religious identity in a nation that was overwhelmingly Protestant. By the 1840s, when many Americans took alarm at the new waves of Catholic immigrants, often impoverished and often Irish, the problem grew severe. In a certain Anglo-American understanding of the growth of free institutions, Catholicism was The Enemy. As a result, Catholics faced not only outright discrimination but even violence for both ethnic and religious reasons. In the nineteenth century, no other religious faith except Mormonism was treated as so fundamen-tally incompatible with the conception of the American nation entertained by many Christians. Catholics had to create their own institutions—churches, schools, hospitals, orphanages, relief services—with little help or encourage-ment from their fellow citizens. Yet Catholic leaders were grateful for the reli-gious freedom that allowed them to do this, and they could not help but appreciate the open, enterprising society that had given immigrants refuge from famine, war, and persecution elsewhere. Still, for Catholic leaders, the first priority was understandably the survival and religious integrity of their own people. Catholic civic engagement was often vigorous but also turned inward. Catholic leadership in the landmark struggles for American freedom was accordingly minimal.

At the same time, Catholic leaders could not ignore the questions that separation of church and state and the American emphasis on participatory democracy and individual rights and responsibilities put to European Catholic traditions of more centralized government and close collaboration between church and state. Thanks to the work of several American Catholic churchmen at the end of the nineteenth century, most notably James Cardinal Gibbons, John Ireland, John J. Keane, Denis J. O'Connell, and John Lancaster Spalding, as well as several later theorists and activists, Catholicism has not only found a secure place in America, but has itself been enriched by notions of human rights, pluralism, and religious liberty emanating from the United States.

The Difficult Balance

Yet the development of American Catholicism has been marked by serious tensions that continue to challenge people who wish to be both fully Catholic and unapologetically American—who wish, moreover, to be fully Catholic precisely when they are fully present in the American public square. Those tensions once centered on the fact that Catholics could not feel quite at home in the American polity: what might have been a particular Catholic contribution to American public life was frequently muted or marginal, and Catholics expended most of their energies within their own ethnic communities and religious subculture. Today the tensions may center on the fact that Catholics can feel almost too much at home in American society: what might be a distinctive Catholic note in American public life is in danger of being diluted and lost as a distinctive Catholic subculture dissolves.

Certainly it took a long time for leaders in this country and in Rome to understand that the principles of the American Founders could be harmonized to a large extent with Catholic social principles. The great contributions of the Jesuit philosopher and theologian John Courtney Murray in this century inaugurated a way of reading the founding as embodying portions of natural law to which Catholics in America could give ready assent.

Murray gave a hopeful reading of the Declaration of Independence's assertion that "we hold these truths to be self-evident, that men have been endowed by their Creator with certain inalienable rights and that among these are Life, Liberty, and the Pursuit of Happiness." For Murray, this bold statement meant at least three main things: there are truths, we can know them, and we, as Americans, "hold" these truths as a basis for our common life together. Though Murray well knew that this highly condensed version of the natural law needed a great deal of unpacking, he was cautiously optimistic that Roman Catholics could find here common ground with their fellow citizens of other faiths in America. Murray's work not only helped shape developments at the Second Vatican Council on questions like religious liberty; he also stimulated a vigorous Catholic engagement with the foundations of American political philosophy.

The Tensions Remain

Along with these positive developments, however, another set of questions arose for American Catholics, especially in recent decades. Catholicism is one of the few world religions with a highly developed system of modern social teaching. That teaching goes a great deal further than the minimalist natural law principles of the American Founding. If Catholic principles like "subsidiarity" may be rather easily harmonized with American notions like federalism or localism, other Catholic principles find little or no place in American thought. For instance, America's highly individualistic ethic clashes in various ways with ideas like the "common good," "solidarity," and Catholic personalism. In Catholic social thinking, the human person is neither an autonomous individual nor a mere fragment of a social mass as in several forms of twentieth-century collectivism. The person is constituted by links to the family, community, and political structure, and to independent sources of moral reflection and action. The person, then, exists in a matrix of relationships that is not given much attention in mainstream American thought. Catholic social teaching, with its highly technical and somewhat foreign terminology, has therefore found itself in some tension with mainstream American political discourse, and this tension has given rise to disputes, even among Catholics, about applicability of Catholic thought in the context of this nation.

Concrete historical developments in the United States have injected paradoxes and ironies into Catholic civic engagement. Besides the tensions long felt (but increasingly resolved) between the nation's founding principles and the Catholic tradition and the gap still remaining between America's individualistic ethics and political discourse, on the one hand, and Catholicism's unfamiliar vocabulary and community focus, on the other, at least three main developments have complicated the picture:

- the emergence of a current of political liberalism from the Progressive Era onward that at many points converged with the Catholic tradition practically but diverged from it more and more culturally and philosophically;

- the nation's growing pluralism and the decline of mainline Protestant cultural and moral hegemony; and
- the waning of the Catholic ethnic-religious subculture in the 1950s and 1960s followed by the dramatic reconfiguration of American Catholicism after the Second Vatican Council.

LIBERAL PROGRESSIVISM: CONVERGENCE AND DIVERGENCE

Explicit Catholic social teaching, although rooted in an ancient theological and sacramental tradition, arose in the nineteenth century as a response to the industrial revolution, to the trauma of transition from a rural paternalism to an urban capitalism, and to the rival worldview of socialism. A parallel development took place in the United States. Appalled (and sometimes frightened) by hordes of immigrants, many of them Catholic, crowded into urban tenements and laboring in the harsh conditions of an expanding, unregulated economy, an unstable alliance of old-stock gentry, grassroots organizers and tribunes, evangelical and liberal proponents of the Social Gospel, and avant-garde cultural rebels sponsored a wide and sometimes contradictory agenda of reform, from economic regulation and trade-union organization to welfare provision and even Prohibition.

American Catholics, precariously exposed on the lower rungs of the American economy, stood to benefit from many, though not all, of these proposals and did not share the deep-seated antagonism to positive government intervention that marked the older Anglo-American liberalism. The Catholic Bishops' Program for Social Reconstruction of 1919 echoed many of these reform proposals and foreshadowed much of the New Deal. Of course, Catholics could not ignore some of the elements hostile to immigrants or immigrant culture in the reform alliances. But far more troubling was the fact that the new reformism, in its revolt against the complacencies of Victorian America, was suspicious of all tradition and religious authority, two hallmarks of the church. Indeed, the philosophical and cultural vanguards of the new progressivism appeared to reject the fixity of truth or morality altogether, even in the nation's founding documents. Many of the fault lines in the church's current efforts to project a distinctive Catholic presence in the public square can be traced to this history of practical convergence and philosophical divergence with a major twentieth-century current of American politics.

THE NAKED PUBLIC SQUARE

In recent decades, the decline of the old Protestant establishment has given rise to another set of questions for Catholics in the public square. Despite the conflicts and outright anti-Catholicism of the past, American Catholics and Protestants shared a common moral vision rooted in Scripture. If Catholics created their own school system to provide a kind of education that was missing or, sometimes, disparaged in the basically Protestant public school system, they still championed the American experiment and the largely sound social ethic they found all around them.

Explanations of the decline of Protestant Christian cultural hegemony are complex and much debated. Some factors are said to go back to the early nineteenth century. Others are tied to the liberal and progressive intellectual currents mentioned above. Others derive from the overreaching typical of any hegemony and from practices of exclusion that eventually discredited attempts to maintain the religious character of institutions that once upheld the Protestant culture. Still other factors are largely demographic, including the shifting profile of the American population, the lower birth rates of mainline Protestants, and the entry of Jews and Catholics into the ranks of the affluent and highly educated. By the 1920s and 1930s, certainly by the 1940s, Catholic bishops had already begun to replace leading Protestant clergymen as the ready spokesmen for traditional morality, but the Catholics were filling a role that had been defined by Protestant forebears. Then, in the past few decades, came the full-scale dismantling of the implicit Protestant establishment.

This dismantling, combined with a growing awareness of the multiplicity of worldviews in American society and the liberal argument that the public sphere should remain scrupulously neutral on ultimate questions, has led to what some observers call a naked public square in which not only Catholicism but all religious influence has been reduced to an extent possibly unprecedented in American history. In addition, it is not clear whether the foundational idea of an America based on "self-evident" truths derived from nature or nature's God retains more than a purely rhetorical place in contemporary American social discourse. By contrast, one recent Supreme Court decision warned against anything that would prevent individual Americans from defining for themselves their own idea of the mystery of the universe.

Exactly how naked is the naked public square, that is, how stripped of undisguised religious presence? The exact degree is a matter of debate, but the clear tendency, along with the decline of that "civil religion" that in the past held Americans together, has presented a whole set of new questions to religious Americans, Catholics not the least among them. The Catholic Church, for instance, runs the most extensive education system, health services, and relief efforts of any American faith group. It was inevitable, then, that it would be centrally involved at local, state, and national level in such issues as abortion, euthanasia, family stability, homosexuality, welfare reform, and economic policies. The church also has developed positions on war and peace, which were brought forward vigorously during the debates over nuclear deterrence during the Cold War and continue to be applied to conflict situations around the world where the United States often acts as the world's only remaining superpower. Under John Paul II, the church has been pressing for restrictions on use of the death penalty. All these issues and more inevitably flow from the church's social thought and practice.

THE POST-SUBCULTURE,

POST-CONCILIAR SITUATION

Lying behind all these discrete problems, moreover, is a deeper question for American Catholics today. How are they to be present in an American public life that increasingly runs hot and cold about public religion, now welcoming, now allergic, now tolerant but only within strict limits? And how are they to achieve this presence while the cohesive Catholic subculture of at least a century's standing transforms itself into some as yet undetermined form?

The church, since Vatican II, has done three things of central importance to this challenge. First, it welcomed an understanding of the church's role that made striving for justice in the social arena an integral part of Christian witness and not, as had often been suggested, simply a preparation for a more spiritual or other-worldly missionizing. Second, it argued that engagement with the public realm is primarily the responsibility of the laity. Third, by calling for a stance toward modern culture marked by dialogue at least as much as by combat or rejection, the church lowered the walls of the Catholic subculture and contributed, intentionally or not, to the assimilation of Catholics into mainstream American culture.

The first of these changes made distinctively Catholic civic engagement more religiously charged than before. What often remained on the periphery of a largely other-worldly spirituality was now shifted toward the center. The positions of pastors, bishops, and the pope on political or social questions could not as easily be set aside as idiosyncratic opinions irrelevant to the sacramental life or the work of salvation. A more conscious response was required, even if it was one ultimately of dismissing the authoritative character of church positions.

The second of these changes, emphasizing the role of the laity, harmonizes with what comes naturally to many Catholic lay people, acculturated as they are to America's remarkable tradition of popular initiatives and spontaneous organization for social purposes. But it appears that the lines of responsibility are not as clear in practice as the Council's principles would suggest. Some American lay people still have the habit of looking to their bishops, clerical organizations, and Rome itself to take the lead on social issues, even though many lay organizations have sprung up in the wake of the Council. Other Catholic laity take almost automatic offense at civic direction from church leaders.

The very energy of lay initiatives has, to some observers, led to a certain incoherence in the Catholic presence in American civic life. Bishops and clergy encourage lay participation but may look askance at some of the forms that this participation takes. In a church that has long been marked by its careful attention to doctrinal orthodoxy and unity with the bishop of Rome, letting go of authority and trusting lay initiative has been difficult. In addition, it is the nature of the American context that groups may form calling themselves Catholic but who work at cross purposes to what the hierarchy may see as undeniable theological and moral teachings. Both clergy and laity find themselves in a delicate situation where the "Catholic" voice is diluted or obscured, where dramatic heterodoxy and mere differences in lay opinion cannot be distinguished. This long-standing tension has been heightened as a result of the revelations, beginning in Boston in 2002, of sexual abuse of minors by priests. Some bishops had already responded to an earlier wave of such charges by appointing lay-dominated review boards, and this became a national policy after the bishops met in Dallas in June 2002. Still, tensions persisted over the emergence of lay groups pressing for changes in church structures or procedures as a result of the scandals. In a few dioceses, bishops who saw these groups as threatening church teaching refused to meet with them or forbade them the use of church property for their gatherings. The news media and victims' advocates stood close watch over the work of the national review panel set up by the bishops themselves to assure implementation of their new national policy for handling allegations of abuse and instituting safeguards against future misconduct. Lay people frequently reacted with frustration at any sign that bishops were not cooperating fully with the panel's work, and some bishops grew similarly frustrated at what they felt were intemperate and unfair reactions from critics. The fact that many Catholics, lay and clerics alike, are vigorously pursuing issues of accountability and governance is likely, like the scandal itself, to have an impact on the Catholic presence in the public square.

The third change raises the question of how Catholics will blend their Catholicism with their assimilation to America. This was not a problem when Catholics mostly lived—by outside pressure and internal choice—in a kind of Catholic "ghetto." The success and acceptance in American society that Catholics have come to enjoy is a welcome development. So is the sense of responsibility and shared destiny that they feel with that society. But as with all other religious and ethnic groups who have come to these shores, integration into the American mainstream has costs as well as benefits. Can Catholic doctors, lawyers, politicians, educators, business executives—to say nothing of schools, colleges, universities, hospitals, relief services—remain both Catholic and American in a United States that, at least at a superficial level, seems to have moved far from the Biblical and natural-law principles that provided a bridge between Catholicity and Americanness?

There is no question that one of the central challenges facing American Catholicism, clergy and laity, liberal and conservative alike, is how to maintain a specific identity in the face of forces, both national and global, both cultural and economic, that seem to be making for a much greater uniformity and far less vigorous and articulated religious participation in public affairs.

Peter Steinfels
Robert Royal

1

CATHOLIC SOCIAL THOUGHT IN THE AMERICAN CONTEXT

These essays explore the fundamental concepts that underlie Catholic social thought and their relevance to American public debate and public policy—the intellectual tools with which Catholics have often participated in the public square. Catholic philosophers, theologians, and social activists share a language drawn from the Catholic social tradition. This intellectual framework is solid, serious, and useful, as the essays by John Coleman and Stephen Pope demonstrate. Yet each author asks, what is really conveyed in the tradition's conceptual framework of "common good," "subsidiarity," "option for the poor," as well as its double rejection of individualism and collectivism? How is this framework, and especially the key notion of "common good," currently being understood or misunderstood? What is this tradition's relation to the American liberal tradition or to other modern lines of social thought? William Galston examines the considerable overlaps between Catholic social thought and liberalism along with some of the divergent paths each takes on certain fundamental issues. Michael Lacey and William Shea look from within the Catholic tradition and its sometimes compatible, sometimes contentious relationship with American liberalism.

THE COMMON GOOD AND CATHOLIC SOCIAL THOUGHT

John A. Coleman

Thomas Aquinas, in his classic treatise on law, defines law as an ordinance of practical reason promulgated by legitimate authority *for the common good*.[1] First, I want to raise up that term, *common good*, not because it is a well-known bromide, easily recognized and assented to, but because so few Americans, even American Catholics (for whom it ought to be a heritage), have much of a clue as to what it actually means. Notions of the common good move deeply against the American individualist grain. And then, second, appeals to the common good, in any precise meaning of the term, are increasingly rare in law or politics. The dominant voices in jurisprudence dismiss as meaningless or authoritarian any appeal—beyond mere rhetoric—to the common good. Third, large-scale institutional and sociological changes in our society make any easy assumptions about a received cultural "sense" of the common good hard to cultivate. Yet these very changes show the utter need for a more vivid conversation about the common good. In this regard, a 1993 document released by the general secretaries of three national religious organizations—the United States Catholic Conference, the National Council of Churches, and the Synagogue Council of America—could speak of the common good as "an old idea with a new urgency." Faced with poverty, lack of jobs, irresponsible sexual behavior, violence, racism and other forces that rend our social fabric, the common good is "an imperative to put the welfare of the whole ahead of our own narrow interests . . . an imperative for a national embrace of responsibility and sacrifice, of compassion and caring, as building blocks for meaningful lives and for a healthy society."[2] Fourth and

3

finally, I will attempt to delineate the common good and defend it against its modern day objectors.

THE COMMON GOOD GOES AGAINST THE AMERICAN CULTURAL GRAIN

Not everyone who cries "the common good, the common good" is worthy of being called a "communitarian" (and not every communitarian believes in something like the common good). Some who evoke the term use it as roughly equivalent to "the general interest," seeing in it no more than the utilitarian individualist's merely additive sum of the greatest good for the greatest number of individuals. For others, it serves as little more than a rhetorical screen for benign inclusiveness with no institutional bite. To be sure, like the other great concept, justice, the common good is meant at times to be an evocative term of greater inclusiveness. Edward Dolesji, executive director of the California Catholic Conference, recently told me that he is chary of using the term, the common good, in lobbying and legislative debates because different constituencies mean utterly varying things by it. No one (including the Catholics who evoke the term), he said, defines it in a way that makes it very useful for giving direction to social policy.

Yet, as sociologist Philip Selznick states it in his wise study, *The Moral Commonwealth*: "The common good is the state of the system, not an attribute of individuals."[3] Americans, notoriously individualistic and dismissive or distrustful of institutions (especially large and national institutions) have had a hard time grasping the concept. In an address to the Los Angeles-based Skirball Institute, sociologist Robert Bellah had this to say about the common good:

> The language of the common good is deep in our heritage, with biblical and classical philosophical roots, but is has not always, perhaps not often, been the first thing that comes into the minds of Americans when they talk about their common values. If one listens to the language of political campaigns and particularly to those things that both parties never fail to mention, one will hear first of all, "freedom." That is our most resonant value, and it is often echoed to mean: "In America you can do whatever you like" . . . Our politicians are enough aware of this problem that they usually quickly follow freedom with the term, "responsibility." Leaving us with the pair, freedom/responsibility implies that our values only concern the individual. . . . That is why there is often a third term tacked on to the two basic ones: community. But community . . . often turns out to mean "a group of people like me; a group of people

I feel comfortable with." Community in this vacuous sense doesn't challenge our reigning individualism, but rather complements it. But language about the common good makes us sit up and think—and that's why you won't find it often in our political speech today.[4]

In his seminal sociological studies of volunteerism and civic participation in the United States, Princeton sociologist, Robert Wuthnow echoes[5] Bellah's point about the vacuousness in the many evocations of community. Most of Wuthnow's respondents use the term *community* rather casually, as if, at first, to suggest that they might have a clear idea where their community is located, but when pressed, the idea refers less to any definite place and more to an emotional feeling of being cared for or of being with people who make us comfortable.

To properly conceive of the common good we must be able to think in terms of institutions and systems; we have to see individuals as inexorably situated, embedded beings, enmeshed in institutions that both constrain and empower them. Institutions, after all, shape the behavior, imaginations, and purposes of individuals. Alas—against all good sociological instincts and evidence for this proposition—Americans generally and religious American only slightly less, have a difficult time construing institutions as positive, even enabling, forces. Nor do Americans easily see that institutions, themselves, are potentially moral entities capable of appropriate forms of integrity, moral purpose, and responsibility—or their distortions. We still too easily parrot Reinhold Niebuhr's wrong-headed title that conjures up moral *man* versus immoral *society*.[6]

Clearly, institutions—families, schools, churches, labor unions, business corporations—are intimately associated with the realization of human goods. To institutionalize is to look for ways to perpetuate and to increase—through rewards, sanctions, and symbolic channeling of human motivation and imagination—determinate patterns of behavior conducive to enhancing social and human goods. Institutions anchor values dear to a society. No one can really understand the language of the common good unless they realize, as the sociologist Steven Hart has put it, that "a good society requires not only individuals who behave well but social structures that create well-being."[7]

CONTEMPORARY PHILOSOPHICAL JURISPRUDENCE AND THE COMMON GOOD

Unfortunately, for the classic Thomist and Catholic understanding of the common good, many influential political philosophers reject as meaningless or nefarious any appeal to a common good. They have four major objections. Briefly, they are:

Objection 1: Because of the inevitable relativism of knowledge and human subjectivity, because all knowledge is seen somehow to be socially constructed, no one can really know *the* or *an* "objective" common good. This first objection attacks any objectivist claims to the good ingredient in the classic tradition of the common good.

Objection 2: While people may be able to construe some disparate public goods and aggregate them, there is no way persons can know what is the good for something as large and amorphous as society as a whole. We can, at best, deal with micro-institutions of society, such as education, the family, health care, the employment arena, etc. But only the market (blind to any intrinsic goods) and free exchanges can determine the state of society as a whole.[8]

Objection 3: Any view of *the* or *a* common good will mean the imposition of someone else's vision of the good on others who do not share it. Appeals to the common good, in this objection, are intrinsically authoritarian and inimical to a free and pluralist society. I take this to be the contention of Ronald Dworkin, especially as he states it in *A Matter of Principle.* Dworkin argues that equal treatment of citizens demands that political decisions must be, as far as possible, independent of any particular conception of the good life. This stringent stance of "neutrality," he claims, is a necessary element in treating people equally. Because different persons, in fact, hold divergent understandings of the full human good, to favor one conception of the good over another is to favor some persons over others and, hence, to fail to treat them equally.[9]

In a similar vein, John Rawls has argued in *Political Liberalism* that "the diversity of doctrines—the fact of pluralism—is not a mere historical condition that will soon pass away. It is, I believe, a permanent feature of the public culture of modern democracies." So far so good! But Rawls then adds a controversial claim that pluralism and diversity make *any* notion of the common good impossible: "A public and workable agreement on a conception of the good can be maintained only by the oppressive use of state power."[10]

It should not be missed that Rawls and Dworkin, in their doctrine of stringent state neutrality vis-à-vis *any* determinate conception of the good life or good society, are arguing for a novel and radical disestablishment. They want to extend the disestablishment of state and church, enshrined in the First Amendment, to a more radical and unsustainable disestablishment of state and morality. In principle, this rule of state neutrality vis-à-vis any moral conception of the good would disallow any attempt—even a free and deliberative engagement through unconstrained public discourse—to evoke a common good. Goods are simply plural, perhaps radically antagonistic (as Isaiah Berlin has argued in his elegant, if perhaps wrong-headed essay, "Two Concepts of Liberty") and can not be aggregated, let alone conjoined in some larger sense of public purpose and good.[11]

To be sure, one strand of the liberal tradition of political philosophy, articulated by writers such as Rawls, Richard Rorty, and Robert Nozick, is increasingly under attack for its inherent "possessive individualism" and a proposed ideal of human agents who are totally unencumbered by any commitments and loyalties.[12] The dominant liberal theory being espoused in the English-speaking world is called "procedural liberalism." It sees society as an association of individuals, each of whom has a conception of a good and worthwhile life, and correspondingly a life plan about which procedural liberalism excludes any socially endorsed conception of the good. In such an instrumental view of society, there is little, if any, sense of a common good and of solidarity. To achieve deeper civic bonds would require a commitment to the pursuit of certain determinate virtues and ideals: safeguards for citizen dignity; a minimal shared sense of history and common cultural identity; and some notion of solidarity with one's fellow human beings and citizens.

At least some liberal egalitarians (William Galston, Will Kymlicka, and Amy Gutmann), however, concede the point.[13] They argue for the necessity of some consensus on the essential virtues of our common citizenry, providing some space for dialogue with Catholic notions of the common good. Galston, for example, in his book, *Liberal Purposes: Goods, Virtues and Diversity in the Liberal State*, explicitly rejects the Rawlsian notion of a total priority of notions of the right over the good. Galston still wants to keep a "thin" notion of the good to operate as our common patrimony in a pluralistic society. In order to allow genuine deliberation and discourse about the republican virtues necessary in a good society, he would open the good to greater thickness than Rawls permits.

It strikes me that there may be some common ground between these liberal virtue theorists and a modern Catholic notion of the common good, which sees, as Brian Stiltner insists, that the common good "is not the province of any particular religious group but of the whole political society."[14] Catholic treatments of the common good typically vacillate between thicker notions of human flourishing and the more modest insistence that "because the definition of the common good refers to the aspirations of persons and voluntary associations, it sets limits to what the state or any single sector of society [presumably, including the religious sector or the church] may do in defining or enforcing the common good."[15] The modern Catholic tradition of the common good, which argues that it is possible for a pluralist society to have a politically legitimate, non-coercive, and substantive common good may have to be much more forthcoming in accepting the inevitability and value of pluralism. Hence, it would have to argue for a thinner notion of a common good that reaches less to total human flourishing than to, precisely and restrictively, the shared virtues necessary to a flourishing of our common life together as citizens. It would have to juxtapose its thick notion of the common good to a more modest notion of the state's concern for public order.[16]

Finally, it should be noted that the anti–common good position of Rawls, and Dworkin, that is, their doctrine of radical state neutrality about all moral goods, may have fed into our contemporary "cultural wars." People who *do* endorse substantive and definitive ideas of the good life strenuously oppose such studied neutrality in, among other areas, school systems, the media, and state sponsorship of art and theatre. By and large, sociological evidence shows that the American people still think that good citizenship demands certain determinate virtues (honesty, hard work, conscientious choice, service) that are not merely procedural. Moreover, critics of state neutrality toward all substantive views of the good claim that the neutralists' view of a purely procedural view of justice is never *quite* as neutral or as *purely procedural* as it claims. The neutralists smuggle in their highly particular conception of an unencumbered self.

Objection 4: The final objection to a notion of the common good comes from a variant of modern economic theory, "rational choice theory." This theory presumes the existence of a rich diversity of preferences and interests in society. Because wants and needs differ, they can not be aggregated or ranked in any rational way. Only a system of market exchange and preferential voting can produce any "right" outcome. When individuals pursue separate goals, they can and do act rationally, but *communal* rationality is thought—by rational choice theorists—to be some idle dream or a dangerous fantasy. We find here a variant of Margaret Thatcher's throw-away remark: "There is no such thing as society."

Rational choice theory in economics has spread, like some devouring Minotaur, beyond its application to economic markets into arenas not so clearly well served by market mechanisms. It has moved aggressively, for example, into public policy and jurisprudence and adds to the forces that would de-couple the law from any sense of the common good. Here, I find Stiltner's characterization of Catholic thought on the common good as a theory of "communal liberalism" very helpful. It is a liberalism inasmuch as modern Catholicism espouses procedures and norms for the protection of human rights and champions freedom and pluralism as positive social goods, in their own right. It is a *communal* liberalism because it suggests a political theory that justifies policies of freedom, tolerance, and pluralism by reference to the good of the political community and its sub-communities, and not simply by reference to the rights of individuals. In response to Margaret Thatcher, the Catholic common good tradition insists that language of the rights of individuals, totally divorced from the sub-communities and the larger political society to which they belong, remains not only one-sided but airy and abstract.

CIVIC CONNECTEDNESS IN AMERICA

What is the institutional climate in American society for any notion of the common good? As wise people should know, every public concept must become incarnated in our institutions if it is to truly thrive and take root. When ideas are encapsulated in institutions, they become "taken-for-granted" background notions of the lives we live. How "taken-for-granted" can any notion of the common good be in contemporary America? A number of social critics, principally Harvard's Robert Putnam, have lamented the erosion of "social capital" in America, the networks of mutuality and trust that bind citizens together. Putnam looks to larger organizational structures, both corporate and non-profit civic organizations, such as the Rotary Club, the Boy Scouts and Girl Scouts, the YMCA, labor unions, etc. Everywhere, there has been a massive erosion (even hemorrhaging) of memberships and commitments in such groups (averaging 12 to 15 percent for most organizations, in the last decade and a half, and with little likelihood of replacement for an increasingly aging cadre of members).[17]

The dominant forms of civic membership have shifted from long-term membership in stable, nationally organized groups toward more local, short-term, ad hoc volunteering in special purpose coalitions and networks. The new forms of civic participation, while real enough, are more ephemeral, issue-oriented, and tied to loose coalitions. People are more inclined to join many shifting networks than to seek a niche and commitments in any one ongoing organization.

These changes in civic participation, as Princeton sociologist Robert Wuthnow argues, are connected to porous institutions, with loose connections and boundaries, which increasingly define our social life.[18] Consider just some of the institutional changes we have witnessed over the last few decades. Roughly one in two marriages in the 1990s ended in divorce, compared to one in four in the 1950s. Out-of-wedlock births in this country have increased from 5 percent of all births in 1960 to 31 percent thirty-five years later. People have weaker ties to extended families, as fewer married Americans live in close physical proximity to their parents, siblings, or cousins. Looser connections to families are tied to geographical and career mobility. Companies and corporations have weaker ties to communities, as leveraged buy-outs and mergers and the fluidity of capital in international markets change their modus vivendi. Workers, too, have more tenuous ties to one another: for example, the percentage of Americans belonging to labor unions has shrunk in the last decade from 16 to less than 12 percent of the workforce.

Work careers are also more ephemeral and short-lived. The average American now works at least three different careers before retirement, spending on average only 4.5 years with any given employer. Only 21 percent of workers over forty-five in the United States have remained tied to one career in their work life. Downsizing and outsourcing of jobs by corporations has steadily increased the number of part-time or temporary workers, without benefits or secure commitments to their workplace. One result of these massive changes is the significant decline over the last two decades in the proportion of Americans who express trust or confidence in larger institutions. More striking, however, has been the erosion of trust in one another.

Robert Wuthnow claims that one way to build up trust is by honest interaction in ephemeral and ad hoc therapeutic and self-help small groups, which have grown apace. About twenty million Americans participate in them. Trust is strongest toward fellow members of such groups. But this bodes ill for how we relate to impersonal institutions, such as the law, corporations, churches, and political parties. Porous institutions make it harder for people to trust one another or to conceive of something like a common good. Longer-lived and national organizations, even when pursuing self-interests, have been historically more liable to enter coalitions with other civic groups in the name of something in line with the classic language of a national interest or common good. In short, the institutional and cultural climates of America abundantly reinforce languages of an unencumbered self: choice, self-interest, personal happiness, and pleasure. Contexts that reinforce values of service, long-term commitment, and sharing are often submerged, relative to those emphasizing gratification.

THE COMMON GOOD DEFINED, NUANCED, AND DEFENDED AGAINST ITS ADVERSARIES

I am not sanguine that the American institutional climate and its individualistic cultural bias, so inimical to a notion of the common good, can be easily conjured away. Yet a concerted effort should be made. The common good is an institutional reality. It looks to creating the societal conditions that will enhance and justly distribute common or public goods. It presupposes that there are at least some goods that are public or common. While the common good is not the mere additive sum of individual properties, it does look, nonetheless, to the dignity and well-being of individual persons. Here again, I find again Stiltner's formulation congenial:

> *The ideal vision* of the common good in the modern Catholic conception is the mutually beneficent relation of social actors, oriented toward protecting and enhancing the dignity of persons and toward supporting the nourishing of diverse and good institutions. What is required to approach this ideal are *procedures* for cooperation and dialogue within a pluralistic, democratic framework and *substantive* norms such as defending human dignity through rights and providing for opportunity for participation in society's common life through its public and voluntary institutions.[19]

I would like to emphasize Stiltner's insistence that the common good is both a substantive reality and, simultaneously, a procedural one. Catholic social thought needs to emphasize this procedural aspect of the common good more than it has. It shares with the liberal tradition a high valuation of human freedom but sometimes limps on imagining the necessary procedural guarantees to ensure freedom. Let me focus, therefore, on three of the core concepts ingredient in any Catholic sense of the common good:

1. it is an institutional reality;
2. it entails some notion of public goods;
3. the common good, in Jacques Maritain's fine phrase, remains personalistic.

John XXIII's, *Mater et Magistra*, defines the common good as "the sum total of those *conditions of social living* whereby men and women are enabled more fully and readily to achieve their well-being."[20] The encyclical echoes Selznick notion that the common good is a property of systems, not of individuals as such. It describes the common good in structural terms.

Some goods necessary for the realization of human dignity or flourishing transcend the arena of merely personal interaction and contract. Thus, such goods, for example, as political self-determination, genuine participation in economic productivity, a healthy environment, enjoyment of one's cultural and linguistic heritage, etc., cannot be directly obtained by individuals acting alone. Such goods accrue to individuals through their participation in the public life and institutions of society. As the Jesuit social ethicist, David Hollenbach, notes, "No one creates a polity, an economy or a culture in private. Individuals come to share in these goods in a way that is mediated by political, economic and cultural structures."[21]

Public goods are the good of the relationships through which the members of the community sustain one another, contribute to one another and constitute a creative center for the ongoing life of the community. Public goods are no one's total private property. They do not properly belong to any one person. They accrue to individuals *only because* and *inasmuch* as they themselves belong to and are part of society. Besides individual rights, there are social rights, such as, the rights to assembly, association, political participation, work, adequate health, housing, education, transportation. Social rights represent claims on essentially public goods.

The common good imagines and enacts the institutional conditions and arrangements necessary to secure the social rights to public goods that seem necessary to live lives of even minimal human dignity and flourishing. One way to find out what might be a public good is to ask, following the political philosopher, Michael Walzer, in his book, *Spheres of Justice*: for what goods should we have blocked exchanges, such that blind market exchanges do not primarily determine their allocation?[22] A short list might include such goods as legal justice; access to political participation; fundamental educational opportunities; access to organ transplants or adoptions; minimally decent health care; the allocation of honors based on excellence in the arts; scholarships.

The institutionalization of access to and distribution of public goods represents the organizational face and indispensable font for a society's genuine commitment to social and distributive justice. The common good, then, in Catholic social thought, must be seen as a corollary of the wider notion of justice. The great tradition of the common good from Aristotle, Cicero, Aquinas down to our own time, insists that even individual flourishing requires a context of the common good in which we can deliberate together in an open and public way about the goods we will hold as public and agree to pursue in common. In this way of thinking, the very ability of people to identify what is good or noble depends on their being part of a community or shared tradition, locked in argument, conversation and dialogue. In that community of tradition, individuals undergo a *paideia* through which they are educated in the virtues of a common citizenship. Without that *paideia*, neither the more abstract moralities of obeying the impersonal law of the state or fulfilling moral obligations based on the exchanges of the market can be sustained. These latter grow from learning reciprocity, self-transcendence, trust and a sense of rooted obligation in what Edmund Burke once called, "the little platoons of society." Both the economy and the polity are dependent on a prior gift of society.

Yet individualists that we inexorably are as Americans, we tend to resist the notion of the common good, because we fear that our personal goals and desires will be swallowed up by some collective, communitarian (or worse still, bureaucratic!) ethos. Hence, it is important to recall that the Catholic tradition of the common good was and is (at least since the first parts of the twentieth century) personalistic. As Jacques Maritain in his classic treatise, *The Person and the Common Good* argued: we exist in and for communities (which are not, as some strands of liberal theory often have it, merely instrumental for personal autonomies). The very capacity for the engagement with community is, itself, a positive perfection of personality. But if the dignity of persons can be realized only in community, genuine community, in its turn, can only exist where the substantial freedom and dignity of the human person is secured. Hence, Catholic notions of the dignity of the human person, based both on human needs and human moral agency, get linked to the common good. These concepts of dignity and freedom protect against any one-sided smothering of human agency by traditions. They are the reason the Catholic theory of the common good is a "communal liberalism."[23]

Philip Selznick resonates with this Catholic notion when he asks us to think of the common good as profoundly systemic, "not reducible to individual interests or attributes yet testable by its contribution to personal well-being":

> The common good is served . . . by institutions that provide collective goods, such as education or public safety. The strength or weakness of these institutions is a communal attribute, not an individual one. . . . Similarly, a major collective good is social integration. When social integration is measured, the measure will take account, at least indirectly, of individual attitudes, behaviors, opportunities and affiliations. And a connection is likely between personal and social integration. People can live more coherent lives and have more coherent personalities when they belong to coherent social worlds.[24]

Let us look again at the four objections that are characteristically raised against any appeal to the common good. The first objection rests on an argument from relativism and subjectivity. It reminds us that any attempt to speak of the common good presupposes some form of a moderately realist epistemology. To be sure, much of our knowledge *is* socially constructed and mediated, but not all of it is. Moreover, we have, at any given time, only an incomplete grasp of the fullness of truth. Any truth we hold must, then, be revisable, based on testable hypotheses or new data. Nevertheless, reality is not simply polymorphously perverse and various, totally tractable to our subjective desires or interests. It "bites" (as it were) back. We can not construct our worlds in just any haphazard way. There is something like an objective reality to which we have some access and which we recognize as something we "discover" and not merely something we "create" or "manipulate."

In all such objections, based on an appeal to relativism and subjectivism, there seems to be an assumption that, to be reliable, knowledge must be foundationalist, unrevisable and absolute. We can, surely, be much more modest in our realisms. Our best estimates of what counts as the institutionalized goods of the system can be experimented with and revised. One does not have to posit, when speaking of the common good, that there is some pre-existing pattern of the good society out there (in Platonic subsistent forms) that one can discern for all time and, then, impose on others. Rather, as Catholic social ethicist, Dennis McCann has suggested, the common good is our interactive pursuit and conversation about the goods we (where the *we* is the set of *all* fellow citizens, precisely as fellow citizens) will pursue in common, the virtues we feel essential toward a flourishing life together as fellow citizens and the institutions needed to enable them.[25]

As John Courtney Murray once insisted, the social compact (what Murray, culling from a medieval document, called the *pactum civilis*) rests on dual pillars. One pediment does rest on the objectivity of the good. The other, however, depends on an agreement, a consensus. Catholic treatments of the common good do a disservice, then, to emphatically stress the objectivity of public goods while totally downplaying the other, important role of societal consensus in constituting the common good. Consensus (and the range of areas where it can be, reasonably, achieved) plays a crucial limiting role on what can serve as the common good in a pluralist society. A putative blueprint for the common good that seriously divides the society and rends the social fabric ceases to be common and may—by reason of its inability to generate a wide consensus—cease to be a true societal good.

I have some sympathy with the second objection which cautions about claiming any very exact knowledge about the desired good for the state of society as a whole. It is necessary, in a preliminary way, to assess the small microgoods of the institutions of society, education, the family, the state, etc., before essaying the larger task of asking what might be the good for something as large and amorphous as society as a whole. Catholic social thought has been rather adept at dealing with some of these institutions, e.g., labor unions, the family, the state. It lacks, as yet, a full analysis of all the micro-institutions of society.

Yet at some point we cannot simply avoid the question of how the various micro-institutions of society inter-relate and find some coordinate good as an ensemble. I do not think concern for a prior careful monitoring of the good of micro-institutions can forestall the judgment day when their interrelated effects (or unintended spill-off consequences) will need to be brought into a balance. In principle, then, the objection is more cautionary than a true veto when talking about the common good for whole societies. This caution will evoke a more modest and revisable assessment of the common good of the whole society. It will also caution Catholics to be aware of the sociological law of unintended consequences. Only someone who denies that a society has system-like properties, however, can press this objection fully.

The third objection, which we met earlier, is deeply rooted in major strands of contemporary liberal theory (but not in all kin of that family). Since different persons in society, in fact, hold divergent understandings of the human good, treating people equally entails publicly stringent neutrality toward any substantive vision of the good or human flourishing, common or particular. With his characteristic wisdom, Selznick responds to these fears that the common good will necessarily mean the imposition of someone else's vision of the good society. "The quest for a common good takes place *within* and not *against* the experience of plurality."[26] Catholic variants of the common good need to be as clear on this point as Selznick is.

It is illuminating to remember that John Courtney Murray's discussion of the common good in his celebrated, *We Hold These Truths*, presupposed a fairly radical pluralism. He even anticipated in the late 1950s the "cultural war" language, entitling one chapter, "Creeds at War." Murray's metaphor for the common good was less one of *imposition* than *conversation*. He spoke of a conspiring together, not from within our plural life-worlds, but across them for the good of the society. And, when, because of some breakdown of civil conversation and/or culture wars, the conversation stops and we start to shout slogans past each other (as we, often, do in contemporary political discourse), Murray's first instinct was to restart the conversation about the truths we do, or want to, or should hold in common.[27]

Opponents of injecting substantive notions of the good into public debate have, it strikes me, at least for the American case, unwarranted fears of societal instability. They tend, alternatively, to downplay or overlook, in Stiltner's terms, "the social alienation that the constraints of" public reason [Rawls' uses this phrase to refer to his stipulated method of a purely procedural sense of justice which must bracket any comprehensive theory of the good from public debate] "might cause or, more positively, the enhanced commitment to the common good that would or might result when citizens are encouraged to speak from their different comprehensive doctrines, including religious ones, on a more regular basis."[28] Thus, for example, more recently people have been evoking a notion of "societal forgiveness"—whose original provenance is, undoubtedly, from religious sources—as a "secular" concept for the healthy or good society. If Rawls' rules were followed such a transfer from particular religious discourse to more general secular usage would never be warranted—perhaps, with some true social loss. Rawls' public reason stacks the deck against those who would speak from their comprehensive doctrines, constraining them, before they speak, with the condition that their arguments should be "reasonable" that is, construed according to the Rawlsian method. It does seem rather arbitrary to decide, ahead of time, what kind of reorientation non-public reasons might have on public reason and the content of justice.

The fears that a commitment to pursue the common good will hamper diversity or pluralism may also be assuaged by the Catholic tradition's characteristic answer to the question: Who has the care for the common good? The state, to be sure, in its concern to provide a framework for security, justice, welfare, and freedom, plays an indispensable role in overseeing the care for the common good. But since society, as such, is never swallowed by the state (strongly enunciated in the Catholic principle of subsidiarity), other institutions —churches, families, private educational and civic associations, business corporations, labor unions—also have a legitimate and nonderivative voice and obligation to look for and care for the common good. The Catholic insistence on subsidiarity is, fundamentally, a plea for pluralism. The plurality of associations is an inevitable consequence of human finitude and a guard against hubris. In sum, pluralism is central to the common good because different communities center on the pursuit of different components of the complex human good; because institutional diversity facilitates extensive participation in social life and because no one association can claim to be the perfect community.

In the end, the pursuit of the common good is not a panacea. Catholic social thought, typically, remains overly sanguine that, at the end of the day, doctrines and conflicts can be harmonized. Yet, clearly, persons will remain divided in their comprehensive views of the good. These divisions will show up and be reflected in conflicts over moral, religious and political issues. No theory can eliminate the conflicting elements from life. Nor should Catholic proponents of a common good expect to do so.

Not much is really gained by trying to finesse away all language of the common good, which will re-emerge, anyway, as a kind of persistent aspiration, especially in divided and pluralistic societies. Much is lost, however, in dispensing with the kinds of questions the common good theory forces us as citizens to ask. The common good theory looks less to some chimera of a conflict-free society (which inter alia would be deficient as a society). Rather, it asks whether all is conflict and whether we might not flourish better as a society if we could pursue the ideals of a more deliberative democracy where, at least in principle, substantive concepts of the good can be raised as a possibly public, if non-coerced, source of our common life together.

NOTES

1. Cf. S.T.I-II, 90 articles 1, 23, in William Baumgarth and Richard Regan S.J., *St. Thomas on Law, Morality and Politics* (Indianapolis: Hackett, 1988), 11–17.

2. U.S. Catholic Conference, National Council of Churches, Synagogue Council of America, "The Common Good: Old Idea, New Urgency," *Origins* 23, no. 6 (24 June 1993), p. 82.

3. Philip Selznick, *The Moral Commonwealth* (Berkeley: University of California Press, 1992), 537.

4. Robert Bellah, "Remarks on Receiving the Skirball Institute Award, 2000," unpublished ms.

5. Robert Wuthnow, *Acts of Compassion* (Princeton, N.J.: Princeton University Press, 1991); *Learning to Care* (New York: Oxford University Press, 1995).

6. Reinhold Niebuhr, *Moral Man and Immoral* Society (New York: Scribners, 1932).

7. Steven Hart, *What Does the Lord Require?* (New York: Oxford University Press, 1992), 150.

8. This seems to be Michael Novak's position in his *Freedom with Justice* (New Brunswick, N.J.: Transaction, 1989).

9. Ronald Dworkin, *A Matter of Principle* (Cambridge, Mass.: Harvard University Press, 1985).

10. John Rawls, *Political Liberalism* (New York: Columbia University Press, 1993), 37.

11. Isaiah Berlin, *Four Essays on Liberty* (New York: Oxford University Press, 1987), 117–182.

12. For these critiques cf. Michael Sandel, *Liberalism and the Limits of Justice* (New York: Cambridge University Press, 1988) and *Democracy's Discontent* (Cambridge, Mass.: Harvard University Press, 1996).

13. William Galston, *Liberal Purposes: Goods, Virtues and Diversity in the Liberal State* (New York: Cambridge University Press, 1991); Amy Gutmann, *Democratic Education* (Princeton, N.J.: Princeton University Press, 1987); Will Kymlicka, *Liberalism, Community and Culture* (New York: Oxford University Press, 1989).

14. Brian Stiltner, *Religion and the Common Good* (Lanham, Md.: Rowman and Littlefield, 1999), 10.

15. Stiltner, *Religion and the Common Good*, 121.

16. The thinner notion of public order as a subset of a broader understanding of the common good derives from John Courtney Murray. For a treatment of this distinction, cf. Charles Curran, *Catholic Social Teaching* (Washington, D.C.: Georgetown University Press, 2002), 228–229.

17. Robert Putnam, *Bowling Alone* (New York: Simon and Schuster, 2000).

18. Robert Wuthnow, *Loose Connections: Joining Together in America's Fragmented Communities* (Cambridge, Mass.: Harvard University Press, 1998).

19. Stiltner, *Religion and the Common Good*, 10.

20. *Mater et Magistra*, # 65.

21. David Hollenbach, S.J., "The Common Good Revisited," *Theological Studies*, 50, 1, (1989), 70–94 at 77. Since I wrote this essay, Hollenbach has published *The Common Good and Christian Ethics* (New York: Cambridge University Press, 2002), which is very helpful on the question of the common good.

22. Michael Walzer, *Spheres of Justice* (New York: Basic Books, 1983).

23. Jacques Maritain, *The Person and the Common Good* (New York: Scribners, 1947).

24. Philip Selznick, *The Moral Commonwealth*, 537.

25. Dennis McCann, "The Good to Be Pursued in Common" in Oliver F. Williams and John W. Houck, eds., *The Common Good and U.S. Capitalism* (Lanham, Md.: University Press of America), 158–178.

26. Selznick, *The Moral Commonwealth*, 538.

27. John Courtney Murray, *We Hold These Truths* (New York: Sheed and Ward, 1960), 103–139.

28. Stiltner, *Religion and the Common Good*, 62.

PLURALISM AND THE COMMON GOOD: A RESPONSE

Jane Mansbridge

Twenty years ago, in *Beyond Adversary Democracy*, I argued that many Americans—and many political scientists—were mistaken in thinking they had described "democracy" when they had described only what I called "adversary democracy"—a democracy based on conflicting interests. I argued that we must move back and forth between modes of decision-making based on the assumption of relatively conflicting interests and modes based on relatively common interests. This is still my position today. As a polity, I believe, we emphasize far too much the politics in which our interests conflict. We try far too little to recognize common interests where they exist and to forge common interests across seeming lines of disagreement.

Since I wrote that book, however, the theories of "deliberative democracy" that have followed have so emphasized the common good that I have felt compelled to stand on the other leg. I find myself pointing out often that good deliberation should not only help forge a common good but should also reveal conflicting interests when they have been obfuscated by spurious appeals to the common good.

In the same vein, I think we need a cautious but committed approach to the common good. We need to recognize, first, that the common good is always contestable. We can never know with certainty what it is in a particular case. This point is the same as John Coleman's first "objection," but differently put. Second, effective appeals to the common good often rest not just on reason, but also, and rightly, on emotion. Such appeals are good, but also dangerous. Third, in conditions of uncertainty, the dominant groups in

19

any society have a great advantage in constructing the reigning understanding of the common good.[1]

I do not think that agreeing with these three conclusions keeps us from acting for the common good as we best know it at a given time. Much of modern life rests on foundational uncertainty. We eat margarine dutifully until we are told that butter is actually just as good for our health. We choke down oat bran, or more recently fiber, until we are told that these substances do not have the powers previously ascribed to them. The ordinary soldier takes the hill not because he is certain that this is the best thing to do, but because he knows that the command to take it is his superiors' best guess at the time. This is, perhaps, the difference between the ordinary soldier and Joan of Arc. Or take a parent who gives up a good job for one that allows him to be home at three when his child comes home from school. You ask him, "Are you *sure* that this is the best thing for your child?" Most parents will say they are not sure, but are acting on their best guess. We can't usually know what is best, just as we can't know what is in the common good. But lack of certainty does not keep us from acting. We consult with one another, deliberate, and make our best guess.

I do not think that Thomas Aquinas subscribed to these points. We differ from Aquinas if we believe that the common good is contestable, that effective appeals to the common good often rest rightly but dangerously on emotion, and that dominant groups will have an advantage in defining the common good.

In another way too we differ from Aquinas. Only since World War II have we had access to a new analytical tool—a tool for understanding one form of the common good that was not available to any earlier writer, including Aristotle, Aquinas, de Tocqueville, or Hume.

It was around 1950 that mathematical theorists first discovered an interactive structure that I will call the "free-rider problem." In its earliest version, which remains important, it was called "the prisoners' dilemma." Later versions were called the "tragedy of the commons," the "problem of collective action," the "common-pool problem" and the "free-rider problem." I like the name the "free-rider problem." These free rider problems have one central and defining characteristic: In them the good is "non-excludable"—that is, no one can be excluded from its benefits. Take the example of military defense. When a group manages to achieve an effective defense against outside attacks, *everyone* in that group benefits, even those who have never contributed to that defense. It is in the nature of a good like military defense that no one can be excluded from its benefits. When we manage to clean up a stream, everyone downstream benefits, even those who have not contributed to the cleansing effort. In such cases, when no one can be excluded from the benefits, it is individually rational for each self-interested individual to "free-ride" on the contributions of others without contributing to the cost of bringing that common good about. This is the "free-rider problem."

The conceptual tool of the free-rider problem, with its distinction between goods that you can exclude others from consuming (like the crops in your own field) and goods from which you cannot exclude others (like the clean water downstream that your anti-pollution device creates), allows an analytic advance almost as important as that made by the tool of supply and demand. This analysis supplants earlier, vaguer theories, which simply asserted that "enlightened self-interest" is congruent with the public good.

Thomas Aquinas, for example, concluded in some passages that individual good and common good are essentially congruent. He wrote: "He who seeks the common good of the multitude consequently seeks his own good . . . because one's own good cannot exist without the common good."[2] This statement is incorrect. It is not true that simply because an individual is part of the public, it is to the individual's own benefit to contribute to that public. In cases where no one can be excluded from the benefits of the public good, it is to each individual's benefit to "free ride" on the contributions of others.

David Hume's argument that contributions to the common good are in each individual's "remote interest" has exactly the same problem. So does Alexis de Tocqueville's argument that contributions to the common good serve "self-interest rightly understood." These formulations are analytically incoherent in a free-rider situation (i.e., with a non-excludable good). When a situation is structured like a free-rider problem, both Hume's and Tocqueville's formulations require an element that neither writer specified. They require that the individuals concerned either follow principle for its own sake, or for one reason or another make the good of other people, or the whole, their own.

Neither Hume nor Tocqueville nor any other writer could explain how, when you cannot exclude others from the good you have produced, individuals motivated only by narrow self-interest could see action for the common good as in their self-interest. It is in neither one's "remote self-interest" nor one's "self-interest rightly understood" to cooperate in a situation structured like a free-rider problem (1) if one's self-interest does not encompass the good of others or adherence to principles, (2) if one's own behavior will not influence others' behavior, (3) if the common good is not an accidental by-product of self-interested behavior, and (4) if others' actions will not reward cooperative behavior or punish its opposite. When there are opportunities to "free ride" on others' efforts, simply being a member of a community that benefits from its members' contributions does not provide sufficient incentive for a narrowly self-interested individual to contribute.

I am emphatically not saying that whenever we find ourselves with a non-excludable common good we should simply give up. When goods are non-excludable (thus creating a free-rider problem), we can always produce a common good by setting up institutions of coercion that will punish those who do not help produce the good (e.g., fines or jail for non-payment of taxes) and then simply let people follow their narrow self-interest. Far more efficient than coercion, however, is getting people to act for the common good by urging them to follow the principle of "fair play" or encouraging them to make the good of the others their own. When people see themselves in community with others, they are far less likely to free ride.

When goods are excludable, by contrast, self-interest combined with the market laws of supply and demand can produce a common good.

Because there are many forms of common good, and many ways to bring about different forms of the common good, my conception of the common good is irreducibly plural.

To sum up thus far, my conception of the common good is irreducibly plural—as well as perpetually in contest, open to dangerous appeals, and subject to expression through concepts that subtly or not so subtly benefit the ruling groups of any society. Efforts to produce a common good must be aware of these dangers as well as the possible benefits.

I agree with Professor Coleman in many ways. I too want to rescue a vision of the common good that can inspire sacrifice, and do so in a way that is compatible with pluralism. He makes the excellent point that appeals to the common good run against the grain of individualism in America. Such appeals need extra effort because of this cultural tendency. I too find it troubling that appeals to the common good are relatively rare these days. Such appeals must be redoubled, and a basis found for them that resonates to the better values of the American people. Finally, I agree that it is not easy to cultivate a commitment to the common good, particularly in response to the objections he identifies so well. And I agree that therefore we must try harder to do so, both by retrieving an understandable sense of the common good and by linking it with the deepest values of our citizenry.

I am, however, a more radical pluralist than he.

In particular, I disagree with him in his implication that the "common good" requires agreement on a substantive understanding of "*the* good."

My own conception of the common good, unlike Professor Coleman's, is compatible with Rawls's neutrality on *"the* good." My conception allows many forms of common good. Some are merely aggregative. Some are related to the function of the polity. Some result only from a coincidence of material interests. Some result from individuals cleaving to a principle, or making the good of others—or the good of the whole—their own.

I can agree with John Rawls, Ronald Dworkin, Bruce Ackerman and Isaiah Berlin on the plurality of "goods" *and* conclude at the same time that schools and other state entities should take a stance on some of these plural goods.

It is highly probable, for example, that we could find close to universal agreement among human societies on the "goodness" of certain human virtues. We might well be able to reach "good enough" agreement on the virtues of honesty, fair play, and certain forms of justice.

But although I think we might well find considerable agreement on the goodness of these virtues, I do not think that we would find comparable *rankings* of these goods from society to society. I am thus far closer to Isaiah Berlin than to Professor Coleman in thinking that there are many different worthy goods, some conflicting with others. Nor would we want simply to assume that these virtues are good, without opening them consciously to contest, and asking when their practice might benefit some groups and harm others.

My commitment to plural, contested, and even incommensurate and conflicting goods does not make me eschew commitment to these various forms of common good. I do not agree with Professor Coleman that "In principle . . . state neutrality vis-à-vis any moral conception of the good would disallow any attempt—even a free and deliberative engagement through unconstrained public discourse—to evoke *a* common good" (emphasis mine). The state can be neutral about the good and we can still agree on the *particular* common good of, for example, not taking the last breeding fish from the common pool. We do not need a moral concept of *the* good to achieve that agreement on a particular common good. To reach the particular concept of the common good we have only to reach an agreement that more fish (which will be able to propagate if we restrict our take) are better than fewer.

Professor Coleman might say that this understanding of the common good is a "merely additive sum of the greatest good for the greatest number of individuals." But I see nothing wrong with this, as *one* form of the common good. The concept has considerable institutional bite.

Consider another example. Most (perhaps all) of us could agree that in most situations honesty is the moral policy. The state need not be neutral in this regard. State schools, for example, can promote honesty as a good for humankind. They would perform that function best if they opened the concept to contest, and asked students to think about both the possibility of uneven benefits to different social groups from its practice and the dynamics of the free-rider problem. (I conclude from such an exercise that honesty benefits the poor as much as the rich, the less powerful as much as the powerful. But that is a longer story.) State schools can promote honesty as a good without committing to a wider and more substantive understanding of *the* good for humankind.

I interpret Professor Coleman as saying that to reach an understandable concept of one or another particular common good we must agree to a "socially endorsed conception of *the* good" (emphasis mine). He implies that to achieve "solidarity" we need a sense of a singular common good rather than many, sometimes competing, common goods.

In short, I argue against Professor Coleman that we do not need a citizenry that can "identify what is good or noble" in what I take to be a singular sense. Rather, we can craft a plurality of common goods for various purposes—including feeling a bond that constitutes part of our identity. We can go beyond procedural commonality. We can go beyond cultural relativism. We can find "good enough" agreement on specific virtues and values, without demanding that citizens share *a* single substantive common good built around those values. I conclude that John Courtney Murray is wrong in thinking that the social compact must rest at least in part on "the objectivity of the good." I endorse the objectivity of *some* goods. We can probably find close to universal agreement that certain material goods and certain virtues are in fact good in the characteristic contexts in which they are typically used and exercised. But this goodness should never be above contest. And, as noted earlier, we will not always agree on the ranking of goods. These many divergent goods do not form a coherent relation with one another that can be reasonably understood as "the" good.

These are subtle differences in interpretation. The elements that unite my own view with that of Professor Coleman are far greater than those that divide us. Coleman quotes Brian Stiltner, for example, as saying that "pluralism is central to the common good because different communities center on the pursuit of different components of the complex human good." My point about ranking is almost identical with this. I would only change the last few words to read "the *many* complex human goods." I think we need not insist on a singular, on *the* good for humankind. And I think that the concept of a singular good for humankind—*the* good—leads us away from recognizing that whatever goods are advanced as common are always contestable, sometimes dangerous, and often deeply influenced by the most powerful.

NOTES

1. Quoted in Lewis 1954, p. 212.
2. Quoted in Lewis 1954, p. 212.

CATHOLIC SOCIAL THOUGHT AND THE AMERICAN EXPERIENCE

Stephen J. Pope

How ought Catholics engage in American civic life in light of Catholic social thought? I will begin by reviewing briefly some fundamental characteristics of Catholic social thought, next offer some observations about our contemporary situation, then argue that natural law discourse continues to be a legitimate way of engaging in public moral conversation within the American context, and finally conclude by offering some suggestions about how Catholic civic engagement ought to be developed in the coming years, highlighting the importance of parish life.

ROMAN CATHOLIC SOCIAL THOUGHT

Roman Catholic social thought is not easy to summarize in a simple and straightforward way, without falling into platitudes and clichés that oversimplify a complex and rich, if not entirely systematic and philosophically rigorous, body of ideas. It includes not only the social teachings of the papacy over the last hundred odd years but also an immense religious, conceptual, and doctrinal heritage, including the teachings of Sacred Scripture, the theological reflections of church fathers like Augustine, Basil, and John Chrysostom, the scholastic synthesis of Thomas Aquinas, and the modern philosophical development of these resources in natural law theories and in the waves of Thomistic revival in the sixteenth, nineteenth, and twentieth centuries. This tradition has hardly produced an unresponsive, unchanging, and monolithic moral code. As John T. Noonan Jr., explains, in the history of Catholic ethics we find "what was forbidden became lawful (the cases of usury and marriage); what was permissible because unlawful (the case of slavery); and what was required became forbidden (the persecution of heretics)."[1]

It is true that Church teaching on practical moral issues like killing, sex, and property are especially subject to variability because they are always so tightly embedded in fluctuating concrete social and historical contexts. Yet the interpretation of general principles such as justice, charity, and the common good have also been closely connected to concrete circumstances and so our understanding of their meaning has evolved over time as well. Even the relatively recent body of papal social teachings exhibits significant diversity, and at times even some internal disparity, concerning, for example, the relation between the unitive and procreative ends of marriage, the role of women in society, and the moral wisdom of capital punishment. So perhaps it is inevitable that authors from different political perspectives will cull favorite doctrines from this large and ranging corpus to enhance their own positions as they conveniently underplay others.

Nonetheless, healthy diversity need not be confused with complete chaos. There are clearly recurring motifs in Catholic social teachings, notably the transcendent dignity of the person, its protection through respect for human rights, and the centrality of the common good. All three motifs are based on a philosophical anthropology that regards human beings as naturally embodied, intelligent, free, and social. These, in turn, are grounded in a theological anthropology of human beings as made in God's image, wounded by sin, and redeemed by grace. In this context, human rights are not absolute claims of radically autonomous individuals, as in radical individualism, but rather, as Kenneth and Michael Himes put it, "claims to goods which are necessary for the person to participate with dignity in the communal life of a society."[2]

These themes have had a major impact on American Catholic public intellectuals, including Monsignor John A. Ryan, John Courtney Murray, S.J., and, by cultural transplantation, Jacques Maritain. The work of each thinker proceeded through a creative synthesis of Thomistic natural law theory and American constitutional democracy. Maritain's French personalism was clearly different from Ryan's Midwest populism and both of these from Murray's precise and historically nuanced analyses. All creatively employed Thomism in their common desire to elucidate and deepen what they identified as a significant and fruitful convergence between the best of American civic values and the natural law tradition.[3]

This common project was based on "moral realism": a positive estimation of the human cognitive capacity to come to moral insight, to provide explicit reasons for choices in civic matters, and to bring these reasons to bear in public advocacy, dialogue, and debate. Underlying their appreciation of the power of human reason was a common metaphysical belief that the structure of being is inherently purposeful, coherent, and intelligible, and that inquiry into its purposes provides guidance concerning the best ways to live and to structure our communities. Along with this metaphysical foundation, they also shared a bedrock religious conviction that God has created us for a purpose and wills that we flourish as virtuous people in good communities.

THE CONTEMPORARY AMERICAN MORAL CONTEXT

In their day, Murray, Ryan, and Maritain were all confident that natural law would be widely accepted by reasonable people operating with good faith. They were able to make this assumption in the midst of a broad convergence of moral themes rooted in what was in mid-century called the "Judeo-Christian heritage." They had reason to think that Protestants, Catholics, and Jews could, in principle, agree on matters of ethics and political morality without also achieving the deepest and most profound kind of religious unity. In practice, of course, such consensus was not always obtained, but at least the principle provided the basis for ongoing public conversation on matters of civic life.

Their view points to a stark difference between then and now. Today "religion" is often caricatured by its critics as taking one of two forms: either as intense participation in a cult-like defensive community characterized by rigid dependence on authority, unthinking obedience, and strong internal cohesion, or, on the other end of the spectrum, as casual membership in a domesticated, therapeutically-minded and quasi-secular social club that gives neither offense nor character to its members. Religion in the former case gives rise to self-righteous intolerance and obstinate fundamentalism; in the latter, to vacuous social conventionality and banal cultural Christianity.

Catholics, of course, can have as many reservations about religion as anyone else. Whereas Ryan, Murray, and Maritain could take moral agreement within Catholicism for granted and then work toward forming a consensus over contested policy matters in the public square, today we face the challenge of building moral consensus within the Catholic community itself. The possibility of building this consensus depends, in turn, on the ability to engage in productive intra-Catholic moral dialogue. This consensus should not be confused with imposed uniformity. Nor can it be created by means of vigorously exerting institutional power, and for at least two reasons. First, because consensus is constituted by shared judgment and shared judgment is generated not by coercion but by persuasive reasoning in an atmosphere of trust and dialogue. Second, because coercive threats and their execution are particularly offensive to the sense of fairness and love of freedom that are characteristically American.

This decay of magisterial credibility is a situation that clearly demands our attention. It affects not only the internal life of the Church but also its influence in the public square. For one thing, people who find it increasingly easy to ignore doctrine concerning sexual conduct would also seem more likely to dismiss the Church's message on a whole range of matters pertaining to civic life and public policy, including the death penalty, euthanasia, the ethics of war, the preferential option for the poor, and ecological responsibility. More broadly, they will be less likely to embrace the kind of broad Catholic social vision that can act as a coherent and morally more appealing alternative to radical individualism. The erosion of the effective authority of the magisterium—its ability to persuade and to exert moral leadership rather than its institutional control—undermines, or at least seriously compromises, its ability to offer a prophetic counterweight to the radical individualism, careerism, and consumerism of American popular culture. It also undercuts its constructive ability to teach the importance of the common good, the global moral interdependence of humanity, and the inherent dignity of the person.

AMERICAN CULTURE AND BASIC GOODS

The moral dangers of American values have been perceptively and widely discussed by many serious observers, among them Charles Taylor, Robert Bellah, Vaclav Havel, and John Paul II.[4] Still it is important not to overreact to the flaws in the American ethos and simply write off our society as morally bankrupt. In contrast to the condemnations uttered by the pre-conciliar, anti-modern ecclesiastical authorities, the fathers of Vatican II developed a nuanced and multivalent attitude to culture that continues to be relevant. They proposed a threefold attitude involving appreciation, criticism, and transformation of modern culture that is flexible enough to be applied in varying ways within different contexts. How the Church responds to American demands for gender equality in corporations or freedom of speech in China may be different from the way it responds to American attitudes toward consumption or reproduction, so a singular preselected mode of response—either entirely negative or entirely positive—is too simplistic to be helpful. A variety of attitudes have to be present in a mature Catholic response to the values current in American cultural and political life.

American society is not simply a wasteland of nihilism. In fact, it has some things to teach Catholic institutions regarding gender equality, the benefits of pluralism, and procedural fairness. Some core American values such as freedom of conscience, the dignity of work, the value of creativity, and the centrality of individual responsibility find a home in Catholicism as well. I would like to argue that the Catholic natural law mode of moral reflection continues to provide a basis for identifying common human goods that any decent political community ought to make available to its citizens, and therefore that it still offers the best conceptual means with which American Catholics can enter into public conversation regarding the moral dimensions of civic life.

Americans want to be protected in their ability to make choices about how they are going to live, but also recognize in practice the existence of some basic human goods necessary to any decent life, including nutrition, health, education, housing, and employment. To be sure, we differ over what constitutes the most noble of human goods, how we are to obtain them, and what exactly it means to live a good life in accordance with them. Americans assume that there is such a thing as human nature, that there are basic goods, and that these goods are not simply arbitrary and idiosyncratic preferences. In our day this affirmation provides the cultural context for Catholic engagement in American public conversation.

CATHOLIC COMMUNITARIAN PERSONALISM

Catholics, then, have good reason to feel a certain ambivalence toward American culture. What might be called "Catholic communitarian personalism" provides a helpful perspective from which to articulate in more detail the reasons for this ambivalence and to craft a constructive response to it. "Personalism" affirms the dignity of each human being as made in the image of God, morally free and accountable, and bearing intrinsic rights and duties. Personalism is "communitarian" when it acknowledges each individual as a "person in relation" who is only able to flourish as a member of a community that makes available the whole array of goods necessary for human life. Since people as social animals spontaneously associate in a wide variety of ways in pursuit of different goods pursued in common, the "principle of subsidiarity" is an important expression of this dimension of Catholic social thought."[5] Finally, communitarian personalism is "Catholic" when its motivation, character, and ultimate term are informed by the sacramental, incarnational imagination that is generated by active participation in the life of the Church.

Catholic communtarian personalism provides a moral vantage point for appreciating the ways in which American values protect the dignity of the person, including the way it sets limits on the power of the federal government. It also supplies a basis for criticizing these values when they lead to the degradation of the person, including those many occasions in which the government shirks its responsibility to protect the most vulnerable. Since the person is a social animal, communitarian personalism interprets the dignity of the person in light of the common good, as well as the common good in terms of the dignity of individuals. Human dignity, as the American bishops expressed it, is "realized in community with others,"[6] but communities can only empower people to realize their innate dignity to the extent that they respect the human rights of individuals. Communitarian personalism sees that there are certain basic goods common to all members of a community whose absence signals a deprivation suffered by all, both the individuals who suffer and the community as a whole.

If this kind of Catholic communitarian personalism were to play a role in American public life, we ought to expect it to generate in Catholic citizens both greater degrees of civic responsibility and capacities to criticize radical individualism and the social "atomism" that underlies it.[7] In the terminology of the social teachings, we would say that the laity ought to embrace a more serious devotion to the common good and to the preferential option for the poor.

CATHOLICISM AND CIVIC ENGAGEMENT

How ought communitarian personalism shape Catholic engagement in American civic life? The distinctive character of Catholic participation in civic life is sometimes construed in terms of political power amassed by Catholic special interest groups, or exercised by Catholic politicians, or concentrated in Catholic voting blocks. Some theorists wish that Catholics would directly apply principles from social teachings in their deliberations about policy questions regarding, for example, physician-assisted suicide or minimum wage legislation. This may be possible on some issues, but because of major demographic, educational, economic, and social changes since World War II, Catholics will be less likely to vote as they did when Catholicism was the ethnically-based separatist religion of the working class. Whether or not there will be statistically significant Catholic voting patterns in the future, the most distinctive and important feature of Catholic participation in civic life will be the quality of its moral engagement and the breadth of its moral vision. This includes four components: its understanding of the nature of civic life itself; its motivation for being engaged in civic life; the basic moral sensibilities underlying its action; and the way it interprets the moral standards used to evaluate such action.

First, Catholics ought to understand civic life as an essential expression of our social nature, as the natural context within which we flourish, and as the arena within which we converse together about how to foster and sustain the conditions for a decent and humanly enriching community. This does not rule out the need for realistic political action, or for the right use of concentrated political power, but it does mean that politics must be regarded primarily as a realm of reasoning together about the common good rather than of employing sheer power to gain advantage over competitors.

Second, Catholics ought to be motivated for this engagement out of a religious love for God and neighbor, a sense of the goodness of creation that embraces the realms of politics, culture, and indeed all things human, and an appreciation for the opportunities for goodness made possible by civic life. Our form of constitutional democracy may not actually be the historical heir of Thomistic philosophy, but there are clearly Catholic reasons for appreciating it. We keep alive, in contemporary form, the hope that the good society makes possible "fraternal community."[8]

Third, Catholic moral sensibilities are distinctive to the extent to which they have been shaped by sacramental life, and especially by active participation in the liturgical, educational, moral, and social life of local parishes. Catholics are formed by being part of a community structured by the paradigmatic personages and events recounted in the biblical narratives and in the history of the Church. By their very character, Catholic symbols—the Incarnation, the Cross, the Trinity, the Resurrection, the Kingdom of God, etc.—inculcate solidarity, compassion, and social justice.[9] Emerging from a universal community bound together in this profound way, the Catholic imagination ought to draw individuals out of narrow parochialism and into a more global context.

Catholic efforts to make claims about the moral dimensions of civic life and even about public morality offer a significant counterweight to the growing tendency in our culture to privatize morality and to reduce claims about "values" to the private prejudices or idiosyncratic preferences of individuals. The very fact that Catholics have religious reasons for caring about the common good and the political order offers a valuable public alternative to the privatization of religion current in many circles today. Given the degree of cynicism about it, Catholic commitment to such conversation is itself an important contribution to American civic culture.

Fourth, Catholics ought to move from these sensibilities to practical decisions regarding the civic order through moral standards that, while clearly generated from Catholic underpinnings, are broadly intelligible to the wide variety of perspectives sharing the public realm in our highly diverse society. Catholics interpret moral norms in terms of the human good; as Aquinas put it, moral precepts are derived from natural human inclinations.[10] The Catholic tradition has held that the basic moral norms governing human conduct are given, in the natural law, which can be grasped in its essentials by reasonable people. For this reason, we can make claims about the moral dimensions of the civic order that are both Catholic in their inspiration, motivation, and interpretation and at the same time humanistic in their articulation.

Appeals to the natural law and its functional equivalents need not entail that all reference to religion be excised from public arguments. In a truly pluralistic civic realm, there ought to be no reason for Catholic citizens to feel an urgent need to "cover their tracks," religiously speaking, in all public forums—as long as, that is, the positions we espouse on public matters can also be expressed in language that appeals to fellow citizens who accept the moral but not the particular religious reasons we have for making them.

Yet given the increased skepticism of our society over the last fifty years, or at least its increased alienation from institutional Christianity, we have to have modest expectations about the extent to which public references to explicitly religious language can be broadly persuasive.[11] Perhaps politicians who make vague and inoffensively general appeals to God, compassion, and integrity will still get a hearing from many Americans, including those who consider themselves "spiritual but not religious," but arguments made in the public square based on explicit references to the demands of Christian discipleship or obedience to the social encyclicals will be less successful.

J. Bryan Hehir rightly maintains that, while distinctively religious language is more appropriate for "shaping the mind of the Church" within the Catholic context, efforts to engage in broad societal debate concerning public policy is best carried out through the philosophical mode of discourse focusing on the implications of the natural law.[12] It is one thing to give religious witness to Christian beliefs in a pluralistic or even largely secular forum, another to invoke biblical images that evoke a latent humanistic agreement about appealing moral virtues or ideals in that forum, and yet still another to make sound and persuasive arguments over hotly contested issues about how to govern that forum.

Yet even our interpretation and application of basic human moral standards is, in many cases, unavoidably influenced by our Catholic identity. Catholic identity can be seen not only in these cases but over the entire range of moral standards concerning justice, courage, and temperance. Since the more encompassing religious perspective includes the moral sphere—i.e., since God wills human beings to flourish—our interpretation of the latter cannot help but be influenced by the former. This is why we should be surprised neither at a significant degree of overlap between Catholics and others on some moral issues (for example, on criteria for a just war), nor at widespread objection to what the Church considers to pertain to the natural law when it comes to others (e.g., on abortion).

THE ECCLESIAL BASIS OF CATHOLIC MORALITY

How, then, are lay people to be brought to the point of engaging in public theology? Sociologically speaking, there are many American Catholics whose attitudes toward civic matters show little resemblance to Catholic communitarian personalism. So we are faced with an important question, namely, how can Catholic communitarian personalism be made a more significant mark of Catholic engagement in civic life?

Lay people are more likely to reflect upon and engage in public life precisely as Catholics when they take their Catholicism seriously, that is, as a core and defining feature of who they are rather than as a sociological marker resulting from the sheer historically contingent accident that previous generations happened to be Irish or Italian or German, or, more recently, Latino. By "Catholic" in this sense I mean not the broad sense of all those baptized into the Church, but rather more exactly those who are active churchgoers, and especially those whose attendance is weekly (this probably means some-

thing between a quarter and a third of all those who are sociologically identified as Catholic).[13] A genuine Catholic presence in American public life
should be seen not primarily in the policy pronouncements of bishops and
cardinals but in the civic activity of the laity that has been generated by living
faith. This depends above all on vibrant parish life.

Practicing Catholics are exposed to the social dimensions of the gospel,
at least implicitly, through church attendance. Sociologist of religion Robin
Gill argues that church attendance correlates significantly not only with
higher belief but also with higher levels of adherence to the church's moral
code. Evidence suggests, for example, that the more regularly a Catholic
attends church, the less likely he or she is to cohabitate or to be married more
than once. One survey in Britain reporting that only 22 percent of regular
churchgoing Catholic teenagers believe that all nonmarital sex is wrong actually showed that Catholic teenagers are more conservative than their peers,
even if the majority do not accept the Church's moral rule.[14] Churchgoing,
then, does make a difference, but it is a relative rather than an absolute difference.

While the sociologists of knowledge correctly argue that churchgoers
tend to change as the general population changes, it is also the case that active
participation in a parish provides the best context for being socialized into a
religious and moral identity that is relatively distinctive rather than uncriti-
cally conforming to the general pattern of the wider culture. This is by no
means to deny that many Catholics, and even weekly churchgoing Catholics,
will conform to popular morality, but only to predict that, statistically speaking, they will be relatively more likely to embrace the teachings of the Church
than those who are not churchgoers. This applies, pari passu, to their appro-
priation of the Catholic social message as well.

On the sociological level, the Church contributes to civic culture in its
sponsorship of parishes as important mediating structures within the larger
network of social relations. Democracy benefits enormously from thriving
parishes, but also from their schools, their outreach programs, and the wide
array of affiliated organizations connected to them like the Knights of
Columbus, the St. Vincent de Paul Society, the Catholic Youth Organization
(CYO), etc.

But more important than their sociological value as intermediate associations, vital and creative parishes nurture the laity in a variety of ways, primarily by offering excellent liturgies, but also by providing an array of
opportunities to become more religiously and morally engaged within and
beyond the parish community. The academic discipline of Christian social
ethics tends to focus so strongly on policy debates or questions of personal

virtue that it tends to ignore the special significance of the parish setting for realizing its themes. Even theologians who advocate "narrative ethics" and "virtue ethics" tend to reflect in the abstract on a theoretically constructed, ideal Christian community populated by moral exemplars of perfect *agape*, not on concrete religious communities in which ordinary people, with all their ambiguities, actually misunderstand one another, struggle over power, and nurse resentments as well as engage in sincere worship, learn about their faith, and serve one another in love.

Maritain held that the transformation of the social order involves not only structural change but also, and concomitantly, "a rising of the forces of faith, of intelligence and of love springing from the interior depths of the soul, a progress in the discovery of the world of spiritual realities."[15] For most people, this "rising," if it takes place at all, happens through the agency of particular holy people and usually in the context of a believing community. The great themes, beliefs, and virtues of the gospel are appropriated first and most widely through personal contact, not through abstract reflection or intellectual argument. The significance of this personal contact is deepened through immersion in "the world of spiritual realities" through symbols, stories, and rituals, which in turn shape our imagination and moral sensibilities.

For Catholics, the Eucharist provides a symbol of the unity between God and humanity, but also of the deep unity of all members of the human family. By participating in the Eucharist, Catholics are encouraged to allow themselves to be formed within a community for social love. To the extent that we are formed by worship within this kind of community, we are imaginatively "primed" both to experience the moral claim of solidarity and to recognize the principle of the common good. Christians who allow themselves to be so formed will care about the common good and work in appropriate ways for its promotion in civic life. They will not be looking for ways to isolate themselves from the troubles and suffering of others or for excuses to escape responsibility for them.

Unfortunately neither the potential symbolic power of the Eucharist nor its social implications have been experienced by many Catholics who are alienated from the Church or who simply no longer attend services. Just as we might worry about people "bowling alone," we ought to also be concerned about Catholics engaged in "praying alone" as a "New Age" substitute for church membership. The decline in churchgoing among Catholics is a serious issue and one of its consequences will be the diminished impact of Catholicism on our civic life.

Perhaps, as Andrew Greeley suggests, "parishes may be stronger than ever."[16] Charles R. Morris concurs: "Fewer Catholics go to church, but parish life is far more vibrant, far more participative, than it ever was in the Church's glory days."[17] Yet, there are indications that many churchgoers do not experience very deeply the symbolic power of the Eucharist or its social implications. All too often "going to Mass" is regarded as a chore or duty, an inconvenience, or habitual routine undergone for the benefit of one's family members or to cover one's bets, as an act of nostalgia or a way of avoiding guilt. The impact of good homilies and prayerful worship is diminished by other factors, especially those presented by popular culture. Be this as it may, it is clear that we need an improvement of parish life, an infusion of energy and creativity into what is too often experienced, especially by young adults in their twenties and thirties, as a place where the problems and struggles of "ordinary people" are not always understood.

Outside of the sacramental, spiritual, and doctrinal context of parish life, the themes, norms, and ideals advocated by Roman Catholic social thought are all too liable to be misinterpreted and assimilated to the dominant mores of American popular culture. Many Catholics still accept John F. Kennedy's view that Catholicism is a matter of private faith having nothing to do with politics. Just as ordinary Catholics sometimes mistakenly take Jesus' injunction to "judge not, lest you be judged" to confirm their own unreflective moral relativism, so Catholic endorsement of the right to private property can be construed as absolute, freedom of religion confused with religious indifferentism, and freedom of conscience to imply the privatization of religion. Received outside the social anthropology and communitarian ethic embedded in its religious life, those who spontaneously reduce Christianity to ethics can easily assimilate Catholic human rights doctrine to the ideology of radical individualism.

So if the Church wants to enable people to overcome what *Gaudium et spes* described as "among the more serious errors of our time," namely, "the split between the faith which many profess and their daily lives,"[18] then parishes need to become more religiously effective centers of worship, knowledge, and love. This is not to deny that some individual parishes function effectively now—only to face honestly the problem that there are also many that do not. To do this they must become places where parishioners are encouraged and trained to take active responsibility for their own spiritual lives and where they see that, in virtue of baptism and confirmation, every Christian is called to a life of discipleship and ongoing spiritual formation.

The top-down flow of official social teachings provides an important intellectual resource for Catholic social analysis and action, but it must be supported by the grassroots, or bottom-up, work done on the parish level. Parishes must be communities where gifted lay people are encouraged to become involved in various forms of ministry and even to exercise major kinds of leadership within the parish itself. This is not to invoke lay involvement as a second-class remedy for the decline in clerical vocations, but rather to apply on the parish level the principles outlined in the Decree on the Lay Apostolate from the Second Vatican Council. We are increasingly recognizing that in some cases this growth leads Christians to devote the charisms bestowed on them by the Holy Spirit[19] to serve the Church through specific forms of nonordained ministry. These engage the laity more deeply in faith as well as charity and therefore, in different but complementary ways, concretely instantiate the social message of the Church. Social justice ministry, religious education, and social outreach all offer special avenues for the dissemination of Catholic social teachings, but no one program should specialize as the "social conscience" of the parish. The Catholic social message should function as a dimension of all parish activities, just as justice is a constitutive dimension of life in the Church.

FOCUSED LEADERSHIP
FOR SOCIAL JUSTICE

Some parishes have excellent liturgies and engaging ministerial programs but give little attention to communicating the social teachings of the Church. This is possible because the social message is a profound but implicit dimension of the Eucharist that can be ignored or minimized. Moral silence can be the mistaken result of an exaggerated attempt not to confuse religion with politics, or of a desire on the part of clergy to stay politically neutral and above partisanship, or of assuming that bishops and the pope communicate the social message of the Church well enough. More scandalous is the extent to which frequent churchgoers in highly Catholic places like Chicago, Boston, San Francisco, and elsewhere continue to hold racist attitudes and exhibit callous indifference to welfare recipients and immigrants. Sincere piety ought to, but does not always, in and of itself, lessen the grip of a vice on one's character—as Newman observed, "Integrity on one side of our character is no voucher for integrity on the other side."[20] So neither spirituality nor worship automatically eradicates racial prejudice and other forms of bigotry, or the fear and ignorance that normally underlie them. Parishioners may believe abstractly in the duty to provide affordable housing for homeless people, but not in their particular neighborhood; in recognizing the human dignity of gay people, but not in their parish school; in racial integration, but not on their block. There is a difference between vaguely supporting a benevolent social vision, viewed from a comfortable distance, and taking concrete steps, even at some personal cost, to approximate that vision in one's own community. This flaw continues to characterize affluent middle-class suburban parishes now as much as it did when parishes in this country were self-contained urban ethnic enclaves of immigrant Catholics.

Experience indicates, then, that churchgoing is a necessary but not sufficient condition for the development for a Catholic social conscience. Pastors, lay ministers, and religious educators must therefore exert more leadership in articulating the social implications of the Catholic faith to their parishes. Parishes, in other words, must not only nourish the religious vision and the spiritual way of life that gives rise to the social conscience of the Church, but also take deliberate steps to educate the laity on matters of public theology and Catholic social teachings. And this agenda, of course, is only made possible when people studying for ministry in seminaries and universities are thoroughly educated in Catholic social thought as well.

CONCLUSION

To what extent can we Americans come to substantive moral consensus in the absence of agreement on deeper religious matters? The jury is out on this question, and may be for some time. Catholics will continue to maintain that we can build a public consensus about the moral dimensions of civil society, one that matches our political consensus on the value of constitutional democracy. As we grow increasingly diverse as a society, such public moral consensus may prove more elusive to attain than might have been predicted by our natural law forebears fifty years ago. Theologian Joseph Komonchak believes that we face "loss of a common belief that a public consensus on anything more substantial than democratic procedures is either possible or desirable." Indeed, the main challenge presented to Catholic social thought in the contemporary American context lies in the "widespread belief that no ethical, much less religious, beliefs or values are more than the products of personal choice."[21]

The Catholic presence in American public life ought to be exercised on a variety of levels to counteract this dangerous tendency. Bishops ought to continue to strive to shape a broad consensus on the moral dimensions of public policy, theologians ought to address broad public audiences, Catholic schools ought to continue to teach the need for ethical principles in politics and society, and Catholic lay people ought to be encouraged to be active in public life in order to infuse it with a humane ethic. Rather than resolving the objections raised by the ideology of privatization only by means of developing a coherent theory of religion in public life, perhaps American Catholics can best make their case by showing in concrete cases that it is in fact practically possible to build such a consensus. That such a consensus can be difficult to obtain in a pluralistic context is evidenced by the obstacles presented to those who would build a "common ground" within the Catholic community itself. In this country the terms for the debate over a huge range of issues, ranging from business and the professions, to sex, marriage, and the family, has been set by radical individualism. Perhaps Catholic employment of the language of human good, community, and responsibility for others can modify the terms of this debate. On a deeper level, perhaps the basic faith that we can obtain such a public consensus and move beyond radical individualism is itself an important expression of American Catholicism. If so, its practice is surely one important contribution we can make to American civic life.

This challenge is complemented by one already mentioned above, namely that of building consensus within the Catholic community itself. This goal is promoted first and foremost not by convening panels of bishops and theologians but by building strong parishes that not only offer excellent liturgies and religious education but also sponsor mature religious conversation among parishioners. If dialogue and consensus building have a chance in our society, one would think they would most likely be found in communities explicitly devoted to faith, hope, and charity. Dialogue will sometimes lead to mutual agreement and, at other times, seek simply to clarify unresolved differences. Within the context of mutual respect such dialogue will lead to greater understanding between interlocutors, stronger bonds within parish communities, and even deeper identification with the universal Church. Local ecclesial engagement, then, might provide a venue for cultivating the kinds of practices and habits of mind that we would like to see involved in Catholic civic engagement in the wider public arena as well.

NOTES

1. John T. Noonan Jr., "Development in Moral Doctrine," in *The Context of Casuistry*, eds. James M. Keenan, S.J., and Thomas A. Shannon (Washington, D.C.: Georgetown University Press, 1995), 194.

2. Michael J. Himes and Kenneth R. Himes, O.F.M., *Fullness of Faith: The Public Significance of Theology* (New York: Paulist Press, 1993), 46.

3. John A. Ryan, *The Living Wage* (New York: Macmillan, 1920); John Courtney Murray, S.J., *We Hold These Truths: Catholic Reflections on the American Proposition* (New York: Sheed and Ward, 1960), 67; Jacques Maritain, *The Person and the Common Good and Man and the State* (Chicago: University of Chicago, 1951).

4. Charles Taylor, *Sources of the Self: The Making of Modern Identity* (Cambridge, Mass.: Harvard University Press, 1989); Robert Bellah et al, *Habits of the Heart: Individualism and Commitment in American Public Life* (Berkeley: University of California Press, 1985); Vaclav Havel, *Open Letters, Selected Writings 1965–1990* (New York: Random House, 1992), especially "The Power of the Powerless," 125–214. See, Pope John Paul II, inter alia, *Sollicitudo rei socialis*, nos. 27–29; *Centesimus annus*, no. 36.

5. As explained by Pius XI in *Quadagesimo anno*, no. 79, the principle of subsidiarity recognizes that "it is a disturbance of right order to assign to a greater and higher association what lesser and subordinate organizations can do. For every social activity ought of its very nature to furnish help to the members of the body social, and never destroy and absorb them." In *The Church and the Reconstruction of the Modern World: The Social Encyclicals of Pope Pius XI,* ed. Terence P. McLaughlin, C.S.B., (Garden City, N.Y.: Doubleday, 1957), 247. See Joseph A. Komonchak, "Subsidiary in the Church: The State of the Question," *The Jurist* 48 (1988), 301–302.

6. National Conference of Catholic Bishops, *Economic Justice for All*, 23.

7. See Charles Taylor, "Atomism," in *Power, Possessions, and Freedom: Essays in Honor of C. B. McPherson*, ed., Alkis Kontos, (Toronto: University of Toronto Press, 1969).

8. Maritain, *Integral Humanism*, 203.

9. Michael J. Himes and Kenneth R. Himes, O.F.M., *Fullness of Faith.*

10. See Thomas Aquinas, *Summa theologiae*, I–II, q. 94, a. 2.

11. Robin Gill, *Churchgoing and Christian Ethics* (New York: Cambridge University Press, 1999), ch. 3.

12. J. Bryan Hehir, "The Perennial Need for Philosophic Discourse," *Theological Studies* 40 (1979): 710.

13. Charles R. Morris, *American Catholic: The Saints and Sinners Who Built America's Most Powerful Church* (New York: Random House, 1997), 307. Sociologists, of course, debate the frequency of churchgoing among American Catholics. Some arguing that only about 28 percent of Catholics regularly attend weekly services (as contrasted with 80 percent forty years ago), while others, like Gallup, maintain a higher figure of about 40 percent. Standard sources are the University of Chicago's National Opinion Research Center <www.norc.uchicago.edu> and the George Gallup Organization <www.gallup.com/index.html>. The University of Michigan's "National Election Studies" <www.umich.edu/~nes/> provides important information on the influence of religious affiliation on political behavior.

14. Robin Gill, *Churchgoing and Christian Ethics*, 53, 59, 172, 200, 203.

15. Maritain, *Integral Humanism*, 89.

16. Cited in Morris, *American Catholics*, 301.

17. Morris, *American Catholics*, 293–294.

18. *Gaudium et spes*, no. 43.

19. See *Lumen gentium*, no. 3.

20. John Henry Newman, "Secret Faults," in *Sermons and Discourses*, ed. Charles Frederick Harrod, (New York: Longmans, Green, 1949), 5,1825–39.

21. Joseph Komonchak, "The Encounter between Catholicism and Liberalism," in *Catholicism and Liberalism*, eds. Bruce Douglass and David Hollenbach, 94.

CONTENDING WITH LIBERALISM

William A. Galston

In his letter of invitation to this conference, Peter Steinfels formulated his charge to me in the following terms:

> While American Catholics have obviously worked out practical compromises with liberal pluralism, even in practice, and more so in theory, it is unclear whether Catholic social thought uses a moral vocabulary and indeed assumes a whole mindset alien to most Americans, including many Catholic Americans. . . . Catholic social teaching seems to offer a comprehensive idea of the good and put forth a vision of a harmonious social and political order. Liberalism eschews such comprehensive visions, is agnostic about the nature of the good, and accepts conflict and competition as more or less permanent, often productive features of society. . . . [We would like you to] assess where and to what extent the Catholic tradition tends to mesh or clash with the various conceptions of liberal pluralism—where you think there might be fruitful engagement—or where you think certain aspects of one tradition or the other are simply going to have to give way.

Let me begin by acknowledging what will soon become painfully apparent—my scanty knowledge of Catholic social thought, much of it acquired in a rush during the past few weeks (although I will admit to devouring the writings of John Ryan two decades ago). The topic is complicated by the fact that the terms *Catholic social thought* and *liberalism* each name a family of positions rather than a single stance, and these family differences become especially significant as proponents move from abstract philosophical principles to concrete public prescriptions.

In the nineteenth century, Catholic social thinkers ranged from outright reactionaries to genuine radicals, with shades of moderate and liberal reformers in between. Today, Catholic thinkers espouse diverse views on subjects such as the merits of capitalist markets and the limits of state intervention. The editor of a recent collection of essays celebrating a century of Catholic social thought acknowledges that

> The authors in this volume represent a decided tilt or bias toward Catholic progressivism, the Catholic left, and solidarity movements for justice in the church. We do not shirk from this choice. Others can celebrate the tradition in their own way.[1]

It is my impression that modern Catholic thinkers are sensitive to this distinction between principle and prescription, and to its implications for both thought and practice. Bryan Hehir asks,

> What authority should be attributed to teaching [i.e., legislative-policy advocacy] which is a mix of principles and policy choices? The [less activist, educational-cultural model of church activism] fears that this mix will mortgage the moral authority of the church. . . . The appropriate response is to distinguish levels of teaching and to espouse a procedural principle for teaching, that is, increasing empirical specificity means declining moral authority.[2]

More generally, a distinction is acknowledged between the church's universal moral principles, which bind in conscience, and its prudential policy choices, which require serious attention from Catholics but do not so bind.[3] Based on my readings, however, it appears that there is a great deal of unity on the plane of moral principle among Catholic social thinkers who disagree vehemently in their political and policy stances.

Matters are even more complicated within the family of liberal thinkers, who disagree both in practice and in principle. The practical differences over issues such as state intervention in the economy, the extent of permissible income redistribution, and the organization of educational systems are well known. Less well known, but equally significant for our purposes, are the increasingly intense theoretical debates among liberals over questions such as the following:

Is liberalism based (or can it be based) on a "comprehensive" religious, metaphysical, or moral doctrine, or must it be decoupled from such commitments?

If liberalism is seen as freestanding, are its principles known through intuition, or do they rest on an assumed consensus gentium which may be local rather than universal?

Is liberalism truly neutral with regard to substantive theories of the good, or does it necessarily presuppose some views of the good and rule out others?

Does liberal civic life accommodate, or rather rule out, public discourse and decisions based on comprehensive religious and metaphysical views?

Is there an authoritative liberal account of the human person, and, if so, does it offer an adequate account of moral motivation?

Can liberal society be theorized on the basis of individual self-interest, or is it necessary to introduce some moral principles that go beyond (and may contradict) self-interest?

May the liberal state intervene to promote a substantive vision of human development, or must it respect individual liberty except when its exercise jeopardizes the rights and interests of other individuals?

To what extent does the maintenance of liberal civic order and unity take priority over claims based on religious conscience, individual liberty, or the rights of parents?

Within the liberal tradition, each of these questions admits of a range of answers. The way in which a particular species of liberalism responds will determine the extent to which it is compatible with Catholic social thought. For example, forms of liberalism that in principle exclude religious discourse from the sphere of public deliberation are at odds with the basic public role of the modern Church. Similarly, it is impossible to reconcile Catholic social thought with the contention of "civic liberals" that in cases of conflict, the claims of individual conscience and religious free exercise must regularly yield to the requirements of citizenship and public order. But other variants of liberalism invoke substantive conceptions of the human good and see rights and duties, liberties and responsibilities, as intrinsically related and recipro- cally limiting. The gap between these liberalisms and Catholic doctrine is far narrower.

Moreover, some of the classic Catholic critiques of liberalism rest on easily dispelled misunderstandings. For example, we learn from *Pacem in ter- ris* (78) that Catholic thought must reject any theory that grounds civic rights and duties, the binding force of the Constitution, or the government's legiti- mate authority, in the individual or collective will of human beings. But most liberal thinkers would likewise reject such theories. Anyone who believes, as did the authors of the Declaration of Independence, that individual rights are prior to government and that their protection is the central purpose of public life would resist grounding rights in human will.

Even those liberals who employ versions of social contract theory see consent as conferring legitimacy on governments and constitutions only when the circumstances of consent comport with moral requirements that force of which cannot be reduced to individual or collective will. For example, when the best-known contemporary liberal thinker, John Rawls, develops "justice as fairness," he insists that our choices lack public legitimizing force unless they occur within circumstances that reflect certain substantive moral views.

Finally, modern Catholic thought makes generous room for the principle of public consent. As John XXIII states,

> It must not be concluded . . . because authority comes from God, that therefore men have no right to choose those who are to rule the state, to decide the form of government, and to determine both the way authority is to be exercised and its limits. It is thus clear that the doctrine which we have set forth can be fully consonant with any truly democratic regime. (*Pacem in terris*, 52)

I do not see how this teaching is fundamentally at odds with the underlying theory of liberal constitutionalism, that governments derive their just powers from the consent of the governed but that the permissible substance of that consent is delimited by the basic purpose of public institutions—the protection of individual rights and the promotion of the general welfare.

This convergence with liberal thought is strengthened by the manner in which modern Catholic doctrine coordinates individual rights and the common good:

> In our time the common good is chiefly guaranteed when personal rights and duties are maintained. The chief concern of civil authorities must therefore be to ensure that these rights are acknowledged, respected, coordinate with other rights, defended and promoted, so that in this way each one may more easily carry out his duties. (*Pacem in terris*, 60)

A final introductory remark concerns the ambiguity of the "liberal pluralism" with which Catholic social thought may stand in tension. At one level of analysis, this phrase can refer to a specific moral understanding, associated with the late Isaiah Berlin among others, according to which genuine goods and values are multiple, heterogeneous, mutually irreducible, non-hierarchically ordered, and (often) inharmonious. The wide range of choice-worthy and valuable human lives reflects the myriad ways in which human beings can choose among, combine, and balance these goods and values. For some liberals (and I count myself among them) this moral understanding offers the most persuasive justification for the basic tenets of liberal social philosophers. But other liberals disagree, either because they prefer some other foundation or because they reject the architectural metaphor entirely and view liberal social thought as freestanding.

It seems likely that Catholic social thought is incompatible with the philosophical account of moral/value pluralism, and therefore with any account of liberalism that takes philosophical pluralism as foundational. To the extent that Catholicism continues to embrace a natural law vision of the universe as cosmos or rational order, it seems committed to ultimate harmony among values and must reject any account of fundamental goods in conflict. And to the extent that Catholic morality takes its bearings from the imperatives of *imitatio dei*, it must subscribe to a theological version of a hierarchy of values, with Jesus' virtues at the apex.

At the other end of the spectrum is liberal pluralism understood in the manner of neo-Madisonian political science, as the division of society into conflicting and self-interested groups. Catholic social thought can certainly begin by acknowledging the fact of interest-group pluralism, but it cannot end there, for two reasons. First, Catholic social thought seems committed to the ideal of social harmony, and to the belief that the legitimate claims of each group can be brought together into a coherent and consistent whole. From this perspective, the clash of social interests is a sign that they have exceeded morally appropriate bounds. Second, Catholic social thought cannot remain satisfied with any account that reduces human motivation to self-interest. A sense of care for others and for the common good is within the moral powers of every human being and every citizen, and is therefore a basic demand of social morality. From this perspective, interest-group pluralism poses the problem, and Catholicism the solution.

There is a third sense of "liberal pluralism" with which Catholic social thought appears entirely compatible. I have in mind the theory, first developed by British thinkers such as Figgis, Barker, and Laski, that social life occurs in a number of associational venues, no one of which enjoys full authority over others. In particular, associations such as faith communities and families are not the creatures of political institutions and not wholly subject to their authority. This theory, which stands opposed to both Aristotelianism and French civic republicanism, leaves space for liberal freedoms of religious conscience and association as well as the distinction between public and private concernments. It is also compatible with Catholic teachings (as I understand them) concerning such matters as the independence of the Church and the authority of parents.

Finally, we reach the version of pluralism that seems most important for contemporary liberal theory and society—namely, deep and enduring differences among competing understandings of what gives meaning and purpose to human life. Many believe that liberalism as a social and political philosophy originated in the post-Reformation wars of religion. Viewed in this light, liberalism represented the effort to reconfigure the relationship between politics and religion such that a multiplicity of faiths could coexist within the same social space. This effort did not presuppose skepticism about religious truth-claims, let alone the relativist thesis that every faith tradition is equally true (or false). It flowed, rather, from the proposition that the human and moral costs of enforcing a single faith (even the True Faith) through coercive state power were prohibitive. More recently, liberal thought has generalized this argument for religious freedom and tolerance to include a wide (though not unlimited) range of differences among non-religious conceptions of the good life.

It goes without saying that liberal public orders cannot reasonably require Catholic social thought to relativize its theological and philosophical understanding of the human good. (Indeed, no individual or group can be required to do so, though some may try.) Nor, most liberals believe, must the bearers—individual or institutional—of Catholic social teachings confine their beliefs to the community of the faithful. The Church, leaders and laity alike, are free to bear witness in and to the larger society and when necessary articulate a critique of that society from the standpoint of "faithful citizenship." What liberalism requires, rather, is that the Church adopt a stance of severe and principled self-restraint in the face of the temptation to impose its beliefs on others through state coercion. As we will see, it is this requirement, the moral bedrock of liberal politics, that most squarely raises the specter of a clash between liberal principles and Catholic social thought.

SUMMARY OF A PROVISIONAL RESPONSE

With these considerations as backdrop, I can sketch my provisional response to Peter Steinfels's challenge as follows:

From the early stirrings of liberalism in the eighteenth century through the mid–twentieth century, the opposition between official institutional Catholicism and liberalism was stark. The clash between natural law-based organicist monism and individualistic pluralism was at the heart of this historic opposition. As David O'Brien puts it,

> The problem of *Quadregesimo Anno* . . . was that its proposed Christian social order would be difficult, perhaps impossible, to implement in a pluralistic society. How could differing interest groups be persuaded to subordinate group interests to the general welfare? More important, who would define the specific requirements of the common good? The church had always regarded the democratic answer of negotiation and compromise as incompatible with natural law. . . . Refusing to acknowledge the legitimacy of pluralism, [the popes prior to Vatican II] could hardly understand the necessarily messy, ambiguous ways of democratic politics.[4]

Since then, the gap between Catholicism and liberalism has narrowed significantly. Much of the movement has occurred on the Catholic side. For the purposes of this chapter, I will take it as given that mainstream Catholicism has made its peace with constitutional democracy, rights of religious conscience, and individual liberties generally. Indeed, this reconciliation is now expressed in the language of principle rather than of regrettable necessity or modus vivendi. To quote O'Brien once more:

> [John XXIII's] list of human rights included both the social and economic rights developed in the social encyclicals and the political and civil rights, including the right to religious liberty, about which the popes had long seemed more doubtful. Because they drew heavily on neo-scholastic philosophical categories, John's encyclicals recalled those of Leo XIII, but now these affirmations of human dignity and human rights were placed in a democratic context: individuals and states had the obligation to share responsibility for constructing institutions in which these rights could be protected. . . . With the changes of the Second Vatican Council, especially the Declaration on Religious Liberty, Catholics could explore the requirements of citizenship (as done, for example, by John Courtney Murray and, more recently, by the United States Bishops) without the inhibitions the older church even at its best had imposed.[5]

Two of the most important reconciliations with liberalism have come in the areas of freedom of expression and religious pluralism. Regarding freedom of expression, the *New Dictionary of Catholic Social Thought* observes that

> In *Pacem in terris* John XXIII abandoned the earlier papal emphasis on censorship and recognized a person's moral right to freedom in expressing and com-

municating his feelings. Though a person may think and speak incorrectly, the pope insisted that a distinction be made between error and the person who errs. Thus, errors must be rejected, but people in error must be allowed to speak so that they might break through their mistakes and make available to everyone occasions for the discovery of truth.[6]

Even more significant is the shift in the sphere of religious pluralism, which implies a fundamental shift in the relationship between the Church and public authority. Hehir notes that

> In the nineteenth century church-state controversies (Gregory XVI to Leo XIII), religious pluralism was an exception to be tolerated when it could not be overcome. . . . In the teaching of Vatican II religious pluralism was . . . the accepted setting in which the church pursued its ministry in freedom, dependent only on its own resources and the quality of its witness.[7]

In our time, accordingly, the freedom of the Church is understood as requiring not a favored, publicly authorized position in society but only the protected ability to be socially engaged.[8] This new understanding of the role of the Church in a pluralistic society is laid out most lucidly in *Gaudium et spes*:

There is a clear distinction between the Church and the political community. The Church's core activities rest on the power of God rather than of the civil authorities. While the Church makes use of "things of time," it is a sign and safeguard of the transcendence of the human person. While the political community and the Church are mutually independent and self-governing, each works in its own way for the good of the person. The service of both church and state works better if there is mutual cooperation. At the least, earthly powers must not impede the liberty of the Church to carry out its distinctive mission—to preach the faith, teach the social doctrine, discharge its human duties, and pass moral judgment on politics as well as social questions when necessary.[9]

Despite these manifold engagements with pluralism, some continue to wonder whether modern Catholic doctrine is yet adequate to the new social reality that it is encountering. John Colemen puts it this way: "Catholic social thought too easily assumes the possibility of social harmony. . . . [It] has not really faced the full reality of pluralism, especially the political implications of living in societies with especially deeply diverging views on fundamental social values."[10]

At first glance, this suggestion is perplexing, at least to an outsider. As we have already seen, the modern Church has abandoned all theocratic claims, acknowledged a separation between church and state authority, recognized the fact of religious pluralism, and endorsed the principles of freedom of expression and freedom of conscience. This would seem to be enough to allow the Church to coexist stably with modern societies containing deep differences on social values. (Of course, the Church claims the authority to declare a unity of fundamental principles binding on the conscience of all its members, but that is not directly a question bearing on public order.)

Nonetheless, there do seem to be enduring tendencies that tug against the principled opening to modern social pluralism. As Hehir points out, in contradistinction to liberal political philosophy, "Catholic teaching holds that society and the state are organic developments rooted in the nature of the person. This premise inclines Catholic teaching to accord a broad role to the state, particularly in pursuit of moral and religious values."[11]

It is not hard to see how this self-confident organicism might spill over into stances that non-Catholics (or even Catholic dissenters) could rightly view as the oppressive use of state power. At the highest religious or metaphysical level, the lingering influence of Thomism may bolster this organicism by leading Catholic thought to give too much weight to the idea of universal rational order at the expense of divine grace and inscrutability as supervening on rational knowledge, and of human sinfulness as a disruption of God's order.

Even if the concept of a singular divine order is maintained, pluralism enters through the range of possible interpretations of that concept—differing theological orientations that develop around a range of theological metaphors. In the Catholic tradition, God has been variously understood as the good shepherd, as the intelligent designer, as an historical journeyer with humanity, or as social liberator. Each of these images finds warrant in canonical texts and human experience; each leads to a distinctive understanding of the person, society, and social action.[12] One may wonder whether the Church fully acknowledges the force of this internal pluralization, which can lead to a wide range of practical stances and prescriptions.

Even if one denies the force of these pluralizing tendencies in the name of an ensemble of knowable and authoritative social truths, individuals and groups are likely to stand in differing relations to those truths. Even if the public order has the right to encourage knowledge of social truth, it does not always, or usually, have the right to repress falsehood. (That is presumably the point of John XXIII's distinction between error and the person who errs.)

There is, however, another crucial distinction, between maintaining error and acting on error. As I understand it, the Church believes that it is not wrong for the state to repress the erroneous action, even when the nature or fact of the error is socially disputed—that is, even when the Church's moral position is not universally accepted. To take a familiar example: while the members of a political community may agree that all persons are entitled to certain enforceable protections, they may disagree about the nature of personhood. The Church teaches that fetuses are persons; others have different views. If the Church were able to persuade a solid majority of American citizens of its position, it might be able to reverse the nation's current constitutional-legal stance and use the power of the state to outlaw abortion. Presumably the Church would feel no qualms about so acting. But those who take their bearings from the fact of deep moral disagreements in society might well have a principled hesitation about taking this step.

On the other hand, sophisticated contemporary liberal theorists (John Rawls is the leading example) distinguish between "reasonable" and "unreasonable" pluralism. State authority may not deploy its coercive power against reasonable positions, because it is possible for the proponents of all such positions to reach rational agreement on the fundamental principles of social order; not so for the unreasonable. Within its own teaching, it would seem that the Church has the right to make the same distinction and to act accordingly. The debate would then turn to competing conceptions of the morally reasonable. One may doubt that there is a neutral position from which to conduct this debate.

CATHOLIC SOCIAL THOUGHT AND LIBERAL THEORY

It may prove useful, in conclusion, to conduct a more systematic comparison between the basic tenets of Catholic social thought and those of liberal theory. As a point of reference, I will use the nine-point account of Catholic social teachings in the *Encyclopedia of Catholicism*.[13] This section of my paper will set forth each point and offer a commentary from a liberal-theoretical perspective.

Point 1: "The foundational concept of the social teachings is the sacredness or dignity of the human person."

Commentary: Many contemporary liberals take human dignity as their point of departure. Some ground that dignity theologically (human beings made God's image). Others proceed in a Kantian manner: our dignity is rooted in our liberty, which is a "fact of reason." Still others ground human dignity in moral intuition, or in a consensus gentium.

The liberal account of dignity diverges from Catholicism in a number of key respects. First, while liberal dignity is compatible with a divine foundation, it does not require it. Second, liberals are inclined to interpret dignity as moral freedom, with few restraints placed on the use of that freedom other than respecting the like freedom of all other individuals. For example, many liberals contend that under suitable circumstances, suicide is consistent with respect for human dignity. Third, liberalism embraces a range of views on the nature of human personhood, some of which include, while others exclude, beings whom Catholics place in the category of persons.

Point 2: "Catholic social teachings draw a direct line from human dignity to human rights and duties. Human rights are moral claims to goods of the spiritual and material order that are necessary to protect and promote human dignity. Duties are responsibilities that flow from the person's status as a creature (duties toward God) and from the social bonds one has in the human community (duties toward others)."

Commentary: Many liberals would accept the Catholic account of rights as encompassing affirmative claims as well as negative protections. It is not clear on its face precisely which spiritual and material goods are required to promote human dignity, but liberals need not disagree with Catholic social thought on the particulars, many of which (e.g., those enumerated in *Pacem in terris* 11–27) liberal thinkers would regard as both familiar and acceptable. Moreover, liberals agree that rights and duties are correlative, that it is logically impossible to claim a right without simultaneously asserting others' duty to respect that right. While all liberals acknowledge social duties, some deny that the person must be understood as a creature and therefore do not acknowledge duties toward God.

Point 3: "A central dimensions of Catholic social philosophy is its stress on the social nature of the person. Society and state are natural extensions of the social nature of the person."

Commentary: Liberals need not, and most do not, deny the social dimension of personhood. No one can reasonably doubt that normal human development requires social bonds, or that many important human goods can only be realized in and through society. At the same time, there is an important ambiguity in the idea of state and society as natural extensions of the person. Society is—as Aristotle himself suggested—a combination of natural inclination (or need) and human artifice (or choice). Not all social and political forms are equally hospitable to the development of the human person. From a teleological standpoint, some forms are more "natural" than others are.

Point 4: "The state-society distinction is a complement to the distinction of the common good and public order. The common good . . . is the complex of spiritual, temporal, and material conditions needed in society if each person is to have the opportunity to develop his or her human potential. . . . The public order is that part of the common good that properly belongs to the state. It is constituted by the goods of public peace, public morality, and the enforcement of basic standards of justice. . . . The effect of distinguishing the terms common good and public order is to limit the role of the state."

Commentary: Liberals are often thought to deny the existence of the common good. And this is true, to the extent that the common good is understood as distinct from and even opposing the good of individuals. Notably, the Catholic view does not do this. Catholic social thought defines the common good as the social space within which each individuals can realize his or her own good. It is a complex empirical-sociological question whether such a social space is possible—that is, whether the conditions for the development of each individual can be harmonized in practice with the conditions of all others. (Catholics may well be more inclined to assume the possibility of harmony than are most liberals.)

Moreover, liberal theory is entirely comfortable with the state/society distinction and with the thesis that important human goods are found within voluntary associations independent of the state. Far from being alien to liberal theory, the assertion of inherent limits to the legitimate role of the state is widely regarded as one of liberalism's defining features. (The location of the boundary between state and society, or between the public and the voluntary, has always been contested and remains so today.)

Point 5: "The state-society relationship is evaluated in Catholic thought by the principle of subsidiarity and the concept of socialization. Subsidiarity . . . seeks to preserve as much freedom in society as possible, by contending that responsibility for addressing social questions should begin with the local or smallest institutional authority and be referred to the state only when it becomes clear that other institutions cannot fulfill the need. . . . The state has positive moral responsibilities and is the ultimate guarantor of the rights of the person in society. . . . Socialization is the product of increasing complexity in society, generated by the growing involvement of the state in the socioeconomic order. [Pope John XXIII] saw this enhanced role of the state as a method of satisfying human rights."

Commentary: This point marks a difference, at least of emphasis, between Catholic and liberal thought. Not all liberals accept the principle of subsidiarity; some believe that to promote a wide range of overarching public purposes, the central state is justified in overriding the authority of families, voluntary associations, and local public authorities. Not all believe that the maximization of social freedom is the single dominant value that should determination social organization. Nor do all liberals accept the concept of socialization; some argue, conversely, that increases in economic and social complexity have outrun the ability of state mechanisms to govern these processes knowledgeably and efficiently. For them, the logical implication of complexity is the reduction of the state's role in favor of markets and voluntary associations.

Point 6: "In the social space beyond the control of the state in society, Catholic teaching locates the role of intermediate associations, often called voluntary associations in Western society. These groups come together by the choice of citizens; while not under the auspices or control of the state, they exist for public purposes."

Commentary: Since at least de Tocqueville's time, intermediate associations ("civil society") have been a leitmotif of liberal social thought. After a period of eclipse in the mid–twentieth century, neo-Tocquevilleanism surged and now stands at the center of liberal social inquiry.

The extent to which intermediate associations are beyond the control of the state is contested, however. Some liberals are more inclined to empower the state to enforce general public norms within such associations, with controversial consequences. For example, some public authorities have demanded the right to enforce principles of non-discrimination against associations that exclude women, while others would deny organizations such as the Boy Scouts the right to exclude individuals on the basis of sexual orientation. The legal and constitutions resolution of these disputes frequently revolves around the question of whether particular associations should be regarded as carrying out public purposes in a manner that bring them within the purview of legitimate state regulation.

Point 7: "Permeating the entire structure of Catholic social teachings is their theory of justice. . . . The theory of justice distinguishes commutative, distributive, and social justice, with the latter category providing the dominant framework for the social teaching."

Commentary: Modern liberalism focuses on theories of justice as well, with a noticeable shift from commutative to distributive questions in recent decades. If it is correct to understand social justice as the fair and equal opportunity to participate in public institutions and social processes that promote a good society, then liberalism embraces social justice as well.

It is important, however, to distinguish between the concept of justice and specific conceptions. Liberals are not in agreement among themselves, either about the appropriate methods for arriving at a determinate conception of justice or about the substantive content of that conception. Some liberals espouse views that overlap with Catholicism's social democratic emphasis, while others move in a more "neo-liberal" direction.

Point 8: "A post-conciliar addition to the social teaching is the 'option for the poor.' . . . The phrase . . . conveys the idea that special attention to the needs of the poor is a moral obligation for individuals, for the Church, and for society as a whole."

Commentary: Some contemporary liberals advance principles that overlap with this Catholic obligation. According to John Rawls, for example, justice demands that generally valuable goods and opportunities be distributed in a manner that maximizes the well-being of the worst-off groups in society. Other liberals have criticized this view, either because it imposes excessive burdens on all other groups, or because it exacts too great a toll on economic growth and individual liberty, or because it ignores the ways in which some of the poor contribute to their own plight.

Point 9: "John Paul II uses the concept of solidarity as a central theme in his social teaching. . . . [He] sees solidarity as analogous to charity; it assumes in his teaching the status of virtue. The principal role solidarity has is to direct the dynamic of interdependence, which is reshaping the socioeconomic life and societies and the international community. In a world of increasing interdependence, a vision of solidarity is needed as the foundation for just relationships."

Commentary: There is a direct analogue in liberal thought to the concept of solidarity—namely, the characteristic liberal tendency toward moral universality that transcends particular attachments and identities. From this universalistic standpoint, it is unreasonable and wrong not to care about the suffering of some fellow human beings, just because they happen not to be members of one's family, tribe, ethnic group, or political community. Liberals disagree among themselves concerning the morally acceptable balance between particular attachments and universal concerns. But all are inclined to attach moral weight to the idea of a common humanity. It was liberals, after all, who took the lead in developing a conception of universal human rights, of the right and duty of the world community to enforce these rights against sovereign states that systematically violate them.

CONCLUSION

If the analysis presented in this paper is even roughly accurate, then one must conclude that the gap between Catholic social thought and liberal theory is much narrower than it was in the mid–nineteenth century, or even in the mid-twentieth. On the one hand, Catholicism has made its peace with constitutional democracy, individual rights, freedom of religious conscience, and the separation of church and state. On the other hand, liberals are less inclined than they once were to emphasize self-interest at the expense of moral motivation, negative liberty at the expense of social justice, or rights to the exclusion of natural duties. Liberals are happy to reject "atomism" in favor of the social embeddedness of individuals—that is, as long as the social nature of personhood is not employed to deprive individuals of personal and political liberties.

Important differences remain, however. Some liberals embrace skepticism or relativism about the human good; some downplay the moral role of the state or seek to exclude faith-based arguments from public discourse; some emphasize the civic prerogatives of the state at the expense of family and associational autonomy. Clearly Catholics must reject these versions of liberalism. Liberals for their part must resist the Catholic use of controversial theses in theology and natural law as the basis of coercive state policy. It is one thing for Catholics reasoning within the premises of their community to reach conclusions about abortion, assisted suicide, and homosexuality that are held to be binding on the faithful; quite another to impose those views on others. Catholics may be affronted by a legal code that permits acts they view as abominable. But in circumstances of deep moral diversity, the alternatives to enduring these affronts may be even worse.

NOTES

1. John A. Coleman, "Introduction: A Tradition Celebrated, Reevaluated, and Applied." in Coleman, ed., *One Hundred Years of Catholic Social Thought* (Maryknoll, N.Y.: Orbis Books, 1991), 5.

2. J. Bryan Hehir, "The Right and Competence of the Church in the American Case," in Coleman, *One Hundred Years,* 68.

3. "Modern Catholic Social Thought," in Judith A. Dwyer, ed., *The New Dictionary of Catholic Social Thought,* 614.

4. David O'Brien, "A Century of Catholic Social Teaching," in Coleman, *One Hundred Years,* 19–20.

5. O'Brien, "A Century of Catholic Social Teaching," 22–24.

6. Dwyer, *The Dictionary of Catholic Social Thought,* 623.

7. Hehir, "The Right and Competence," 63.

8. Hehir, "The Right and Competence," 59–61.

9. Summary of *Gaudium et spes,* 76.

10. Coleman, "Neither Liberal nor Socialist: The Originality of Catholic Social Teaching," in Coleman, *One Hundred Years,* 39.

11. Hehir, "The Right and Competence," 64.

12. Dwyer, *The Dictionary of Catholic Social Thought,* 623–625.

13. "Catholic social teachings," in Richard P. McBrien, ed. *Encyclopedia of Catholicism* (New York: HarperCollins, 1995), 281–282.

CATHOLICS AND THE LIBERAL TRADITION[1]

Michael Lacey and William M. Shea

Over the last several years, many Catholics have lamented their state of political homelessness. They want to know where they belong in today's debates over public policy and political philosophy. Those are the debates that, in John Courtney Murray's phrase, shape "the growing end of history," by giving a renewed sense of overall direction and purpose to the workings of government in society. However politically homeless Catholics may feel in today's politics, empirical snapshots show they are all over the lot. They can be found at the upper levels of all three branches of the national government. They represent a sizable presence in both political parties, with perhaps a slight tilt still lingering in favor of the Democrats, sometimes for reason of shared memories. They are prominent in the leadership of both liberal and conservative circles, and among the pundits as well. Nancy Pelosi and Henry Hyde, Ted Kennedy and Don Nickels, the late Daniel Patrick Moynihan and Antonin Scalia, Pat Buchanan, William F. Buckley, and E. J. Dionne Jr.—all are members of the same universal church.

And then there is the pluralism inside the mind. Consider the following beliefs held by the two of us and perhaps others as well, but motley enough in their contents to provoke concern and accusations of inconsistency from many quarters in today's political landscape.

ANSWERING THE LITMUS TESTS

We don't think taxes are too high, government is too big, the market should rule, or that the Declaration of Independence and Bill of Rights are infallible.

58

We are not against bureaucracy; it does big jobs that can't be done otherwise, and has a certain moral worth that we ought to think about more deeply. Among other things, public bureaucracies are tools for the pursuit of social justice and the common good. As much as we gripe about the paperwork, the public needs protection and the touch of leveling that comes with regulation, as the damage wrought by robber barons, old and new, makes plain enough. We are not for guns in the hands of citizens. We don't think the individual has a right to kill himself or help someone kill himself. We do think that abortion is a social evil as well as a sin, that no one has a right to it, and that child and spouse abuse are not private matters but sins, and should be treated as crimes. We don't think divorce is a generally good idea; it is a sadness in most cases.

We don't believe humans are perfectible, but that bit of wisdom calls for moral realism, not complacency or dropping out. Too often it is used *tout court* to ridicule the hopes of reformers: "Don't waste your time on politics and government," say the worldly wise, "the results will only break your hearts." We believe in the radical moral equality of human beings, each one made, as we were taught, in the image and likeness of God. We do not believe, however, in radical social equality, equality of outcome, either as an ideal or a goal in public policy. We believe that while moral and social equality are different things, they are related things, and there are limits to how much inequality in the material goods of life people should put up with. Precise discriminations may be impossible, but consider the extremes. More than one-third of the economic assets in America are held by 1 percent of households, and two-thirds by the richest 10 percent. How could anyone believe that this setup is part of the providential order, not to be tampered with?

Is it still considered gauche—awash as we are in new revelations about the gargantuan scale of the "infectious greed" that spread to God knows how many boardrooms—to fret about the merits of the sky-is-the-limit executive compensation schemes or the special protections that ought to be accorded to employee pension funds? We believe that as a practical matter the "preferential option" for the poor should be kept in mind as a kind of "true north" indicator, a useful starting point for navigating the treacherous waters of public policy. It should not be dismissed as soppy altruism when the community needs altruism with teeth. We believe it is wise to work toward greater measures of social equality in education, housing, health care, and other fields of policy, and we would be happier than we are if the Bush administration thought about its slogan "to leave no child behind" with a bit more depth and imagination than it has shown so far.

We believe warmly in progress and the need for it, not the automatic kind of economic fantasy, but the hard-won kind that comes only from struggle and collaborative creativity, and always threatens to come undone unless well tended. (Only yesterday, it seems, there was growing bipartisan enthusiasm for undoing the foundations of our social policy and "privatizing" Social Security.) Making progress is the proper aim and measure of politics, and so progressivism, too, is a good thing, a useful ideal. It calls for steadiness of purpose, taking history seriously, and a constructively critical attitude toward public affairs. The late Bernard Lonergan, S.J., our top pick as the most resourceful Catholic mind grappling with the fundamental problems of modernity over the past half century or so, was always puzzled by those who thought it was easy to see through the myth of progress. His own effort to think through the subject concluded that human beings have a moral obligation, indeed, a theologically sanctioned obligation, to do everything they can to pursue progress and forestall decline, the corollary of that pursuit and the cost of failing in it. We agree.

We don't believe in individualism pure and simple. As anyone who has thought hard about the subject will agree, there is nothing simple about it. We don't think autonomy is the trumping moral ideal (authenticity and integrity are more like it), or that individual rights should be the irreducible legal category, as in arguments for assisted suicide, abortion on demand, or the legalization of psychotropic drugs. We don't believe in the claims of community pure and simple either, and for the same reason. It is a hard subject. At any given time most of us are members of many communities, each of them more or less imperfect. Group bias—be it the snobbery of families, racism, the harder forms of multiculturalism, sectarian extremism, the contempt of the academic class for conventional religion, the belief that the poor have better moral reflexes than the wealthy or vice versa—all forms of the group phenomenon are as subtle and stubborn as the individual forms. Attention has to be paid to both kinds.

We think people are called to suffer and die for one another and with one another and for the communities to which they belong, and that self-transcendence in love is the basic moral and religious meaning of human life. The phrase may seem at first highfalutin, but it accurately describes the phenomenon, and the phenomenon itself is not a rare thing. It is a common, garden variety experience. We see it when things are working well in the family, on the job, and in all the larger communities in which we participate. We think that the church and the government are crucial to our humanity and its flourishing, and that both need constant watching and criticism because they are run by people like us. They are not the enemy any more than the family is. We are supernaturalists where we should be (there is a point to it all and we are pulled toward it) and not where we don't have to be (appearances of the Virgin and devil possession). We are thoroughgoing naturalists whenever possible.

Theologically speaking, we are not "radical orthodox," any more than we are classic neo-orthodox (we leave that to Stanley Hauerwas and Michael Baxter). We think there are important overlaps in language and hope between Christians and secularists, and that we can communicate across the distinct languages we use in religious and secular communities, and between religious traditions. The choice we favor is reason and faith, not reason or faith. There need not be an essential contradiction between a divinely guided orthodox Catholic Church and the secular, sinful, lost world around it that is not a church. The "world" (Johannine sense) is in the church and the church needs saving, too. Witness "the scandal"! Do we need more proof of the presence of the world in the church?

We are not antistate neoconservatives or Americanists who believe that by virtue of its political arrangements our country is closer to God than are other nations and peoples, and we don't think God smiles more broadly on us than on them. We don't think that today's free-enterprise capitalism is a stripped-down version of Christianity in disguise. We are not evangelical Christians or even evangelical Catholics who believe that for the world to work right, it must be Catholic or Christian. We do believe that the gospel must be preached, but how it is done is all important. We don't believe that religious conquest or homogeneity is part of that gospel. Catholicism and evangelicalism have both been blessings to history; both blessings have been mixed. For too long in both its Catholic and Protestant "moral majority" versions, the impossible dream of a renewed Christendom, of one true church in one just state, has distracted religious people from thinking responsibly about politics, as even popes now agree.

LIBERALISM AND COMMUNITY

But enough about who we are not. Who are we? We think of ourselves as Catholic liberals of the communitarian kind. We won't say it is a match made in heaven, but we do believe that Catholicism and liberal communitarianism as it is developing today, both in academic circles and as a fledgling political movement, have much in common and good reason to keep in touch. Communitarians want to recover the feel of real life, from which we have drifted away, in our politics. They know that the choice between an abstract individual, on the one hand, and an abstract community, on the other, is a bogus choice. While it values freedom, as all modern "isms" must, communitarianism is alert to the costs of liberty, and insists on judging the claims made for individualism against the background of the often implicit needs of the communities that make up the fabric of social life.

As a tendency in academic philosophy and political theory, the "communitarian turn," of which we speak, began to take shape in the 1980s. While it was hardly a Catholic project (most of its leading figures—Michael Sandel, Amatai Etzioni, Philip Selznick, Robert Bellah, William Galston, Benjamin Barber, Alan Wolfe, and Jean Bethke Elsthain, for example—are not Catholic), Catholic thinkers, such as Charles Taylor, Mary Ann Glendon, Alasdair MacIntyre, and E. J. Dionne Jr., have been prominent in its development from the beginning. All of these writers have been engaged in an attempt to reevaluate our many-stranded liberal tradition, and to reinvigorate its most important insights.

The communitarian project is not a conservative movement, though most of its adversaries would frame it that way. For some critics, left and right, the fusion of commitments to both the individual and the community, which is characteristic of communitarian thought, is a basic contradiction. For liberals such as Patricia Ireland or Kate Michelman, president of the National Abortion and Reproductive Rights Action League, or for Libertarians such as Milton Friedman, Charles Murray, or members of the debate teams at Washington's Cato Institute, for example, the choice is not bogus, but genuine and forced by the way things really are. We think otherwise. When American Catholics signed onto the modern liberal tradition in a big way in the 1930s, it was the communitarian elements of the tradition that caught their attention and earned their loyalty. The old siren song of laissez-faire economics and rugged individualism made no sense to them. The nation-building ethos of solidarity that lay behind the Social Security Act and the Wagner Act (with its encouragements to unionism and protection against the exploitation of management) along with many other proposals, then and since, seemed the proper kind of liberalism to the Catholic ethnic and laboring communities. Free-market capitalism, as Andrew Greeley has shown on many occasions, has never been attractive to most American Catholics, and it still isn't, despite the migration of many into the Republican Party.

Much has happened to the liberal tradition since the communitarian shaping given to it by progressivism and the New Deal—from the antiwar and Civil Rights movements to reparations and multiculturalism, the women's movement, free love and gay liberation, the pro-choice crusade, modern environmentalism, animal rights, and many other new causes (how quickly they come to feel old!), all of them championed more or less skillfully by academic spokespersons. The two of us are old enough to have lived through all these different cross currents and eddies of public thought and feeling, and at times it has seemed very confusing, sometimes even objectionable. Looking back, however, this much seems clear: a fight was going on over the proper meaning and grounds of the liberal tradition. The political and intellectual community that made up midcentury American liberalism gradually succumbed to factionalism, was splintered and pulled in various directions. This happened not only politically in the Democratic Party but also philosophically, in tandem with changes of fashion and argument (too complicated for brief summary here, even of the polemical kind) that arose and were given expression in academic life.

The most recent stratum of communitarian thinking arose from these political and academic changes. The quarrels between liberal communitarians and liberals of other persuasions over the true bearings of the liberal tradition itself have been bitter, as only arguments *en famille* can be. Nonetheless, the proponents of communitarian ideas have sought not to repudiate the liberal tradition (it is much too complex and valuable a thing for that), but to prune it, correct its abuses, and provide amendments where they are necessary. Like the neo-orthodox theologians of the middle of the last century (Reinhold Niebuhr and Paul Tillich, for example) in relation to the theological liberalism of that day, communitarianism aims at revitalizing a tired movement. As the neo-orthodox writers reminded liberal Protestants of Original Sin and the need for redemption, so communitarians remind their fellow liberals that the world is a community of communities and not simply the backdrop for individual achievement and its satisfactions.

Communitarians do not want to turn the clock back on the Civil Rights movement or the women's movement, but they have not been afraid to tally up the costs to the moral commonwealth of apparently neverending waves of liberation so intent on overcoming various establishments that they have lost any hope of a broad and genuine community of mind and spirit. They are sharply critical of doctrines of moral relativism as corrosive of the foundations of political order and justice. They have been vigorous in their opposition to the hard forms of multiculturalism and the absolutist ideas that sometimes color the politics of gender. They are not against rights, but insist on distinguishing rights from wants and grounding them in credit-worthy public reasoning. They have chided the unexpected reticence of those who fancy themselves liberal spokesmen but who can't quite muster all three cheers for the common good, fearing that something ugly and repressive might be imposed in its name. Communitarians believe that a good argument might end in an even better conversation about strengthening the community's ties, and that conversation itself is the bond that is threatened by ideologies, including some forms of contemporary liberalism, such as take-it-or-leave-it free-choice politics, or hardheaded, single-issue politics of the right-to-life type, or extreme versions of free-speech doctrines whose advocates cannot in conscience preclude shouting "fire" in a crowded theater, much less banning child pornography from the Internet.

The need for responsibility in a rights-mad, individualist culture has been the leading theme in communitarian thinking, and the lack of any workable theory of responsibility within much of today's popular liberalism (and popular conservatism, too, it must be said) is what drew communitarians together in the first place. When the communitarian network was established in 1990 by Etzioni, Galston, Glendon, and others, they created its quarterly journal and made a point of giving it the title: *The Responsive Community: Rights and Responsibilities.* They speak of theirs as a "centrist" philosophy, intended "to restore social responsibilities and a commitment to community, without Puritanism or authoritarianism." While the movement disclaims any ties to party politics and the network includes some conservatives and Republicans in its number, most communitarians are Democrats and have been prominent in the effort to pull the party back to the center and away from the allure of fringe politics and ideological purity.

Despite the great and obvious gains for humanity that modernity ushered into history (democratic government and unconstrained scientific inquiry chief among them), the moral environment of modernity has been hard on all the bonds of traditional community—on family ties, on ethnic and religious affiliations, even on social class and the norms of the learned professions. Communitarian policy thinking aims to shore up the fraying bonds of community. Those bonds include not only shared outlooks and values, but shared institutions as well, among them the institutions of government. These are counted as assets of community, not the outposts of alien tribes, and they are to be used for the solution of a special class of problems, those which cannot reasonably be handled by individuals or private associations alone.

Communitarians stress the importance of doing whatever is possible to maintain a thriving civil sector, meaning the whole kit and caboodle of non-governmental human associations, from families and bowling leagues, to churches, unions, and corporations. But they don't accept perspectives that pit government and civil society against one another as natural enemies, the way conservatives like to do. They are the same at the source: people like us. Thus liberal communitarians seek a certain kind of competence in the public sector. They look for responsiveness, cooperation, and the closer integration of government and society, not their separation. If the common good requires new roles to be played by government, such as making qualified daycare widely available, for example, so be it. If a dose of privatization of what was previously public makes sense, such as turning over the provision of government services to private corporations operating on contract, in trash collection, for example, or, to give the idea a different and more controversial twist, the use of tax dollars to provide vouchers for children to attend religious schools, then try it and find out. But do find out, and don't make a fetish or a cure-all out of the term itself. What counts is the quality of the modern way of life taken as a whole, and for this to be good we need knowledgeable and responsive governance, a communitarian ideal. You can't get either without public oversight and well-informed political discussion about the ways we actually live and work.

The liberal communitarians have had little to say as yet about problems of religious identity and tradition, but Catholics who take seriously the social teachings of the church (the natural-law tradition on family and social justice, subsidiarity, public responsibility for the social and economic safety net) are likely to find their concerns and general way of talking congenial. The great religious traditions are alike at least in this: All of them would find the ideal of untethered individualism and the idolatry of personal choice wide of the mark of righteousness, if not repellant. For this reason they have been the main vessels of communitarian values throughout history, and are likely to remain so. As we well know, religious communities can be tribal in their focus and narrow in their intellectual and spiritual horizons. Getting over this without losing the faith is the challenge of modernity. The religions have been ill at ease with one another, but even less comfortable with the ramifications of the ideas that gave rise to modern secular culture, which sometimes appeared to be all selfishness, hustle, and impiety. Gregory XVI and Pius IX condemned the modern world for putting unbearable pressure on the church, and Pope Pius X could speak of Catholic modernism as "the synthesis of all the heresies." The same kind of thought has crossed the minds of clerics in the other traditions.

Popes haven't thought or talked that way for a long time. *Mater et magistra, Pacem in terris,* and the post–Vatican II social encyclicals have returned time and again to the need for both solidarity and subsidiarity if we are to achieve a genuinely responsible political order. Indeed, the interplay of solidarity and subsidiarity—both themes being mainstays in the church's natural-law tradition—makes up the idiom that gives Catholic social thought its distinctive communitarian cast. Subsidiarity is a way of thinking about the ideal of responsiveness in the social order. It speaks to the morality of giving and receiving help. It points to the complex requirements of cooperation among the "higher" and "lower" associations of life in society, and the need to provide help without harm up and down the line—to furnish welfare support for those who need it, for example, without financing a caste system and undermining fulfillment of the obligation to look after ourselves and our own. Finding and holding that line can be difficult, and subsidiarity asks a lot from each of us. It can be understood minimally to say: Ask for help when you need it, give when asked, but don't spoil yourself (or anyone else), take care of your own business, and don't be an intrusive busybody.

Solidarity, on the other hand, cautions against complacency and getting lost in your own business. Pope John Paul II speaks of it as a virtue to be cultivated through reflective participation in society and politics. He describes solidarity as an overriding will to community in keeping with our intuitions of the divine will. "It is not," he says, "a feeling of vague compassion or shallow distress at the misfortunes of so many people, both near and far. On the contrary, it is a firm and persevering determination to commit oneself to the common good." Thus understood, solidarity is an open-ended sense of moral obligation that helps us to see the "other" as one of us, and works to prevent communities, including religious communities, from closing in on themselves. The post–Vatican II papacy has carefully championed the sacred dignity of all human persons, not just Catholics in good standing. The new tone and the cautious apologies evident in the Vatican's attempts to repair rifts with the world's Jewish communities, to reopen talks with other Christian groups and with secularists, to dispel some of the old biases against science—these are public exercises of the virtue of solidarity.

We think Catholics could learn a good deal from liberal communitarians, and that Catholics have something to offer communitarians also. In their thinking about the linkage between rights and responsibilities, about the role of commitment in forming it, about the importance of particulars in trying to live up to universal values, about social justice as a distinctive kind of political virtue that requires more than simply treating people fairly, the communitarians are reviving questions and approaches to them that were once on the agenda of Catholic scholars and activists working in the natural-law tradition prior to Vatican II. (On treating people fairly historically speaking, many white persons treated black persons fairly in face-to-face relations, without making a dent in the structure of race relations, and the problem lingers in the distinction between personal and "institutional" racism, the latter showing up not face to face but only at the level of statistical inquiry.) Such communitarian ideas have also been on the agenda of *Commonweal* since its inception. As understood all along by these Catholics, the natural-law tradition held that universal values were real, that there is a kind of innate moral knowledge in all human beings, whatever their culture or condition, and that despite all the variations of customs and mores that history or travel reveal, true standards of justice exist and are not merely made up. They are accessible to everyone through the responsible exercise of their minds.

In the olden days of Jacques Maritain, John Courtney Murray, and lesser lights, Catholics called for others in secular society to join them in the search for shared answers to shared problems along these natural-law lines. No one of great stature on the secular side of things seems to have paid much attention, perhaps because the natural-law style of thinking was suspect as too denominational and merely Catholic. The communitarians represent another chance at serious collaboration with non-Catholic thinkers, a process that can begin only by getting better acquainted. For those who want to do so, we would suggest reading Philip Selznick's recent little book *The Communitarian Persuasion* (Woodrow Wilson Press), a concise but comprehensive, accessible overview of liberal communitarian thought on all the big questions at stake in public philosophy. We would also recommend clicking on the Communitarian Network and their journal, *The Responsive Community*, at their Web site (www.gwu.edu/~ccps/rcq/index.html).

Beyond the affinities of the social teaching of the church and the outlook of the communitarians, Catholicism offers a few more things that only the church can offer. It recognizes and celebrates publicly the sacramentality of human life in community and nature. It distinguishes the sacred from the profane, the really real from the deceptively real. The church promotes the moral and religious conversion of citizens and leaders, encouraging everyone to keep heads up and focused on the big picture. It prizes life, cradle-to-grave, something the government and culture, given their secularity, tend to fudge. Finally, while the state cannot and should not recognize the grace and call of God in the life and death of Jesus of Nazareth (theocracy and even establishment are not options anywhere anymore), at least the church can literally and metaphorically keep the crucifix in the air before it. It reminds us that both setback and failure in the quest for the just society are only moments in which we learn again what we knew all along, that the Reign of God is a gift, not an achievement.

NOTE

1. This essay originally appeared in *Commonweal,* October 11, 2002, and was part of a project funded by the Lilly Endowment.

2

CATHOLIC INSTITUTIONS IN THE AMERICAN PUBLIC SQUARE

Institution building is one of the most characteristic activities of the Catholic Church in the United States. Its presence in the public square is visible not simply in the church steeples that dot urban landscapes, but in primary and secondary schools, colleges and universities, hospitals, clinics, and nursing homes, social service centers, orphanages, and shelters. The work of these institutions form a significant part of the civic presence of the Catholic Church. Their funding and regulation, part of a long and sometimes contested relationship with federal and state bodies as well as nongovernmental groups, thus become highly relevant to that presence.

The project commissioned several detailed studies of Catholic civic engagement by Catholic institutions. Those included in this volume are the place of the parish in the public square, the activities of several state Catholic conferences, that is, bishops' conferences in New York, Wisconsin, and California, and the challenges facing Catholic health care providers.

THE CATHOLIC PARISH IN
THE PUBLIC SQUARE

Philip J. Murnion

A prefactory note: "If I had more time, I would have written you a shorter letter."—Benjamin Franklin.

"Now that Bishop Untener has worked with all his priests on their preaching, are the homilies better?" "Yes, for one thing, they're shorter."

The following is called an exploration because it ranges far and wide over the subject. I needed to set down the many aspects of the question in order to focus on the subject. If I had more time, I would have been able to edit it down, but beg the indulgence of the readers who can surely focus on the main points.

A PROFILE OF PARISHES

"The parish is for most Catholics the single most important part of the church."

This is the opening sentence of a document on parish life published by the U.S. bishops in 1981.[1] Even more dramatic terms have been used about the Catholic parish in the United States: "The American neighborhood parish is one of the most ingenious communities that human skill has ever created."[2]

Certain pastoral theologians have challenged this judgment. They follow a logic that distinguishes between worldviews that one sociologist of religion calls "cosmopolitan" as contrasted with "local."[3] "Cosmopolitans" are people for whom the home community is but one of many communities, and perhaps not their primary community. Their work, their social life, and their lives as citizens and consumers all lay outside the home community. "Locals" are people for whom the community around home is the primary and embracing community. I say doubters about the continuing importance of

71

territorial parishes "follow a logic" because, while it is logical that territorial communities, originating in a rural life, hardly relate to contemporary urban and suburban life. Yet reality defies that logic. The territorial parish persists as the primary way that Catholics express and deepen their faith, give sacred meaning to birth and marriage and death, find community and support outside their families, and enter into public life. In fact, even the majority of cosmopolitans who remain active members of the church are almost as likely to be affiliated with their home parish as locals are.[4]

Parishes also represent what has come to be called "social capital": they provide people with "social skills," and offer people opportunities to be involved in various forms of public life. They create "ties to fellow congregants that can be used to mobilize energies."[5] The skills range from basic educational skills to more complex skills for participating in and leading public projects. The opportunities range from programs internal to the life of the parish to those in the larger community. As the Reverend Eugene Rivers, a Protestant minister, notes: "The Catholics have an organizational structure that lends itself to putting troops into the field."[6] It is the whole culture of the parish, more than its programs, which relates parishioners to the wider world.

Parishes contribute to the public life and common good of the country. This is not sufficiently appreciated by the American public. I saw this when, in preparation for a visit of John Paul II to the United States, the *New York Times* and other media researched the role of the church in the cities on his itinerary. One of the reporters called me about Newark, New Jersey. He was astonished to find the extensive way that the church contributed to the needs of people in inner-city Newark, especially through parishes and their schools. "Isn't the church in Newark the most outstanding example in the country of Catholic involvement in the city?" he asked me. He had a quote and was looking for a mouth to put it in. I had to tell him that what he had found in Newark was just as true in New York, Philadelphia, Detroit, Chicago, and most of America's inner cities.

COMMUNITY, MINISTRY, AND LEADERSHIP

Community. The differences in community—size and composition—are enormous. The average parish has 2,500 members.[7] This is approximately ten times the size of the average Protestant congregation. But a quarter of parishes have fewer than five hundred Catholics, and a quarter have more than 3,000

Catholics.[8] Further, *community* means very different things in urban, suburban, and rural parishes. Once I speculated with the bishop of a rural Midwest diocese that the majority of parishioners in the small towns probably attend Mass. "Not only that," he replied. "The pastors know who's missing and they know why they're missing." The effects of size are paradoxical. Researchers agree (though without much supporting data) that large parishes, especially in urban environments, generate less parishioner responsibility to contribute to parish life. On the other hand, our own studies find that in larger parishes there are greater numbers both of ministries—opportunities to participate—and ministers.[9]

Two other critical aspects of community are the economic condition of the people and the size of the local Catholic community. In San Antonio, for example, poor and working class Hispanic Catholics are a majority. San Fernando Cathedral can take the Christmas *posada* ceremony into the streets and incorporate the officials and official buildings into the event. The same phenomenon is at work in Los Angeles.

Community means something else still in the 1,800 of 19,000 parishes which are "personal" parishes. They are defined not by territory—the norm in the Code of Canon Law (c. 518)—but by constituency: a particular ethnic group, the university community, a military installation, or some other community. Even the territorial-personal categories are not airtight. Many Catholics take part in personal parishes even though they do not belong to the founding community, and many territorial parishes are effectively personal parishes—the members are largely of the same culture. One further important point: for the past fifty years, bishops have moved away from the practice of establishing personal parishes for new immigrant groups, responding to the integrationist emphasis in the culture. This has posed a challenge for parishes with significant Hispanic, African-American, Haitian, and Asian subcommunities.[10] Parishes remain an important means for integrating immigrants into the society, whether in separate parishes, or through offering special language services in a territorial parish.

Parishes differ also in *ministry.* Pastors in a survey reported an average of four organized ministries in their parishes, but the busiest parish reported fifty-nine organized ministries (for example, ministries to youth or to the aged, or for adult education). Parochial schools represent a significant investment of resources. After a period of school closings, now halted, about one-third of the parishes have parochial schools. This is a remarkable story of resilience.

The kinds of ministries continue to change. The Rite of Christian Initiation of Adults (typically and lamentably referred to by the initials RCIA, and then referred to as a "program") is largely responsible for the sharp turn-around in the numbers of adults becoming Catholic. Though this number plunged from 145,000 in 1960 to 75,000 in 1974, engagement of parishioners in the whole process led to the baptism or reception into the church of over 160,000 in the late 1990s.

Following the general shift of the church toward greater participation of parishioners in the rites and ministries of the parish, many other structures and ministries have been adopted: peer ministries for groups like the bereaved or divorced and separated; pastoral and finance councils; and parish participation in congregation-based community organizations and other ecumenical activities.

Parishes also differ considerably in *style of leadership*. Leadership here refers to both the pastor and the others who exercise leadership. In a study of Chicago congregations of various faith groups, it was evident that the leader of the congregation—rabbi, priest, minister, imam—set the direction for the congregation.[11] That study simply confirms what was already apparent about the impact of a pastor on a parish. In poetic terms, "The priest is the heart of the parish."[12] In more prosaic terms, two things are true: if parishioners boast of the quality of their parish, the next sentence out of their mouth is praise of their pastor. Second, if people are having difficulty or dissatisfaction with their parish, the finger is pointed at the pastor.

Increasingly, other ministers play a role in parish leadership. The staffing of parishes has changed dramatically. Now there are almost 30,000 lay persons serving as paid pastoral ministers (not counting school or support staffs), at least on a part time basis. This does not include the vast number of parishioners who provide leadership on a volunteer basis. Ten percent of the parishes have no resident priest pastor, and in about 500 of these, day-to-day pastoral care leadership is entrusted to a sister, a deacon, or lay persons.[13]

SHIFTING CONDITIONS OF PARISH IDENTITY: MEMBERSHIP, STEWARDSHIP, DISCIPLESHIP

The elaboration of communities, ministries, and leadership is matched by diffusion in what it means to be "good" Catholic, a "faithful" parishioner. What it takes to be a good Catholic has effectively become hard to determine—not officially, mind you, but effectively. Many, perhaps most, Catholics insist that they are Catholic regardless of their adherence to official teaching or participation in church life. Study after study finds enormous diversity in beliefs and practices of Catholics. Furthermore, most Catholics appear reluctant to judge how Catholic anyone else is: though about half attend Mass in the course of a month, four out of five believe that one can be a good Catholic without taking part in this central action of the church.

At one time, membership in a parish was sharply defined—the baptized Catholics living within the boundaries of a territorial parish or who belong to the community for which the personal parish was established. Now, while the majority of active Catholics still participate in their home parish, in principle they feel free to choose their parish, what it means to belong to a parish, and what obligations they have to their parishes

In order to facilitate communication with parishioners and to foster commitment by parishioners, parishes now typically encourage registration. This may make it easier to keep track of and to communicate with parishioners, but registration cannot be construed as a measure of commitment.[14] It may as likely be an expression of entitlement—to a baptism, marriage, funeral, enrollment of children in the parish school. Pastors themselves may encourage this thinking by withholding service from parishioners who do not register, in spite of the fact that canon law endows all Catholics who are within the parish boundaries with membership. In other words, both "sides"—pastors and parishioners—are subtly redefining the membership method from that of a parish (all those within the community) to that of a congregation (a self-selecting group). I need to restate that in practical terms: parishes remain parishes, yet a congregational impulse is lying beneath the surface and it affects the level and kind of commitment and participation.

Finally, in recent decades about half the parishes have formed what are variously called "small Christian communities," "faith-sharing groups," or simply "small groups." Parishioners meet in groups of a dozen or so, usually in homes, and typically following a guidebook. They pray together, "share faith," and consider the implications of their faith for their life. This is an effort to personalize both belief and belonging and thereby build up the community of the parish.

YET AND STILL

Parishes remain the most pervasive way that Catholics express their faith in public and are led by their faith and fellowship in to public life. The parish still tries to be the kind of community described by Pope John Paul II in an address to French bishops:

> In close coordination with other pastoral groups, it is essentially the parish which gives the Church concrete life, so that she may be open to all. Whatever its size, it is not merely an association. It must be a home where the members of the Body of Christ gather together, open to meeting God the Father, full of love and of the Savior his Son, incorporated into the Church by the Holy Spirit at the time of Baptism, and ready to accept their brothers and sister with fraternal love, whatever their condition of origins.[15]

Furthermore, the evangelizing role of the parish, says the pope, inevitably has social dimensions:

> If we are fully imbued with the grace of faith enlivened by hope and inspired by charity, there is no happy or sad aspect of village of neighborhood life which can fail to move us. Thus evangelization will take different forms in social solidarity, family life, work, neighborly relations. An isolated witness has its limitations, but witnesses stimulated by the community will be better able to share the "hope that does not disappoint us, because God's love has been poured into our hearts through the Holy Spirit who has been given to us" (Romans, 5:5).[16]

It is the very richness of community and mission that enables the parish to make a contribution to public life. As Andrew Greeley wrote:

> [The neighborhood parish's] overlapping network of religious, educational, familial, social and political relationships has created what my colleague James S. Coleman (who is not Catholic) calls "social capital," a social resource in the strictest sense of the word because it comes not from individual investments but from relational patterns.[17]

I must admit, however, that while parishes are essential to the life of the church and to the ways that the church fosters involvement in public life, they are not adequate. Movements, organizations, and regional efforts have always been a necessary complement to parishes.[18] Catholics were engaged in community life through the Jocist groups (CFM, YCS, YCW) the Legion of Mary, the Catholic Worker Movement, the St. Vincent de Paul Society, Catholic programs relating to the labor movement, Catholics Interracial Councils, and a whole host of other programs. We lack the inspiration and direction of such groups at present, with unfortunate consequences for the church's involvement in public life. Furthermore, the more economically, socially and politically diverse the Catholic community has become, the more difficult it is to determine programs for public involvement that relate to the majority of Catholics and their parishes.[19]

PARISH, PERSON, AND WORLD

A former professor of mine offered a good illustration of the danger of exaggerated sociologism: A researcher, explaining how control is maintained in prisons, concentrated so much on the relationships developed between the guards and the trusties that he forgot to mention that the guards carried guns. We could make the same mistake about parish life, concentrating on specific parish programs so much that we neglect what is at the heart of the parish. A parish is by definition public: it takes people beyond the privacy of family into relationships not of one's choosing. This is especially true of the normative parish, the territorial parish. Its members are all baptized Catholics who live within its boundaries. It even has obligations to those who are not Catholic within its boundaries, and to Catholics who do not live within the boundaries. Participation in parish life is participation in public life.

A Sacramental Self

The first way parishes introduce people into public life is through infant baptism—a rite that says many things about a person. It says that birth and life have dimensions far deeper and wider than meets the eye. It says that the child belongs to the local community of the parish, the universal community of the church, and the communion of saints that transcends time and space. (The relationship to the communion of saints was more clearly expressed when all parents gave their children the names of saints, such as the saint honored on the date of birth.) It says that life and personhood are essentially relational, and that each of us is at once sacred and flawed. The child is blessed, but in need of being formed in the faith, and the parents are to be the "first and best teachers" of the child. Infant baptism is testimony to the sacred character of all life—no one merits baptism: no feature of race, age, intelligence, prosperity, or gender earns or denies the sacred character of each person. It says that the deepest, most spiritual aspect of our lives is essentially tied to the physical, material, and familial aspects of our beings, and vice versa: the physical, material and familial aspects of our lives have an intrinsically spiritual dimension. What Cardinal Joseph Bernardin articulated as the "consistent ethic of life" is first expressed in infant baptism.

In familiar terms, baptism conveys the sacramental and communal character of life. What begins in baptism is carried forward in the sacraments and sacramental character of parish life. Sacraments are the spine of a parish, providing shape and structure to all else. Throughout life the parish reminds us of the need and opportunity for personal transformation. James Q. Wilson is convinced that religion is not the source of morality—many people who are not religious are moral—nor the main source of moral sanctions. "Religion's chief contribution to morality is to enable people to transform their lives." The very notion of transformation is a little examined but central linkage between sacramental life, moral obligation, and conception of one's place in the world. These ground a whole perspective to life of the power and obligation to shape the very elements of life and world.

Throughout the celebration of the sacraments and the celebration of the Eucharist, in the preaching and teaching, in the symbols and hymns, parishioners are reminded that they are members of the Body of Christ, temples of the Holy Spirit, called to discipleship. As followers of Christ, they are to be guided by three terms that are a constant refrain: love, sacrifice, and transformation. Time after time after time, love of God and one another is proposed as a way of life. In a culture of entitlement, the rites and words of parish life set forward sacrifice, in imitation of Christ, as the necessary means to love and life. And the transformation of self and world are put forward as the ongoing challenge of discipleship.

From birth to death, the parish says that persons are sacred, relational, and responsible. The whole person is embraced in the theology of church and parish—the physical, emotional, voluntary, and intellectual aspects of the person. All are involved in Catholic understanding of conversion and initiation, and the processes of conversion and initiation are important clues to a church's understanding of person and membership. In past decades, emphasis was placed on the intellectual and voluntary aspects: people were *instructed* in the faith and membership was in the *practices* of faith and morality. More recently, other aspects of person, conversion, and initiation have been emphasized. The adult catechumenate, for example, locates initiation in a context of community—the Sunday Mass, the parishioners who serve as companions and catechists for those seeking membership, and a grouping of catechumens—so that relationships are emphasized from the beginning. Parishes are increasingly using prayerful retreats as preparation for the parents of children to be baptized as well as for young people preparing for Communion and confirmation.[20]

In general, a more fully rounded approach to conversion is evident in a variety of programs of preparation for the sacraments, continuing formation (especially in the many forms of small communities in parishes), as well as in promoting the church's social mission.

As I noted previously, parishes are key communities for introducing immigrants to the wider culture. They do so, first by extending the familiar and secure environment of the home culture to immigrants as they adjust to the new culture. When national parishes were typical for new waves of immigration, they did this by affirming the culture of origin and the worth of the individual, at a time when acceptance in the wider culture was tenuous. In recent decades, emphasis has been placed more on integration, because of a shift in priorities in the country and the lack of clergy from the immigrant group. When we look at how parishes equip parishioners for public involvement, we will consider whether the present strategy is as effective regarding recent immigrant groups as the earlier strategy was for their predecessors.

A Sacramental World

"Mourning and weeping in this vale of tears."
"The earth is full of the goodness of the Lord."
The first expression was part of the closing prayer at every Mass prior to Vatican II. It expressed well the struggle of a largely immigrant and struggling Catholic population. We no longer say this. The second phrase is a frequent refrain during Mass at present, and better expresses the current stance of the majority of U.S. Catholics. In fact, the words and rites of the parish keep balancing the two perspectives. Parishioners are constantly reminded that the world is, like themselves, at once sacred and flawed, God's creation and in need of our creative efforts if it is to be the Kingdom of God.

Besides defining and expressing the identity of the individual as sacred, relational, and responsible, parishes define the world in ways that will affect one's involvement in the world. The basic Catholic perspective is that person and world are both sacred and sinful, precious in the eyes of God and flawed, deserving of reverence and in need of direction. The Catholic approach in this and other matters is essentially a "both/and" one. In the past, parishes sometimes violated this view by so emphasizing temptation, sin, and the need for forgiveness that normal appetites were made to seem ineluctably sinful. Yet, there was abundant opportunity for forgiveness. In more recent times, though I know of no research on this, preachers may be reluctant to present hard sayings on sexual or social morality, and the ministry of forgiveness has been greatly altered. Some would say it has been diminished because few people regularly use the sacrament of penance. Others might argue that forgiveness has been made more abundant but less costly, because of the penitential rite at the beginning of each Mass and the seasonal celebration of a communal rite of penance, in which confession is directly made to God rather than to the priest as representative of the community. What is thought to be a communal mode of celebrating the sacrament may actually be rather individual.

It remains true, however, that the parish, in its whole conduct of life, encourages the view that the world is a place for growth and development, for the exercise of personal responsibility and mutual charity, and for carrying forward the creative and redemptive work of Christ. In fact, according to an international study, Catholics are more likely than others to see the world and human nature as basically good.[21] It is neither inexorably evil nor good. The world and its works are where we must individually and collectively work out our salvation with the help of the Spirit.

One exception may be noted. Parishes typically do very little to recognize and celebrate the religious and spiritual dimension of work, of people's occupations. As home-based communities, parishes tend to focus on home and family related concerns. Aside from the vocation of marriage and the vocations to priesthood and religious life, parishes do not celebrate the vocations of the people. At a time when many people find their identity in their work and determine the value of their lives by their accomplishments in the work place, which is separate from home, this gap between parish and work may seriously erode the significance of parish for people's lives.

RESPONSIBILITIES AND OPPORTUNITIES

There are specific ways that parishes equip parishioners for engagement in community life and public action. It may be helpful first to summarize the research about parish involvement and public involvement.

Church attendees in general are more likely to give money and time to voluntary organizations, including those with no evident connection to churches.[22]

Religion and, more directly, Mass attendance and participation in parish life increases the likelihood of participation in public life.[23] Attendance is also related to voting in presidential elections.[24]

Catholics are more likely to see the world and human nature as basically good.[25]

Catholics are least likely to describe themselves as politically conservative and most likely to attend religious services.[26]

Catholics who attend Mass are more convinced that government has a role in addressing the problems of the poor and weak.[27]

Catholics who attend Mass and who see God as a loving person are more supportive of government care for those suffering from AIDS.

Catholic women, and especially married women, are more likely to be involved in public life than the men are and their involvement tends to be in educational and "informal" activities.[28]

Catholics have less of a role in church worship activities than Protestants and have less use of civic skills in church even though they are more likely to attend church.[29]

Catholic Mass-goers are twice as likely to accept the church's social teaching than other Catholics.[30] That teaching includes individual responsibility regarding social justice, the role of government in ensuring care for those in need, and the right to organize in pursuit of economic and political rights.

Catholics Mass-goers more fully accept church teaching on sexual morality.

Equipped for the Work: Human Development

The focus in recent discussions of the capacities the church brings to its social mission is often too narrow. Church ministers think of the resources of diocesan social action offices, pro-life offices and other offices or committees directly targeted on social issues. Yet, apart from Catholic hospitals, colleges and universities, and diocesan social services programs, parishes have broader capacities for affecting social life and Catholic participation in social life. Especially important here are the parochial elementary schools and, in a few instances, parochial high schools. There are 6,375 parish elementary or middle schools, enrolling over 2.5 million children. In principle, these schools provide a vision for life, basic educational skills, and cultivate habits for life— both the habits we call virtues and those we can rely on as skills.

More than 13 percent of children enrolled in parochial elementary schools are not Catholic.[31] The importance of Catholic parishes for equipping people for economic life has been evident to business leaders in the cities, whatever their own religious identities. They respect parochial schools for equipping young people with the skills and disciplines needed for employment. They have demonstrated this respect by contributing to school support programs, both privately mounted campaigns and such diocesan programs as the Inner City Scholarship Fund of New York, the Big Shoulders Campaign of Chicago, and the Fund for Educational Development in Newark. Non-Catholic business leaders frequently chair these campaigns.

I want to underscore the significance of enrolling non-Catholic children in parish schools. Parochial schools were originally established in the nineteenth century not only to ensure basic schooling for immigrants, but formation in faith and church membership lest the Protestant-run public schools lead the youngsters astray. When the major waves of immigration came to an end, Catholics became assimilated, and, in many areas, Catholics moved out of the cities where the schools were located. One option was to close the schools. The fact that school enrollment was opened to non-Catholic children is a remarkable shift in purpose and in the relationship of the church to the larger society. A similar shift occurred in Catholic health and social services, which was more understandable because these services were now substantially supported by public funds and insurance reimbursements. Support for the schools remained the responsibility of the church and those whose help the church is able to secure. Given the contribution of the schools to the public good, even apart from enrollment of non-Catholic children, it is not surprising that many people look to vouchers for public funding. This story of conversion from an institution built to take care of "our own" into a more general public service needs to be told.

A second, related area of human development is the ability of parishes to enable new immigrants to enter into American society. While the parochial schools at one time largely charged no tuition because they were regarded as the common concern of the whole parish, most now do. For this reason and for other reasons not fully explored, many Hispanic children are not enrolled in these schools. The schools are not doing for many recent immigrants what they did for prior immigrant groups: equipping them for life in society and engaging them in the life of the church.

Education in Catholic Social Teaching

The parish provides ongoing education in Catholic social teaching, both in preaching and in its various educational programs. It also provides opportunities for people to consider the links between this teaching and their own lives, as well as for the evaluation of candidates for public office, and the development of public policy. Catholic Social Teaching in the form of papal and episcopal documents has been broadly developed in the past half century. Popular texts and pastoral guides exploring this teaching have been produced for use in parishes. An example is the document the U.S. bishops produce every year as a guide for evaluating candidates for public office. Almost 100,000 copies of the 2000 guide, *Faithful Citizenship,* have been sold. This represents a small percentage of the 60 million Catholics, and no one knows how much these guides influence the voting behavior of those who use them. Nonetheless, resources like this have been published and inform preaching, the work of parish ministers, and the "social concerns committees" of parish pastoral councils. In addition, social teaching and social responsibility have increasingly become part of religious education texts at every level of Catholic education. Another more direct way of linking social teaching to political life has been "candidates' nights" in parishes. Admittedly, a decided minority of parishes sponsor these events. But parishes typically urge parishioners to vote, to study the issues.

Individual or Collective Action; Political or Economic Arena

There is a significant split in the church regarding the best way to bring the church's social mission into the public arena and the best way to engage Catholics in that mission. Diocesan social action offices and the programs they direct toward parishes tend to focus on projects that organize people to affect public policy and the action of public and private institutions on individuals and communities. These are community organizations, organized labor, legislative networks, consumer boycotts, and the like. The constituency to be organized is largely those who lack adequate power to achieve their goals.[32] The focus is almost entirely on what people can do when they are organized and not on the life, stresses, or efforts of individuals.

Some more recent programs take a quite different approach. These are the various faith-work programs designed to help individuals relate their faith to their work life. I think of the Jesuit Woodstock Business Conferences, Heart-to-Heart in Akron (a remarkable development of groups of those in almost twenty different occupations such as law, nursing, criminal justice, teaching and the like), Opus Dei, Legatus, and other programs. These efforts provide support for Catholics trying to maintain their integrity in the workplace, balance the obligations of home and work, and endure the stress of the workplace. The focus is almost entirely on individual responsibility and virtue, and what the individual can do with little or no attention to organized action. When it comes to economic justice the first see the political forum as the best place to further justice; the second see the efforts of people within the business world as the best leverage for change.

PARISHES AS CORPORATE ACTORS IN THE PUBLIC ARENA

Parishes are not only collections of individuals; parishes are also corporate entities that act in the public arena. They do this first by their very existence, by their defining of the world in terms of territory and/or constituency. The bells that still ring out in some parishes are a herald to the entire neighborhood or town of the presence of a way of life. Parishes are also corporations subject to the laws affecting non-profit corporations, buildings, and programs. Parishes can be anchors in an otherwise changing neighborhood, maintaining community, services, and resources as others are withdrawn from the neighborhood. Many parishes act more directly in the public arena, precisely as parishes. Below are a few examples of parish public service projects:

Direct services to those in need: social services, health care, shelters and food pantries, care of the elderly, counseling, etc. Half the parishes in the country report having organized social service activities.

Organizing people to work together in pursuit of their rights, the needs of their communities, and the common good through community organizations, legislative networks, etc.: About a third of the parishes have organized an effort explicitly to promote social justice. A recent survey found 130 community organizations involving parishes and other faith communities. This means that Alinsky-style organizing in local communities have greater influence with regard to the public and private forces affecting their communities than individual citizens, and even individual congregations, could have. Typically, Catholic parishes are essential partners in these community organizations, and the Catholic Campaign for Human Development is one of the funders for every one of them.

Legislative networks are more recent efforts by the Catholic community to engage Catholics in the legislative process. Typically organized in relationship to state government, the networks inform Catholics about issues being debated in state legislatures (and occasionally in the Congress), and encourage them to contact their representatives in support of the position adopted by the State Catholic Conference. They work through the medium of the parish and other diocesan communications, as well as through a specially developed mailing list.

Economic and community development projects: Parishes are also involved as developers and sponsors of publicly assisted housing, credit unions, and certain economic development projects. These can be job-training programs and even job development projects. Obviously, this occurs in poor neighborhoods and towns. The projects usually require public funding and/or foundation funding. From the 1950s to the 1980s, organized efforts by parishes tended to operate through grass roots community organizing, or in various forms of housing sponsorship with the use of public funds (especially housing for the elderly). During the seventies, disagreement developed between those who saw community organizing as the best vehicle for change and those who looked more to community and economic development efforts.[33] In recent years the gap has closed between the two as community organizations began to get directly involved in community development efforts. The best known of these efforts are the Nehemiah Housing projects of the Industrial Areas Foundation community organizations in Brooklyn, the South Bronx, Baltimore, and elsewhere.

Direct advocacy with legislatures, government services, and private agencies: Parishes not only encourage parishioner involvement in advocacy—social justice lobbying—but also act through their own offices and staffs. They contact legislators, public officials, and private agencies to secure assistance for those in need.

Convening people across economic and racial lines, between cities and suburbs, or among those in church ministry, public officials, representatives of organized labor, and others: Parishes that are involved in their communities have significant capacities to convene people who could not, or are reluctant to, meet with one another. They can forge relationships among people, getting them beyond stereotypes to an appreciation of their common ground and common interests. At a simpler level, a parish can serve the public interest by making its resources available to community groups—its buildings for meetings, its bulletins for communication, and its computers and reproduction machines for producing materials.

Faith and Community Action

Faith and community action programs differ in terms of how explicitly they relate to and invoke faith as the origin and context of the work they do.

They lie along a continuum from those that are quite explicit (what we might call evangelical), those that are less explicit about the faith of the program or of the recipient but arise from and are clearly intended to build up the church (what we might call ecclesial), and those that are quite secular, operating according to secular or professional norms and standards. In general terms, the church's social mission for most of the twentieth century was developed in a community of faith which was confident about its faith. Those grounded in the faith and church needed only to acquire the resources and skills to provide service to its fellow believers. As the century wore on and professional skills were fully adopted, the challenge now became to understand how clearly guided the projects were by the faith, and how directly related they were to the church.

This discussion usually focused on Catholic educational and health care institutions. But community organizing, more directly related to parishes, is also part of the challenge. When Monsignor John Egan began working with Saul Alinsky in community organizing in Chicago, the parishes had no doubts about their rootedness in faith and their desire to build up the church and extend its mission. Involvement in community organizing was simply an expression of the corporal works of mercy, indeed of the second of the great commandments; love your neighbor as yourself. As time went on, the relationship of community organizing to the life of faith and parish became more problematic: how does community organizing's appeal to self-interest relate to a gospel way of life? Does the organizing effort build up the parish, or does it simply draw off leadership from the parish? Is the organizing an expression of the community of the parish or does it simply become another organization in which few parishioners are involved? What criteria are used for determining desirable goals and appropriate actions? These questions remain largely unresolved and are as much a concern today as they were when raised over twenty years ago. Similar questions arise about something as simple as a parish food pantry. Parish staffs on Manhattan's Lower East Side have wondered about this simple service: What does simply dispensing food do for the person in need? Should the effort be more directly evangelical or at least more connected with efforts to change the person's situation? Or will that impose unwanted piety on the recipients—as in those soup kitchens where one had to hear the sermon before getting the soup? What does the distribution of food do for the whole parish community?[34]

Faith-Based Organizations: The Pendulum Swings

Many efforts that are called "faith-based" are only indirectly so. They might better be called church-based or congregation-based. Faith as the origin, criterion, and ultimate purpose of the activity can become very dim indeed. At the same time, public service as an expression of faith, irrespective of the faith of those with whom a parish works, needs no more justification than the great commandments.[35]

An important shift occurred in the sixties. Parishes as such could not secure public funds from poverty programs instituted at this time. They had to establish legally separate organizations. Often public funding was granted only because the public officials could count on the institutional stability and reliability of the church as a member of the new "poverty programs," but at least a fig leaf of independence from any one church or religious organization was required.[36] This had the effect of separating the program from many of the other dimensions of church life—the ability of churches to shore up and strengthen broader personal, familial, and community commitments and standards. Many corporations adopted a similar approach. In the early 1970s I approached the community funding director of a major national bank headquartered in New York. I was looking for funds for community projects of the twenty-eight parishes of the South Bronx. When the officer realized the purpose of my visit, he erupted with what seemed like disdain: "You're looking for funds for the church? We don't fund the church!" "Even when it is the only effective network of institutions in the community?" I asked. "That's right!" he insisted. Recently, the tide appears to be turning, as "faith-based" organizations are looked upon favorably by many social engineers, public officials, and candidates for public office. This shift itself needs consideration.[37] A few cautions:

A. Subsidiarity: Sometimes the shift is defended as an example of subsidiarity, but this can be misconstrued as meaning action at the lowest possible level. Subsidiarity calls for action at the level best able to address the issue at hand.

B. Government as actor: Government is often not only the best but the only actor able to address certain issues or achieve certain outcomes— for example, the enactment of minimum wage legislation or the Earned Income Tax Credit. The promotion of the role of the parishes and other church institutions in alleviating the plight of the poor and vulnerable cannot be an excuse for government to avoid its proper role.

C. If the interest is in hands-on service, we might hope that faith-based groups will be more effective (as is argued by DiIullio, among others), but this remains to be proven. Within the Catholic community itself, there is need for considerable discussion about what is appropriately distinctive about our health and welfare services.

In spite of these cautions regarding the growing interest in shifting government services to faith-based organizations, Jim Wallis argues pragmatically: "Who is better able to provide the vision, direction, credibility, longevity, trust, and, of course, organizational constituencies" for human services? The ingredients faith-based organizations provide, he writes, are: message and motivation—an ethic of and opportunities for love and sacrifice; a countercultural and prophetic voice; and institution and constituency—the resources, relationships, and organizational capacities for delivering services.[38]

AN ECCLESIOLOGICAL EPILOGUE

At present there is a competition in play among models of the church. The basic types now range from a loose community of occasional participation (what Greeley calls "communal Catholics") to a church shaped by centralized authority and devotional piety. In between is a variety of types, one of which is a very socially conscious approach to church, best exemplified in socially-active poor parishes and liberal magnet parishes, i.e., those that attract liberals because of an egalitarian style of relationship between clergy and laity, good preaching with a social dimension, and well-developed and participative liturgy. At the center of the continuum lies the parish that is, by definition, pastoral. By pastoral I mean those things that go into an effort to be accountable to official teaching and norms, but accommodating to local cultures and individual needs; attentive to the demands of personal piety and morality as well as to social morality and spirituality; authentic in teaching and worship, and pragmatic in its programming. The parish has a sense of mission, combined with a desire to be inclusive even of those whose participation and commitment is tenuous at best.

The liberal and conservative extremes tend to be ideological—intentional in their ecclesiology. The others are not—they are the result of individual or pastoral impulses and instincts that take the parish in particular directions. It could be argued that after decades of a model that was decidedly militant (on behalf of the poor immigrants and against the threat of communism), a period in which inclusion was the primary motivation (of Catholics and the church in the culture and society, and of the people of the parish in authority and ministry), parishes are in search of a shared mission that would set priorities for their internal life and shape their approaches to culture and society.

At a recent inter-American meeting on parish life in Mexico City, representatives of widely different parishes from fifteen countries found themselves in agreement about the basic direction for such a shared mission. The phrase that captures it best is "missionary community." "Missionary" meant both extending the mission of Christ into all aspects of culture and society, as this is spelled in the Council document *Ad gentes*, and reaching out to the most marginal persons in society. "Community" is both the goal and the means toward achieving that goal—the whole approach of parish life is to engage people in various kinds of communal relationships and efforts, working against both the individualist and the professionalist tendencies of the time. Such an ecclesiology would directly relate the internal community of the church to the engagement of parishioners and parish in the building up of a more just and humane society.

NOTES

1. NCCB Committee on the Parish, *The Parish: A People, A Mission, A Structure* (Washington, D.C.: USCC Publication Services, 1981).
2. Andrew M. Greeley, *The Catholic Myth* (New York: Macmillan, 1990), 154.
3. Wade Clark Roof, *Community and Commitment* (New York: Elsevier, 1978).
4. A more complex analysis of the relationship between parish and territory might be had by applying the thinking of Anthony Giddens regarding space and time in modernity. See his *The Consequences of Modernity* (Cambridge, Mass.: Polity, 1990) and *Modernity and Self-Identity* (Stanford, Calif.: Stanford University Press, 1991).
5. Robert Wuthnow, "Mobilizing Civic Engagement: The Changing Impact of Religious Involvement," in Theda Skocpol and Morris Fiorina eds. *Civic Engagement in American Democracy* (Washington, D.C.: Brookings Institute, 1999), 331–363.
6. "Addressing Youth Crime: An Interview with Eugene F. Rivers," *America*, September 30, 2000, 22.
7. More precisely, 2,496 members according to the 1997 study: Philip J. Murnion and David DeLambo, *Parishes and Parish Ministers* (New York: National Pastoral Life Center, 1999), 11. The number is extrapolated from pastor responses to a survey. The Center for Applied Research in the Apostolate (CARA) puts the total at 3,085 and the average total "registered" parishioners at 2,175; cf. Bryan T. Froehle and Mary L. Gautier, *Catholicism USA* (Maryknoll, N.Y.: Orbis Books, 2000), 51.
8. Froehle and Gautier, *Catholicism USA*.
9. The National Pastoral Life Center study, *Parishes and Parish Ministers*, found that the larger the parish the greater the number of parish ministers, and that these additional parish ministers increase parishioner involvement regardless of the size of the parish. Furthermore, this general trend is also true regarding parish social ministries, i.e., the programs to foster social justice. In short, the more resources in a parish, the greater the participation of parishioners in internal church life and parish social ministry.

10. Bishops appear to be making an exception for Vietnamese communities: they are establishing Vietnamese parishes. The exception appears to be based on the fact that the Vietnamese have their own priests while the various Hispanic/Latino communities do not.

11. This was the Religion in American Life project carried out under the direction of Lowell Livesey at the University of Illinois.

12. Greeley, *The Catholic Myth*, 147. Actually Greeley locates the primary influence of a parish in the leadership of the pastor/priest, and the primary influence of the priest, especially on the young, in his preaching.

13. See Murnion and DeLambo, *Parishes and Parish Ministers*. Another feature of this development is that four out of five of these new parish ministers are women. This means that soon, if not already, women will outnumber men in parish ministry. "Feminization" of ministry is occurring in other churches as well.

14. Construing registration as a measure of commitment was perhaps evident in the Notre Dame Study of Catholic Parish Life, which referred to registered parishioners as "core Catholics." See, for example, a report from the study, Joseph Gremillion and Jim Castelli, *The Emerging Parish* (San Francisco: Harper and Row, 1987).

15. John Paul II *Ad limina* Address to a group of French bishops, *L'Osservatore Romano*, February 5, 1997, reprinted as "Planning for Parishes," *CHURCH*, Summer 1997, 43–46.

16. John Paul II *Ad limina* Address, reprinted as "Planning for Parishes," *CHURCH*, Summer 1997, 43–46.

17. Greeley, *The Catholic Myth*, 155.

18. It is also true that movements depend on parishes for contact with a broad range of Catholics and for staying power.

19. The convergence of religious and social needs in the past also made many Catholics members of the Democratic Party.

20. There has been a trend since the sixties to offer what are called "conversion experiences" for young people and adults, weekend "encounters" of prayer and fellowship, of personal testimony and group sharing, which leads to strong emotional experiences in the course of the weekend. An opposite viewpoint is represented in the Neo-Catechumenate, a program in parishes which stresses the need for active Catholics to be more deeply grounded in the tradition and teaching of the church. This is an extended training process carried out over many years and segregating the participants from the general community of the parish.

21. The study was called the International Values Study and Andrew Greeley prepared the U.S. report on the study. This finding is mentioned in Andrew Greeley, *Religion as Poetry*, 149.

22. Wuthnow, "Mobilizing Civic Engagement," 335.

23. See Greeley, "The Other Civic America: Religion and Social Capital," *The American Prospect*, May/June, 1997, 68–73. Also Wald, Wuthnow, etc.

24. Wuthnow, "Mobilizing Civic Engagement," 353.

25. Greeley, *Religion as Poetry*, 149.

26. Wuthnow, "Mobilizing Civic Engagement," 340.

27. Greeley, *The Catholic Myth*, 78.

28. Wuthnow, "Mobilizing Civic Engagement," 342.

29. Sidney Verba, Kay Kehman Schlozman, and Henry E. Brady, *Voice and Equality: Civic Voluntarism in American Life* (Cambridge, Mass.: Harvard University Press), 32–33. The writers speculate that the reasons behind this are: the fact that Catholic congregations are larger than Protestant one, that fewer Mass goers have active roles in liturgy (I seriously wonder about this), that the Catholic parish is more hierarchical and centrally controlled

than the locally controlled Protestant congregations, and that women have a lesser role in Catholic parishes.

30. See James Davidson, et. al, *The Search for Common Ground* (Huntington, Ind.: Our Sunday Visitor Press, 1997), 63 ff.

31. The data comes from the National Catholic Education Association. Included as "parish schools" are inter-parish schools. Many dioceses have responded to dwindling enrollment and straitened finances by merging schools with the contributing parishes sharing enrollment and responsibility.

32. David Ramage, a leader in social ministry for the Presbyterian Church in the latter half of the last century and an astute observer of social programs, once observed that community organizations work best in communities which not only have something to gain but have something to lose. They do not work so well, he concluded, with the poorest people and communities, nor with well-to-do communities.

33. The two approaches at one time distinguished the Catholic Committee for Urban Ministry organized by Alinsky-supporter Monsignor John J. Egan of Chicago, and the National Center for Urban Ethnic Affairs, organized by Monsignor Geno Baroni, a priest of Washington and later deputy director of the Department of Housing and Urban Development.

34. For a related discussion, see Ronald J. Sider and Heidi Rolland Unruh, in E. J. Dionne and John J. DiIullio, eds., *What's God Got to Do with the American Experiment?* (Washington, D.C.: Brookings Institute, 2000), 132.

35. This discussion of how explicit faith and church are to be in the exercise of the parish's public mission is the action counterpart to the discussion of how explicitly religious the church should be in framing its approach to public policy. The more evangelical explicitly frame public policy discussions in faith-terms, while the more typically Catholic "Programs in Housing Sponsorship," or "Stopping White Flight."

36. One priest from a Catholic Charities office on a visit to HUD regarding a contract for an ecumenically sponsored, low-income housing project was pulled aside by the HUD official before the meeting to obtain assurance that, no matter how ecumenical the sponsorship, the Catholic Church was going to stand behind the project. The church's stability in the community was an important guarantee of the soundness of the project.

37. See Dionne and DiIullio.

38. See James Wallis's essay in Dionne and DeIullio, *What's God Got to Do with the American Experiment?,* 147.

WHAT DO STATE CATHOLIC CONFERENCES DO?

William Bole

For years, in church circles, Catholic social teaching has been dubbed "our best kept secret." That a compendium with this title has sold thousands of copies through several editions since 1985 is one indication that this corpus of social doctrine has become less obscure in recent years. (Authored by fellows of the Center of Concern in Washington, its latest publisher is Orbis Books.) Catholic institutions, from universities and charities to national and state organizations of bishops, have played a critical part in amplifying these teachings to American Catholics and others within hearing distance. Of these institutions, probably least known—even among those in the Catholic know—are state Catholic conferences, which represent their bishops in the public policy arena. Most of these organizations, at work in thirty-three states and the District of Columbia, did not exist before the Second Vatican Council, and some have only recently adopted agendas that reach across the expanse of Catholic social teaching. The state conferences now find themselves occupying a more decisive place in American Catholicism's engagement with public life. That is due partly to the devolution of responsibilities (such as welfare) to the states as well as the evolution of causes within the states (criminal justice reform, for example).

Like other institutions of Catholic social teaching, state Catholic conferences aim to bring such principles as the rights and dignity of the person, a preference for the poor and vulnerable, and solidarity, into the public forum. Grounding this mission are assumptions about the encounter of Catholicism with culture, a generally sociable outlook epitomized in the Vatican Council's declaration that the "joys and hopes, sorrows and anxieties" of the modern world are those of the church (*Gaudium et spes*, #1). Such a hearty sensibility requires confidence in Catholicism's ability to nurture a broad conversation about public morality and the social good, the civil discourse championed by John Courtney Murray (with no small caveat: that the conversation hinged on some consensus about the moral foundations of social life).

Looking to upend these assumptions are some neo-orthodox Catholic intellectuals, notably a younger band of theologians and historians. Skeptical of any real harmony between Catholic tradition and the American political experiment, some critics have soured on the search for a public philosophy (a project dissected by historian Glen W. Olsen in the summer 2000 edition of *Communio*). Holy Cross Father Michael Baxter of the University of Notre Dame has lampooned what he styles as the enduring motif of Catholics coming to the rescue of America; he would rather make sure Catholics themselves understand the social theology (*Our Sunday Visitor*, April 27, 1997). In recent years, this yeasty debate over the so-called Murray project has also given rise to a fresh project of public theology, highlighting what Michael J. Himes and Father Kenneth R. Himes describe as the "essentially public nature of religious belief" (*Fullness of Faith,* Paulist Press, 1993). The authors call for a substantially theological offering to the nation's larger discourse, surpassing the more secular philosophical and natural-law categories applied by Murray.

Closer to the ground are questions about methods and models of Catholic action, approaches that break more or less into three parts: legislation, education, and organization. Before the Vatican Council, Catholic organizations, both ecclesiastical and lay, most notably gravitated toward the latter two modes. They focused on forming the lay social conscience and helping Catholics flesh out the social doctrines in their own secular settings (trade unions and professional associations, for example). Frequently, the church also exercised a convening role, a classic though scarcely remembered example being the business-labor-government conferences on industrial problems organized by the bishops' social action department during the complacent 1920s and for several decades after. Since the Council, Catholic social justice activities (particularly of official church agencies) have leaned heavily on legislation.

Further, some would say Catholic social action has become more noticeably clerical, or institutional and professional, in the post–Vatican II era. While lay-led organizations such as the defunct Association of Catholic Trade Unionists characteristically took center stage in defining moments of the past, since the Council the bishops and their organizations have assumed the most visible roles. Monsignor George Higgins, the late dean of American Catholic social action, has pointed to an irony in this shift. "At present, despite our greater theological awareness of the church as the 'people of God,' we tend to emphasize the role of church professionals—be they clerical or lay—in promoting justice and defending human rights," he wrote in his 1993 memoir, *Organized Labor and the Church: Reflections of a "Labor Priest"* (published by Paulist Press and co-authored by this writer).

State Catholic conferences offer a fresh lens for viewing these currents, or undercurrents, of the church's convergence with American public life. Are the conferences lending Catholic assets, institutional and intellectual, to an encouraging search for the public good? Are they making a difference in the broader discourse, as well as legislative outcomes? How do they divide their energy between lobbying legislators and educating people in the pew? What are they primarily seeking to sway—legislation or the public moral discourse? (And is that a distinction with a difference?) What do they tell us about the Catholic comfort level in contemporary American culture and the hindrances to genuine Catholic participation in political life?

A WELL-KEPT SECRET

As one of the church's better-kept secrets, state Catholic conferences have attracted sparse interest among writers and researchers. The only known work of any comprehensive measure is an altogether dated doctoral dissertation in canon law, completed in 1971 by Michael J. Sheehan, then a priest of the Dallas Diocese, now archbishop of Santa Fe, New Mexico. At the time, Sheehan tallied twenty-four state conferences, only three of which predated the Vatican Council. (New York's is the oldest, founded in 1918; Ohio's was launched in 1945; New Jersey's bishops started a lobby group in 1947 that Sheehan considered the equivalent of a Catholic conference. One conference, in Michigan, was launched a year into the Council.) The number rose gradually during the last three decades of the twentieth century to a high mark of thirty-four.

Unlike the U.S. Conference of Catholic Bishops, state conferences are considered non-canonical. They are voluntary, and the advantages of such a cooperative body are less clear-cut in states with only one diocese. (They are not chapters or formal affiliates of the national conferences.) Still, the state conferences haven't saturated the ecclesiastical market. A comparison of lists and directories indicates that seven states with more than one diocese (from

Virginia and Tennessee to Oklahoma and South Dakota) had no statewide organization for public advocacy as of 2000.

Sheehan was keen on the conferences then, and is now, as visible leader of the New Mexico Catholic Conference. He believes the conferences have proven effective in organizing the voices of bishops in diocese-rich states as well as those, such as his own, with only a few dioceses. In a telephone interview, he gave heavy credit to his conference for the passage of legislation in New Mexico prohibiting the procedure known as partial-birth abortion, in early 2000. The year before, the Catholic Conference helped spearhead an extensive coalition against capital punishment. "We even had the ACLU in with us," Sheehan notes, referring to the American Civil Liberties Union, one of the church's chief adversaries in the abortion struggle. In a non-legislative drive, the New Mexico conference has also corralled opposing interests in a desert struggle over water rights, holding several workshops that pulled together miners, environmentalists, and small farmers. Giving his impression of state Catholic conferences in general, Sheehan adds, "They've gotten stronger in my time. Currently the bishops have great confidence in the value of these conferences."

While the agencies have clearly become more popular among prelates (who are known to boast about their statewide operations over cocktails during national meetings), they remain fairly obscure otherwise, certainly among most of the laity. Frank J. Monahan, who directs the Office of Government Liaison of the U.S. Conference of Catholic Bishops, utters the usual sentiment: "They're really doing the business of the bishops, behind the scenes. They're not the face of the church. The face of the church are the bishops, in their dioceses. They're working quietly with the government. They're not high profile, or intended to be high profile." (The National Association of State Catholic Conference Directors, which meets twice yearly, has an Internet site—www.nasccd.org—with links to seventeen Catholic Conferences.)

Existing at the pleasure of their bishops, Catholic conferences take on different institutional personalities and procedures from state to state. The rough rule of thumb is for a conference to have one full-time staff member for each diocese in the state, notes John Huebscher, who served a two-year stint as head of National Association of State Catholic Conference Directors in the late 1990s and directs the Wisconsin Catholic Conference. This means the conferences ordinarily range from virtually one-person operations (with office help) to slightly double-digit staffs, notably in New York, New Jersey, Pennsylvania, Ohio, Illinois, and California. In between are conferences like

Huebscher's in Wisconsin, which has four staff members in a state with five dioceses. The extraordinary case is the Michigan Catholic Conference, which has over three dozen staff members, largely because it administers employee benefits programs for the dioceses there.

In many ways, state Catholic conferences, especially the larger ones, mirror the high-tech thrust of today's lobbying operations. Carol Hogan handles press relations and other tasks for the California Catholic Conference. Answering questions by e-mail, she gave this bracing account of normal operating procedure in Sacramento:

> In the course of any two-year California legislative session, 5,000 to 6,000 bills are introduced. All those bills are scanned; approximately 800 to 1,000 of them will fall within our customary concerns. We follow those bills throughout their "legislative life" using a computerized tracking system that also allows us to assign a "priority status." Each bill will be labeled as: *major, significant, monitor,* or *track* [her emphasis].

The customary concerns are reverence for life, religious freedom, human and civil rights, economic rights, education, and family life. California's bishops, during their semi-annual meetings, identify the important issues, often in consultation with moral theologians. The conference also arrives at positions through meetings with diocesan ministry staff and "collaboration with like-minded lobbyists."

As in California, boards of bishops generally call the legislative shots, but the conferences allow different degrees of input from others. In one laudable and elaborate example, New York has a thirty-member Public Policy Committee consisting largely of lay people who work in church ministries statewide (and a few in the wider world). With subcommittees that deal with issues such as criminal justice reform, the policy committee advises the bishops on which legislative proposals to line up behind or against.

Another development is the fairly broad agenda pushed by state Catholic conferences. Although a few conferences are absorbed in one or a few struggles (as in the case of gay marriage in Hawaii), most would want to encompass the social teachings along with the consistent ethic of life articulated by the late Cardinal Joseph Bernardin. Their research and analysis of policy issues have grown to reflect broader experience and expertise, which has come with what is generally viewed as a distinct improvement in executive leadership over the past decade and a half. The larger conferences tend to have specialists in areas such as education, pro-life concerns (increasingly about assisted suicide), social welfare programs, and health care delivery, people with professional experience in those areas. By and large, the directors are lay people who have backgrounds in law, public policy, education, social services, and similar fields (in and out of church institutions).

WIDE AGENDA, SPECIFIC TARGET

Catholic conferences as a whole have embraced a now-familiar package of issues including partial-birth abortion, tuition vouchers or other indirect aid to private schools (which once characterized the agenda of some conferences), welfare reform, immigration services, and affordable housing. Tapping the expertise of Catholic Charities agencies, the conferences will often push programs such as job training, child nutrition, and help for unwed pregnant women. Frequently the issues have a regional flavor, as with the argument over water rights in New Mexico and calls for housing aid to migrant farm workers in California and Oregon. Some advocacy is parochial or offbeat, often owing to institutional interests like those of Catholic cemeteries, which get a lobbying hand from the conferences in regulatory matters. Some concerns have been previously undetected in the Catholic conscience. For reasons found in any parish hall on bingo night, the Catholic Church has little distaste for gambling as such. In Illinois, however, the Catholic Conference issued in December 1999 a thoughtful reflection raising questions about the social and human costs of riverboat gambling (as well as about the parish bingo operations). In Wisconsin, the bishops' conference, for the first time, has taken an "enough-is-enough" stand on expansion of casinos.

A new cause is the defense of religious freedom in Catholic institutions, one of several topics discussed by state directors at their 2000 summer meeting in Wisconsin. For example, several state conferences have found themselves pleading for "conscience clauses" in legislation requiring all employers to provide coverage for contraceptives in prescription drug plans. A few have fought off proposals pressuring Catholic hospitals to provide reproductive services incompatible with Catholic moral teaching, a dispute stemming largely from the mergers with non-Catholic hospitals. In California, the legislature passed a contraception-coverage bill that makes no exception for many religious employers. With back-up support from the Catholic Conference there, Sacramento's Catholic Charities filed suit in the summer of 2000 to block the law.

By all accounts, state Catholic conferences assign their resources primarily or overwhelmingly to legislative concerns. In California, Hogan estimates that the conference staff spends 40 percent of its time on directly lobbying the legislature, through office visits, telephone calls, letters, and other approaches. Another block of staff time (20 percent) goes to tracking bills and communicating positions to diocesan staff. (Hogan says the conference has positions on literally "hundreds of bills" currently in the legislature.) The remaining effort is given to holding conferences, interacting with the press, providing dioceses with information about federal programs, collaborating with kindred organizations, and running projects requested by the bishops (at least some of which seem legislative-related in one way or another).

How the conferences divide their time between lobbying legislators and educating people in the pew is a question that elicits varied responses. For instance, when asked, Hogan replied tersely by e-mail, "Our charter is to lobby for the church's position in the public policy arena, to assist diocesan staff in their work, and to represent the bishops in the public square. We do not have direct contact with 'people in the pew.'" In fairness, that would be a heavy order in California, where there are approximately 9 million Catholics in 1,300 parishes and 12 dioceses (including two archdioceses), according to her figures. On the other hand, in New York, where Catholics number over 7.3 million (almost half the population), the bishop conference reports that it has expanded significantly its efforts to educate ordinary Catholics in recent years. The impressive vehicle for this is the Public Policy Education Network, formed with the idea that "our presence in Albany must be supplemented by active grassroots efforts of Catholics lobbying their legislators at the local level," according to Rick Hinshaw, associate director and spokesman. The network aims ambitiously to shape a common Catholic legislative agenda in a diverse state with struggling rural areas, distressed inner cities, and rich suburbs (a unity that has often eluded the Catholic Conference in California).

For some conferences, the legislative year is highlighted by "lobbying days" that call together church activists, once a year, for prayer, social analysis, and lobbying. New York is exemplary: a thousand people turned out for its daylong policy forum in March 2000; California has recently copied the model. These are strictly Catholic affairs, but officials of the conferences will also speak of their collaboration with other faith groups. Observers, though, do not have an impression of extensive ecumenical participation by these organizations, as a rule. More likely noted are exceptions such as the Oregon Catholic Conference, which has little choice but to act ecumenically in a state where Catholics rate one-tenth of the population and all faith groups together do not make a majority.

Overall, the conferences fit neatly in a legislative pattern of social advocacy. This does not necessarily mean they see their role entirely as government liaison (which Sheehan cautioned against in his 1971 thesis). Like the U.S. Conference of Catholic Bishops, some state conferences are pursuing a more spirited outreach to the laity. Still, as illustrated in New York, the usual rational behind this education and organization is legislative: to mobilize lay people behind the bishops' statehouse agenda. This is quite different from seeking to help the laity grapple with issues as Christians in secular settings, yet it does spread the word about Catholic social priorities.

EVOLVING WITH THE DEVOLUTION
OF GOVERNMENT

The so-called new federalism has made state Catholic conferences more consequential and occasionally more visible.

As social welfare responsibilities have devolved from the federal to state and local governments and all the way down to churches and food pantries, the more alert conferences have staked out a creatively ambiguous position in public debates. They have cautioned against a rending of the safety net and the shirking of legitimate responsibilities by higher levels of government. At the same time, they are helping to accelerate the process of devolution by demanding that faith-based organizations be given a wider place in the delivery of government social services. In that way, the conferences appear to be pushing beyond the familiar false choices of partisan polemics, between the public and private, federal and local. California Catholic Conference executive director Edward "Ned" Dolejsi alludes to Catholic social teaching and especially the doctrine of subsidiarity: "I don't think we could sit here and be total critics of what has transpired" in the new federalism. In some instances, the state and county governments have "rolled up their sleeves and figured out how to solve problems, work with faith groups, and encourage personal responsibility. On the other hand, you lose a certain accountability," explains Dolejsi (who was executive director of the Washington Catholic Conference for nine years before coming to California in 1997). On that score, he says that in 2000 the conference pushed the state to tap $590 million of federal money for child health insurance coverage. Under the devolutionary design, the legislature needed to come up with a plan in order to qualify for the funds. It did not, and left the money on the legislative table.

Huebscher in Wisconsin goes with the spirit of Catholic social discourse when he observes, "What devolution does is force the community to have a serious conversation about the nature and location of society's responsibilities." He believes that the doctrine of subsidiarity could help nourish this debate, while acknowledging that the conferences nationwide have work to do in clarifying the principle, originally formulated in 1931 by Pope Pius XI (*Quadragesimo Anno*, no. 79–80).

Basically, subsidiarity underscores the need to tackle problems at levels closest to the people involved (unless the people at those levels are unwilling or unable to solve the problems). "If there is one area where we have more teaching and explaining to do, it's around subsidiarity. It's often seen as just a theory of local control, but it's more nuanced than that."

These political trends have given state conferences a more strategic place in Catholic social advocacy. The U.S. Conference of Catholic Bishops and other national organizations, including the Catholic Health Association, have been eager to forge links with the state conferences, recruiting some directors for seats on boards and committees. Still, doubts have aired about the readiness of national staffers for the devolutionary challenge. Richard J. Dowling serves as executive director of the Maryland Catholic Conference and was elected president of the National Association of State Directors in 2000. He argues that the national conference has a lagging understanding of devolution, as well as of the evolution of issues within states. Dowling is quick to say the conference has lent pivotal help in reacting to legislative eruptions in states—for example, whenever the specter of assisted suicide arises. He adds, however, that the national conference has fallen far short of a nationwide legislative strategy within the states. (So, it would seem, have the state conferences as a group). And so, "It's a kind of crazy quilt" of Catholic policy advocacy in state legislatures, as Dowling sees it.

As the debate over devolution suggests, state Catholic conferences clearly have Catholic assets to bring to public concerns. How effectively are they able to leverage these resources in the marketplace of ideas? The recent experiences of three conferences point to some particular openings, as well as some hurdles.

IN NEW YORK, CHASING THE GHOST
OF NELSON ROCKEFELLER

The New York State Catholic Conference has made repeal of the state's draconian drug laws a priority. Basically, these laws (enacted in 1973 during the days of Governor Nelson Rockefeller) imposed severe minimum sentences on drug offenders, removing judicial discretion. In so doing, the so-called Rockefeller laws became the precursor of mandatory sentencing laws enacted by a majority of states and the federal government. In New York, someone convicted of selling as little as two ounces of cocaine or heroine, or possessing four ounces, gets a minimum sentence of fifteen years in state prison. The reforms endorsed by the bishops and others would give judges the discretion to hand out lighter sentences than currently mandated. Judges would also be able to defer prosecution by ordering offenders into drug treatment programs.

In taking their stand, the bishops of New York's eight dioceses acted on a recommendation by the state conference's criminal justice subcommittee, which includes prison chaplains as well as lay Catholics involved in these ministries and issues. The conference has collaborated with one of the most credible opponents of the drug laws, a Catholic layman and lawyer named John Dunne who, as a Republican lawmaker, was an original sponsor of the Rockefeller laws. He went on to become an assistant attorney general in the U.S. Justice Department under the first President Bush, and now works in private practice while directing the bipartisan Campaign for Effective Criminal Justice, in Albany. Dunne says he supported the laws out of frustration with the failure to curb drug abuse and trafficking, noting that treatment programs at the time were notoriously ineffective. However, the stringent laws have not only failed to deter drug crime, but have also swept into prison many offenders, including mothers of small children, who belonged in treatment and counseling programs. Not incidentally, studies indicate that the techniques of addiction treatment have vastly improved over the past three decades.

The bishops laid out the Catholic position in a two-page statement issued on June 14, 1999. In it, they spoke as "pastoral leaders" and "moral teachers" in witnessing to the harsh effects of the Rockefeller laws on families. Calling the statutes "well-intentioned" in their time, the statement said the laws often keep non-violent addicts, who pose no threat to the community, incarcerated for long periods. The bishops pointed out that their own pastoral and clinical experience (through church-run programs) has taught them that treatment for alcohol and drug addiction can work, and does reduce the rates of recidivism. Providing these alternatives to imprisonment, they asserted, would advance the "common good and social justice for all."

Though peppered with these phrases of Catholic social thought, the statement was strongly secular in its language and arguments. One line, "The cry for justice in our society seems to clash, at times, with the plea for forgiveness," had a theological ring. Otherwise, the bishops relied on their pastoral credentials, appeals to basic fairness, and empirical studies.

While no one expects near-term success in this reform drive, the New York State Catholic Conference approaches it with the confidence of an experienced player in legislative debates. In 1999, for example, the conference lobbied successfully for more spending on alternatives to abortion—not a new cause for the bishops. In the 1980s, three years of lobbying bore fruit in the creation of the Prenatal Care Assistance Program, which funds some of the alternatives. In their triumph, the bishops fought off a push to include abortion funding in the program. (Former Governor Mario Cuomo eventually sided with the conference on this point.) In the last legislative session, the conference also had a large hand in erasing New York's "Learnfare" program, which threatened to cut off public benefits to mothers whose children skip school too often.

Late in the spring of 2000, the New York conference single-handedly spurred a useful debate over the fate of former welfare recipients. With a modest survey by Catholic Charities suggesting that some former recipients in Long Island found it harder to pay rent and buy food, the conference called on state government to determine conclusively what has become of those who left the rolls. That made headlines statewide, although true to the faint organizational profile of most conferences, the accounts mostly referred to "the bishops" rather than the conference per se. The *New York Post* (June 1, 2000) provided the exception to an otherwise positive press, charging that the bishops seemed "mired in the past," that is, in the welfare mentality. In a statement on welfare reform three years earlier, New York's bishops had argued that the standard of success must be a reduction of need, not simply reduced assistance. While restated in the debate over former recipients, this theme didn't filter into press accounts.

Dunne has seen the conference in action since his decades in the state legislature (1966 to 1989). He hasn't always agreed with the positions, but he gives the organization very high marks as a social-justice lobby. "They move around well [in state government]. They're well thought of. They win their share and lose their share," he says, adding that the conference is a critical piece of the coalition aiming to repeal the Rockefeller laws. "Their real strength lies in the fact that they are a continual presence. They're a moderate presence. They're a player." As Dunne has observed, the preferred language of the conference is secular rather than theological. "Their arguments are more on the ethical and moral level rather than scriptural or [beholden to] church tenets," he observes, arguing that a more theological approach would probably have "a very negative effect" on lawmakers.

Simply by virtue of speaking out against the apparent injustice wreaked by the Rockefeller laws, the Catholic Conference in New York is moving Catholic assets into the public square. These assets are institutional as well as moral and theological. The policy points of the bishops are traceable in part to the church's experience in prison ministries, as well as drug and alcohol rehabilitation programs. In this case, the institutional presence is helping to provoke a discussion that needs to be joined at the state level.

Could the conference make a heftier contribution to political discourse on this point? Should its arguments be more markedly Catholic or religious? Could it more lucidly convey the moral dimensions of criminal justice reform? The conference does have resources it could tap in the renewed theological reflections on crime and punishment. It could, for instance, borrow from a lengthy meditation published by the Wisconsin Catholic Conference in September 1999. That statement attached themes such as sin, grace, and redemption to a conception of justice as primarily restorative rather than retributive. In legislative testimony (January 25, 2000) on this and other criminal justice issues, the conference invoked core themes such as the God-given dignity of human life, but did not extend any clear bridge or mediating principles between these faith convictions and its policy conclusions. The same could be said, to a lesser extent, about the conference's 1997 statement on welfare reform.

The New York State Catholic Conference would seem to have space to safely explore a deeper discourse in both theological and natural law terrain. (One can almost hear Michael Baxter howling in the distance about Catholic social thought "losing its distinctiveness" and becoming "bleached out" in the public transaction, as he was heard to say in another context, reported by *Catholic News Service*, March 17, 2000.) Still, Dunne's caution about the use of dogmatic language in the statehouse should not be disregarded. This Catholic conference shows a conviction that the church's social language must not be foreign to a pluralistic society, and especially not to the New York State Legislature.

IN CALIFORNIA, WEIGHING PRINCIPLES AND PROPOSITIONS

In September 2000, California's bishops took a vow of neutrality in an airwaves war (fought in television commercials) between teachers' unions and a Silicon Valley millionaire over Proposition 38, pro–school voucher voter initiative. It was not a vow of silence. In making their statement, the bishops took a forceful public stand on a key prerequisite of the common good and the overriding need for a civil discourse that is civil.

At one time, a tuition voucher initiative of almost any size or shape might have won the backing of a Catholic conference. That still might hold in some states. In California, however, the conference has compiled a set of criteria for such proposals that includes a core value of contemporary Catholic social teaching: the preferential option for the poor. "We believe that a special preference for children and families who are economically poor or in poorly performing schools should be a key element of a voucher proposition," the bishops said in their statement of neutrality. "We are deeply concerned that the poorer children in our society are already at a perilous educational advantage, especially as we move forward in the technology age."

The Catholic conference concluded (with the help of an independent analysis) that the benefits of Proposition 38 would accrue mainly to affluent families whose children already attend private and parochial schools. That is partly because these schools in California report only about 32,000 vacant seats. Timothy Draper, the initiative's main funder, kept his own counsel on how to craft the ballot proposition, and thus ended up with one that seemed counterintuitive to voucher supporters. The trend in several cities has been to target vouchers to poor students or poorly performing school districts, for reasons both political and educational. Proposition 38 would have given a $4,000 voucher to all of California's schoolchildren for tuition in private schools. The voters overwhelmingly rejected it.

Between the lines of the bishops' statement was another reason for laying low in the Proposition 38 crossfire: the whole process of making law at the ballot box. Conference officials say the bishops are wary of this dubiously deliberative process. "Don't get me started on that," Ned Dolejsi said in a telephone interview when asked about it. "They're very blunt instruments that don't lend themselves much to a quality conversation about the public good." That was one of the oblique messages in the bishops' commentary, which bemoaned the negative television advertising that has pitted the two systems of education (public and private, for lack of what the bishops would consider better terms) against each other. "We urge that negative campaigning about Proposition 38 be recognized for what it is—the enemy of the common good and the educational needs of all of California's children."

The conference, though, cannot be accused of moral absolutism on this score. Last year, it tried to mount an initiative requiring that parents be notified when a child chooses to have an abortion, but failed to amass the roughly 700,000 signatures needed. (In California's bustling initiative business, signatures are going for a dollar a head or more.) The bishops have made their most vigorous stands on life-and-death propositions such as physician-assisted suicide (which lost in the 1990s) and expansion of the death penalty (approved by voters in the spring of 2000). Also in March 2000, they emerged from battle over Proposition 22 (defining marriage as between man and woman) bruised but victorious. Consistently enough, the California conference has fastened these positions to specific themes of Catholic social teaching, as well as reflections on Judeo-Christian heritage and secular definitions of the common good.

The California Catholic Conference betrays the typical eagerness of post–Vatican II Catholicism to join in a search for common understandings about public morality. Such a posture would undoubtedly face a heavy cross-examination from some neo-orthodox advocates. Where does this search lead in a political culture that proposes to assist in suicide, expedite executions, and uproot the tradition of marriage? How fruitfully can Catholicism engage with the public if the public no longer shares the church's most axiomatic assumptions, not least of which is the conviction that morality is public, not merely private?

A further question is implicit in the new clustering of religious freedom issues, particularly attempts to impose mandates on Catholic hospitals (to perform procedures such as in vitro fertilization) and other church-related institutions (to cover contraceptives). State conference directors tend to view these not only as incursions into the free exercise of religion. They also see a stepped-up drive to diminish the public role of organized religion in measures that usually target charitable agencies, hospitals, and universities, the most public of religious institutions. (They seem to stretch a point by arguing likewise about barriers to private-school aid and government contracts for faith-based organizations.) How could the church interest the culture in a profound moral conversation if the culture can barely tolerate the full exercise of religious conscience in church-related institutions?

For Dolejsi, there is a more than casual connection between the public character of American Catholicism and legislative salvos like California's new insurance mandate, which absorbed considerable staff time in the losing bid for a "conscience clause." "We are the most prominent church with a public theology that manifests itself with an institutional presence," he explains. "When society begins questioning whether there's a place for organized religion in a very pluralistic culture that spins itself out politically in a lot of ways. An obvious target is the Catholic Church, because we're so public . . . and we're big." Such suspicion might seem to bolster the contention that Catholic leaders should call off the search for a public philosophy (at least as conceived in the Murray project and its spin-offs). Catholic conferences, however, show little inclination to close the church's window on post-modern culture. In their more impressive moments, they have lucidly linked their stands on institutional issues (such as contraception mandates) to public moral priorities (for example, the more urgent call to extend adequate health care to all). These challenges emerging in the states further an impression of the church as simultaneously engaged with and estranged from a culture of compulsory pluralism.

IN WISCONSIN, SPEAKING TO THE PUBLIC
AND TURNING TO THE LAITY

The Wisconsin Catholic Conference has been distinctive in its contribution of Catholic insights to the public exchange. The conference's 1995 statement on welfare reform fitted its positions within a framework of justice that involves fidelity to relationships (more theologically, fidelity to the relational demands of God's covenant). In this ethical and biblical frame, a key question becomes how the reforms foster the human right to participate in society and thus act on responsibilities to family, community, employers, and the general good.

In testimony to the Wisconsin Senate Committee on Labor (August 19, 1999), Huebscher submitted for consideration the theme of the "indirect employer," as sketched in the 1981 papal encyclical, *Laborem exercens*. This mediating principle emphasizes that the responsibility to treat workers justly is not limited to those who hire them. A former legislative aid who worked for a dozen years in the Wisconsin legislature on both sides of the aisle, Huebscher explained to the committee: "All of us are 'indirect employers' in that we take part in and benefit from economic arrangements that define how workers are treated. As 'indirect employers' we have a duty to fashion policies that help meet the needs of workers that may be beyond the capabilities of the private sector." The testimony was in favor of defining a "living wage" in the state, beyond the mere minimum. Huebscher pointed out that the slogan of Wisconsin's widely noted experiment in welfare reform, "only work should pay," will ring true only if work actually pays—with wages that support families. The state senate did not act on the proposal, though the conference has a sizeable list of legislative accomplishments it can tout. (David Yamane points out in his paper, "Negotiating the Prophetic and Political: Faith-Based Political Advocacy in Wisconsin," that the Wisconsin conference is clearly "the most influential and respected religious advocacy organization in the state.")

The conference did not talk dollars and cents, or even directly about the legislation, in its testimony—a choice that reflects a practice of self-restraint in legislative corridors. "I think there's a temptation to want to be a player in the sense of affecting the nuts and bolts of a policy proposal, and that's not our strength or our mission," Huebscher argues (granting the exception of institutional issues such as cemetery regulation). "That moves us away from our strength, which is talking values and themes . . . [and] keeping focused on the bigger picture." He adds, "We have to apply these themes to concrete situations. But the closer you get to them, the more you get away from those areas of competence, which is identifying the principles and questions that have to be asked. So you have to be careful."

This larger focus also ushers the conference out of the statehouse and into other precincts of Catholic social action, particularly the mission of the laity. In 2001, the conference task force on the status of work in Wisconsin marked the twentieth anniversary of *Laborem exercens* by holding forums that drew on encyclical themes as well as empirical studies and personal experiences. "This isn't business as usual in the church," notes panel member Tim Reilly, a permanent deacon and business consultant who formerly led a large manufacturing firm. He was referring to the process, which he sees as part of a generally balanced approach by Wisconsin's bishops to public pronouncements. The conference used a similar process in hammering out stands on welfare reform, casino gambling and criminal justice.

This taskforce model may have more to do with drafting ecclesiastical statements than with invigorating the independent role of Catholics in social settings. But the approach does demonstrate a turn toward the laity and beyond legislative discourse, apart from obvious implications for the way the church arrives at public positions.

IN CONCLUSION:
BEYOND THE STATEHOUSE

Like other religious legislative advocates, leaders of state Catholic conferences are plainly aware of the pitfalls in this public ministry. A few of those interviewed used identical words in alluding to the temptation to become a "player" and soft-pedal the gospel message because of the legislative thrust. As Dowling of Maryland warns, "You get so involved in the game that you forget who bought you the uniform and what number you're wearing." Still, there seems little debate over limiting the mission of these organizations to a lobbying agenda. Huebscher makes a larger-than-usual distinction between tending to legislative details and fostering a public conversation about the social good. Yet even he argues, "If we did nothing but legislative advocacy, we would still be relatively unique, because most of our advocacy is for someone else, the unborn, poor children," and others without a voice.

Would state Catholic conferences make a more meaningful offering to the social interchange by turning toward other modes of Catholic social action? Would they ultimately have a deeper impact by working more regularly through the laity and a broader mix of social movements and institutions? These questions are probably a bit less than fair. The mandate the bishops have given the conferences is to monitor and influence legislation. Further, the conferences merely reflect trends not only in Catholic social action but also the greater interplay of Catholicism and American society. As a practical matter, the bishops could work more logically through the laity when the laity was aligned in an array of Catholic associations that paralleled institutions of American society (in labor and the professions, for example). These support beams of an older, thicker Catholic culture began to splinter as Catholics came into their own as Americans and the church opened its window on the modern world.

Still, it is worth pointing to a variety of social strategies that fall outside a strictly legislative model. Among the pressing ones: helping pastors preach about biblical justice in the pulpits, programs aimed at helping Catholics connect the principles of the church's social teaching to their everyday lives and work, and convening business and professional leaders to address the moral dimensions of their work. Others include facilitating greater collaboration between churches and labor unions, particularly in the organization of low-wage workers and the promotion of global work standards, and encouraging alternatives such as employee cooperatives, community-based agriculture, and housing land trusts. The cultural effects of technologies ranging from the Internet to genetically modified organisms and artificial intelligence also await a Catholic social engagement.

The very thought of so far-flung a mission could make the conference directors dizzy. Their staffs are not getting any bigger, for the most part, and they probably are not finding it any easier to push Catholics onto the social playing field. As a whole, with modest resources they have molded a presence in state capitals that seems easily comparable to that of the U.S. Conference of Catholic Bishops in Washington, even as they remain one of the church's well-guarded secrets.

THE LIMITS OF COALITIONS AND COMPROMISES: THE CALIFORNIA STATE CATHOLIC CONFERENCE

Edward E. Dolejsi

In the March 7, 2000, presidential primary election in California the voters approved Proposition 22 by a 62 to 38 percent margin. This surprising result was the culmination of a nearly two-year project of a formal and public coalition of groups, including the Catholic Church in California. The coalition was created to protect the traditional definition of marriage and provide a legal barrier to the legalization of same-sex marriages in California.

In December 1999 a formal and public coalition of groups, including the California Catholic Conference, "pulled the plug" at the eleventh hour on an effort to qualify a constitutional amendment ballot initiative that would have required parental notification for a minor abortion to be legally performed in California.

In October 2001, the governor of California vetoed a bill that would have allowed terminally ill prisoners who were no longer a threat to society to receive a compassionate release to their families for their last days. A formal and public coalition of groups, including the Catholic conference, saw its best efforts thwarted at the last stage in a long and complicated legislative process that had unfolded over two sessions.

These are three of the hundreds of stories of coalition politics, large and small, that unfold each year in the halls of federal, state, and local government in the United States. Some of the stories have successful political outcomes for the coalitions, some do not, and some are but single steps on the way to the revision, passage, or defeat of laws in our various political entities.

State Catholic conferences through their directors and staffs officially represent the Catholic Church in thirty-three states and Washington, D.C. Through their efforts on behalf of the Catholic community, the church is invigorated as it engages the rough and tumble world of politics. It also has the opportunity to have a role in humanizing the people and processes that form and shape our laws.

In statehouses all over the country my colleagues orchestrate and live the reality of significant Catholic Church involvement in political coalitions. I have asked them to share reflections based on their experiences. They have provided many examples of public and private arrangements where Catholics act as formal and informal partners with groups as predictable on some issues as Focus on the Family, and as unlikely, because of our differences on other issues, as the American Civil Liberties Union.

In certain states with progressive populist traditions, like California, Washington, and Oregon, the usual statehouse political processes are augmented, and occasionally skewed, by public initiatives and legislature-instigated referenda. These situations provide interesting twists in and of themselves, but when these high profile campaigns unfold a larger spotlight is shone on the Catholic Church's role in formal and public coalitions. In reflecting on the role of the Catholic Church in these cases I will engage some of the fundamental questions that determine whether such coalition participation is a good and appropriate strategy for the Catholic Church. I approach the topic as a practitioner, and offer comments from that perspective only.

PERSPECTIVES AND PRINCIPLES

In 1987, as a rookie Catholic conference director in Washington State, I was embroiled in a battle over policies about how the state would allocate funding to counties for persons who relied on general assistance. The dynamics of the process were emotional. Eventually a decisive moment occurred when the opportunity to prevail against significant political odds emerged. The lives of many poor and working poor women and children would be drastically affected by a legislative victory. The Catholic conference had joined a large and public coalition with likely and unlikely partners, including the National Organization of Women. An endgame step in the lobbying process involved leveraging an individual legislator's decisive vote through some possibly questionable, although not illegal, tactics. In my desire to win and be an effective member of the coalition, I sought the counsel of Archbishop Raymond Hunthausen about the delicate next steps. As I began to explain the choices, he stopped me and said: "Ned, it's your decision. Just remember we are the church while this is unfolding, and we will be the church when it's over. We must always behave like the church." That sound advice remains my guide to this day and informs every complex choice I make in the sometimes messy world of politics. By the way, we were able to influence the coalition not to take the questionable action. We eventually did prevail on the bill.

Our charism as the Catholic Church is not to be a political actor. We can be significant, dynamic participants on particular issues and in certain venues, but we do not, and should not, play the political game with the same abandon and vigor as many others, some of whom we may work with in coalitions.

Forming and working with coalitions is as natural as breathing for those who want to be politically viable and influential. Powerful, well-heeled private and public interests seek out those of common mind to see who can best help them, how, and when. For-profit or nonprofit organizations, moneyed interests, substantial political donors, and even contribution-restricted government entities, all play politics using coalitions as an effective means to achieve their goals. The thirty-four state Catholic conference directors may have differing styles and guidelines for participation, based on their ecclesial and political histories, but all of them are also involved in coalitions, and my brief survey of these colleagues confirmed that their experiences generate diverse reflections.

Let me describe formal and public coalitions and distinguish them from the many informal coalitions in which we constantly participate within the political process. Formal and public coalitions are formed most often around such high profile legislative policy and budget issues as right-to-life, economic justice, homosexual rights, tax reform, and the death penalty. Coalitions of this type are almost de rigueur on public referenda campaigns. Recent examples of such coalitions involved school vouchers in Michigan, homosexual marriage in Hawaii and Nebraska, and assisted suicide in Maine and Oregon.

Markets, media, manipulation, and money are facts of modern American social, economic, and political life. The church exercises her ministry in the midst of this culture. We raise funds for our buildings, our institutions, and our ministries. We understand how the systems work. Candidates and parties need to raise and spend enormous amounts of money to shape public opinion. Coalition participants also need to create formal organizational structures to shape public opinion or to influence significant legislation.

Sometimes a single individual or entity substantially underwrites the effort and calls all the shots; this was the reality in the failed 2000 California voucher initiative. The main proponent provided the majority of the capital and therefore decided what the initiative's content would be and what strategic message would be communicated. Many potential partners, including the church, chose to remain neutral on that initiative.

Formal and public coalitions have certain characteristics. There is usually a formal structure of organizational representation and a clear process for making decisions on political strategy, fundraising, and creating and disseminating public messages. Most coalitions operate on the assumption that decisions will be made by consensus or by another predetermined process. At times there may be a fee for a seat at the table. This can involve a minimum initial financial contribution or, especially in the case of public referenda, a commitment to secure significant amounts later.

In the case of 2001's Proposition 22, "The Committee for the Protection of Marriage" consisted of representation from evangelical, Catholic, and Mormon churches, as well as a number of secular political organizations. Eventually the larger committee worked through an executive committee and political consultants to design the political strategy, conduct the polling, create the message, and organize the fundraising. There may also be many administrative details that must be handled professionally in order to meet rigorous state campaign finance disclosure and reporting guidelines.

Informal coalitions are usually short-term working arrangements with much lower public profiles. In my Washington State and California experiences, I saw that these working groups come together quickly, operate more casually, and don't involve large sums of money or complicated reporting requirements. These informal partnerships focus their time and attention on legislative message refinement and sharing the lobbying workload. Occasionally the coalition as a group may engage the media. Most participants and our "elected targets" understand the nature and operation of these groups and expect that there is a single issue that garners the support of these different organizations. It is usually easy for these coalitions to disband or, if necessary, for one group to easily extricate itself. Some conference directors would probably not even consider these to be real coalitions.

However, all coalitions, formal or informal, emerge in response to, and are subject to, the deadlines of either a legislative time frame or the confines of the electoral process.

The reasons for joining formal and public coalitions are usually clear and simple.

It is a way to multiply and optimize the financial and human resources needed to prevail on a public policy issue.

It is a way to demonstrate broad support for a particular position on a controversial measure.

It can broaden the impact on policymakers who may be influenced by one group rather than another.

It can and does attract press attention by demonstrating sheer numbers for a position or piquing the interest of the press at the unlikelihood of these groups working together. The incredulity that the press may feel at "strange bedfellows" also can lend an authority to a shared position.

It can mobilize significant educational efforts targeted at diverse constituents.

Depending on the coalition participants, behavior, or message, these coalitions can reinforce or highlight the "moral dimension" of a particular issue.

Practical Decisions and Perils

"The Church makes a poor coalition member," according to my colleague and friend John Carr, Director of Social Development and World Peace of the United States Conference of Catholic Bishops. He backs this claim up with humorous anecdotes that describe our need for control, our snail-like decision-making processes, and our general unwillingness to compromise on practice and issues. Beneath the humor lie serious observations about our deep institutional reality and the degree to which we can compromise our beliefs and values. We are not a membership-driven organization, self-interested trade association, public interest research group, or a special issue advocacy group. These groups, by virtue of their purpose and tax status, involve themselves in politics differently than we do. They make endorsements of candidates' political contributions, and engage in electioneering tactics. We can't, won't, and don't engage in these behaviors.

Internal Church Dynamics and Decisions on Coalition Participation

There are many internal decisions that a state Catholic conference of bishops or an individual diocesan bishop may face in deciding whether or not to engage in a formal and public coalition. The moral importance surrounding a specific issue is always the focus of initial analysis and dialogue. When the moral imperative for the issue is fairly obvious, the considerations quickly take a more practical turn. In our California Catholic Conference (CCC) process, the following questions assist us in our assessment:

Is this the best legal vehicle? Are there other options available?
Is this the optimal political moment?
Are the right partners present and active? Are these partners trustworthy?
Can the Catholic community be mobilized on this issue?
Are the needed resources available or will they be?
What are the expected financial, human and system resource contributions of the Catholic Church? Do we have those resources?
Can this effort actually prevail?

Other questions of concern unique to each local church may be added to the deliberations. Expectations for personal involvement on the part of church leadership and other members of the coalition may be a cause for added discernment. It is important to note that there are no objective right answers to these questions. But generally, the discernment explores the moral import of the issue, weighs the practical considerations, and tries to clearly understand the implications of the political context and consequences for the church. Bishops and lay leadership may see the answers to the questions listed above differently. Thus the internal process to determine and keep a united decision to participate is no easy task. The dynamic may take months of internal conversations and negotiations, in an attempt to achieve solidarity among the church leadership. For coalitions seeking immediate and responsive partners, we may not be their first or best choice.

The California Catholic Conference has an unwritten expectation that there will be no position on public initiatives until the measure has garnered enough signatures to actually qualify for the public ballot. In California there are always many ideas and proposals offered. Our bishops believe that the church's primary role is to inform, comment, educate, and influence matters of morality when those issues are clearly in the public decision process, and they choose to reserve the public exercise of authority and expertise until that is the case. This approach, albeit sometimes controversial or disappointing to potential allies, has served the bishops well. This policy is occasionally set aside if the moral import of an issue is high and the prospects for success are good.

In the second example used in the opening of this paper, such a determination was made. The CCC formally joined the "Committee for the Protection of the Family" in an effort to secure 670,816 valid signatures of registered voters by January 6, 2000, to place a constitutional amendment on the ballot for the general election in November 2000. Our interest in changing California law to ensure that parents would be informed of their daughter's life-and-death decision to have an abortion is consistent with our perspective on family life and generates significant concern in our church leaders and members.

This case provides a good example of what can transpire when the Catholic Church, as a partner in a formal and public coalition, does not thoroughly process and execute its internal decisions for support and action. The larger coalition was not able to fundraise effectively in the signature-gathering phase or make reasonable provision for the election-phase funding. Likewise, the coalition leadership counted unduly on a partisan dynamic to deliver the initial goal of qualification for the ballot. These were the main factors in defeat. However, as the conference director responsible for assisting the bishops with their deliberations and participating on their behalf in the leadership of the coalition, I have engaged in appropriate "second-guessing" of my leadership and decisions in this matter. In December 1999, to the disappointment of many dedicated and zealous grass-roots participants the coalition leadership "pulled the plug" on the effort. We were then about 200,000 signatures short. Through our organized parish efforts the Catholic Church had been instrumental in delivering about 250,000 of the 1 million total needed. The responsiveness of our parish-based pro-life volunteers was stunning. They worked long hours on short notice to personally present the petition to their fellow parishioners. But not all dioceses had organized effectively to educate their clergy or to participate in the signature-gathering efforts. Our hope had been to deliver 400,000 to 500,000 signatures. In California, signature gatherers can be paid per signature. This necessitates having sufficient financial resources to purchase the requisite number to guarantee ballot qualification. Although we had been clear that our contribution at this stage of the campaign would be to organize this volunteer effort, our coalition partners continued to press me to secure direct church donations to help with the effort to purchase signatures. Coalition fundraising, while spirited, fell significantly short of the amount needed. A gubernatorial election and partisan races and issues steadily siphoned off contributions from likely donors. We had begun the first phase of the campaign without putting a competent finance committee in place. When the right people did not step forward, the prospects of eventually securing the $10 to $12 million necessary to be competitive with the pro-abortion rights groups in the actual election seemed unrealistic. The project was doomed to failure. A last-ditch effort to find the money for the purchase of signatures was called off. Some of the coalition leaders felt strongly that in our weakened condition we ran the serious risk of losing the general election and negatively affecting the will of the people on this vital issue.

This experience clarifies another set of very important considerations. Our people had been called to action. They had worked tirelessly. We had failed. Many felt betrayed. They were disheartened. Any future decision to mobilize this network would need to be carefully determined. We would need to have everything in place and the prospects for successful ballot qualification ensured.

Some conferences of bishops actually have written policies that limit and/or proscribe their involvement in such formal and public coalitions. One conference's policy prohibits ceding to coalitions the authority to bind the conference on any issues. Obviously, when our need to control reaches that level, we might not be the most responsive of partners for potential colleagues

Our tradition's 2,000 years of promoting a vision of the human person created with dignity, inextricably connected in community, gives the Catholic Church unique perspectives on participating with others in efforts at cultural transformation. The Catholic Church has long maintained strong philosophical and theological consistency. We understand that the church is "in this world but not of it." Being a hierarchical institution has permitted the church to survive through some of the incredible and embarrassing political ventures pursued by society and the church over the centuries. But this hierarchical nature also encourages, some may say predestines us, to exert significant control over the group dynamic and strategy of coalitions. Sometimes our participation in coalitions is strongly desired precisely because we are viewed as being able to deliver a constituency through exercise of authority in our structure. The extent of our "need to control" is dramatically affected by the local ecclesial dynamics in certain states, and the historic and current demographic reality of Catholicism in that civil jurisdiction.

As a case in point, in California there are multiple layers of complexity that influence our need (not speaking here of our ability) to control the agenda in coalition efforts. California has nearly 34 million people. It is the sixth largest economy in the world. The juxtaposition of personal wealth and poverty is startling. We have no single ethnic majority; we are multilingual and multiracial. The county of Los Angeles has more people than forty-four states and the city of Los Angeles has a larger population than twenty-two states. We have forty-six media markets and a booming Spanish-language media. The Archdiocese of Los Angeles has over 4 million Catholics in three counties. We have a cardinal, an archbishop, two archdioceses, ten dioceses, two ecclesial provinces, twenty-two active bishops, and the largest concentration of Catholics and Catholic resources in the western hemisphere. We experience palpable North/South/Central Valley social and civic identity. There is a beautiful history of Catholic participation in the formation of this state. The church has been an essential part of creating the "soul" of California. The presence of so many faithful Hispanic, Filipino, Asian and other Catholics contributes to making us, at 24 percent, the largest single denomination. We operate one of the state's largest networks of private education, social services, and health care. But the church operates in a secular and, at times, hostile political climate. We have a significant influence on local civic efforts, yet our institutions are constantly challenged because they are distinctively Catholic. Decisions affecting our need to control the agenda of coalitions to which we belong is influenced by this complex and, at times, confusing mixture of realities. It forces us to be very intentional and strategic about our public interventions. There is a heightened sensitivity to the actual media costs and the judicious use of our financial resources.

I want to add a few words about our ability to control the agenda, message, strategy and activities of formal and public coalitions.

The 1991 campaign to defeat Initiative 119, which proposed to legalize physician-assisted suicide in Washington State, is a case study of rationales that define the ability to control the message and the agenda of a coalition. If the Catholic Church, for moral, historic, public relations, or practical considerations wishes to control or exert substantial influence on the activities of a coalition, this will usually involve contributing healthy sums of money, or delivering system-wide educational efforts, adding moral authority, lending institutional expertise, or all of the above. The exact mix of these "control levers" is often determined by what the other members view as the church's essential contributions to the success of the effort.

Others in the coalition on Initiative 119 provided fundraising enthusiasm and expertise; the Catholic bishops provided extensive moral authority, educational outreach in the parishes, and secured the involvement of Catholic health care organizations in the effort. We substantially influenced the message and its delivery. We have developed multistate political expertise and message sophistication on this topic that adds to our value as a coalition member in any venue where the issue arises. This issue always elicits our strongest political response.

In the first example, of Proposition 22, for the Protection of Marriage, the Catholic Church was among the first organizations to pledge substantial funding for the campaign through early diocesan contributions. This quick monetary support sent a strong positive message to other funders. But it also, importantly, enhanced our ability to work with the Church of Jesus Christ of Latter Day Saints and others in "controlling" the message of the campaign. The Catholic conference emphasized that this campaign would not use messages that attacked the personal dignity of homosexual persons, or any image or argument that could be characterized as "homophobic." We were adamant that this would not be tolerated during the campaign because it would be inconsistent with Catholic teaching on the homosexual person and our institutional interest in affirming the current definition of marriage in state law. For us, this was about protecting the current definition of marriage and only that! We were fortunate to eventually have the polling data confirm that such a message was also the key to a winning strategy. The early Catholic Church endorsement and funding also bolstered the confidence of many other groups and donors.

Even so, the Catholic Church paid another price in challenges to our own sense of community and internal solidarity. Most of our Catholics fully supported the decision to endorse and provide funds for this initiative. However, many parents of gay and lesbian children, clergy, religious, and volunteer leaders in diocesan ministries with gay and lesbian people expressed their pain at the church's funding. They recognize Catholic teaching regarding the person, family, marriage, and sexuality. And while not all disagreed with our support of the initiative, many experienced the decision to fund the initiative as hurtful. Leaders in California's gay-rights movement certainly appreciated the significance of the Catholic Church's actions. They initiated an incessant campaign, targeting the Catholic Church for "imposing our values" and raised the usual bogus issues around the separation of church and state.

The political dynamics and real motivations of all the partners in a potential coalition can be a minefield, full of reasons for future poor decisions and possible negative publicity. The ostensible goal of all partners is usually the passage or defeat of a piece of public policy. Coalition members share a common sense of what is right and what is in the common good. But passage or defeat of legislation is often not the only or most important goal of all the potential coalition partners. A good example is the Parental Notification for a Minor Abortion Initiative. Many coalition members had strong partisan identifications and agenda. Their decisions about which issue to engage were affected by considerations regarding the power of an issue to speak to their constituents, to rally their troops, to raise their political capital, or embarrass and disadvantage the other party or candidates. Even the actual choice of which election to choose for a particular measure, or the specific timing of a piece of legislation, may have special partisan interests attached by coalition members; these are in addition to the usual concerns about which election optimizes the chance for success. But these are not our agenda. A very practical part of initiative campaigns is to be on "slate mailers" of candidates and parties. This can present some unique challenges and occasional embarrassment for a church that engages such a wide variety of political issues but does not engage in partisan or candidate politics. In California we recently declined early participation in a coalition around one of our key issues because many of the proponents appeared overly interested in the partisan advantage to be gained.

In the case of the coalition opposing the legalization of physician-assisted suicide, it could be argued that by forming a coalition we "watered down" the effectiveness that we might have realized as only one of many organizations speaking separately. Would the many voices, rather than the one coalition voice, have been more effective? Did some of us not work as hard as we could have individually? Did we rely too much on the work of a few? A further reflection on this issue for us as church is whether we weakened the impact of our own special faith-based plea for compassion.

INTERNAL COALITION
PRACTICAL DECISIONS

What are some of the dynamics and decisions that confront the Catholic Church in the actual operation of formal and public coalitions?

One of the first thoughts is always "who is in this with us." For many in the secular arena, this is an overt political consideration or a practical political consideration based on prevailing power relationships, previous experiences, or goals. While those reflections are also part of the church's decision, there are also one or two other prior considerations. Is there any ecclesial inappropriateness and possible scandal associated with being at the same table as any of the partners? We recently declined an invitation to be part of a large statewide coalition of groups promoting universal access to health care insurance. We were expected to be on a steering committee with Planned Parenthood, which has championed defining abortion as "prenatal care" in California law and its budget. To be in a coalition with the proponents of unfettered abortion rights is incongruous, and today impossible. However, Catholic Charities USA and the national Planned Parenthood Federation held a successful joint press conference several years ago. They stood together to oppose a proposed "cap" on welfare benefits that would punish mothers having more than two children. Catholic Charities spoke out because it believed that such a policy pressured women to have abortions. Planned Parenthood spoke out because it would limit a woman's "reproductive choice." Both organizations believed they could maintain their integrity, stand together, and call attention to the inappropriateness of such a policy. Sometimes creating such cognitive dissonance in the minds of politicians and the media by such a partnership can be a powerful force in the political dynamic. However, walking the fine line between causing scandal and achieving dramatic results is a difficult and risky business.

In politics there are many friends and no enemies. Eventually we all need each other. However, many of today's friends are tomorrow's opponents. Another serious political consideration that now influences my own decision to join coalitions—even informal legislative ones—is a growing need to limit how much future opponents may come to know about our internal operating style through our work together in coalitions. The longer the association in a coalition, the more intimate is the exchange of knowledge about an organization's political strengths, weaknesses, and propensities.

One such weakness of the Catholic Church needs attention. Polling data demonstrates that Catholics who attend our churches on Sundays and absorb the Catholic media maintain a consistency of opinion on the bishops' positions on serious social issues. Much has been written about this. But we are also keenly aware that our parishioners are not particularly informed or involved in the world of politics. The directors of Catholic conferences are anxious to work with others to address educational and organizational efforts to empower lay Catholics to put their faith in action in their professions, as citizens and as voters. The USCCB, diocesan offices, and Catholic conferences have developed quality programs and materials, but we have not substantially addressed the systems necessary to motivate, educate, and train our sisters and brothers.

In a different vein, we chose to be part of a California Coalition for the Protection of Religious Freedom. It was necessary for us to make sure that no religious group was left out if they share our interests in religious freedom in public opinion and law. The ACLU is part of this coalition. We have been on the same side as the ACLU on legislation to limit the use of the death penalty, and on the opposite side on the issue of homosexual rights. This coalition has provided us the opportunity for dialogue, to challenge their penchant for championing individual rights at the expense of the right to religious freedom. Working together has helped us forge clarity around our differently held positions and to truly identify our organizational priorities.

As a coalition we have discovered that, while all of our colleagues in organized religion share a mutual understanding of the free-exercise clause of the federal and state constitutions, they do not share our perspective on the establishment clause. From this formal coalition has come the opportunity to know and respect other people of faith in the political world and to engage in meaningful dialogue with groups who oppose us on specific issues. Our desire to be listened to seriously by others requires us to acknowledge and respect the others' right to be heard.

In formal and public coalitions the decisions and actions on the use of financial resources is always fraught with challenges for the church. On some high-stakes political ventures, like public initiatives, it can be sobering for church leaders and deflating for coalition members when the actual costs are calculated and the actual Catholic contribution is presented. This mutual reaction has doomed some efforts and chilled some possibilities for the future. After a review of the amount of money needed and our prospects for securing it, we recently made a decision in California not to attempt a ballot measure on restricting the use of the death penalty.

Some particularly problematic aspects of making financial decisions in coalitions are the specific political choices that need to be made. Is it morally appropriate to spend donor funds to buy the silence or involvement of some groups? In each campaign, monies are expended for consultants. Are they the right ones? Will they act ethically? Decisions need to be made about which advertisements to run, what the message will be, and whether the images are acceptable. When the process involves manipulating public opinion by playing to emotions and prejudices, it enters the gray area of truth in advertising. The Catholic Church may find itself close to being declared a public liar! Public accusations to that effect, even lawsuits and regulatory action against the coalition, have accompanied each of the anti–assisted-suicide campaigns in Washington, Oregon, California, Michigan, and Maine. The Hawaii campaign against gay marriage also drew such criticism. On the plus side, the Catholic Church's presence in these and other coalitions has influenced positive choices and limited the negative zeal of others. When involved as leaders in coalition decisions, the Catholic Church understands the special fiduciary responsibility it accepts for donors' funds. It is our aim always to bring a commitment to truth and fair play that ennobles our own and our colleagues' effort, as well as the cause.

A fascinating side issue debated in some Catholic conferences is the source of funds for many of these high-cost public referenda campaigns. Some argue for no direct Catholic Church funding, only our moral and educational engagement. Others argue for direct church donations to campaigns, as in the case of Proposition 22. In California during the anti–assisted-suicide initiative campaign, there were direct donor solicitations and the collection of campaign funds at most Catholic parishes on Sundays. Some argue that we should be instrumental in forming Catholics into special interest political funding PACs, or that the funding of campaigns should be done through existing Catholic ancillary organizations. All of these ideas will no doubt continue to be explored over the next few years, particularly in states like California, Oregon, Washington, and others where there is an extensive and expensive use of public initiatives.

Faced with so many challenges, many of my colleagues respond differently to being part of a coalition. One describes it this way: "I have found it easier to initiate a coalition than join an existing one or one that is forming. Then you can shape the group consistent with conference principles and goals. I have found that if you are willing to lead and are creative about it, others will follow. We have initiated coalitions over the years on pro-life, death penalty, tax reform, and welfare reform."

Others colleagues in state Catholic conferences have begun to ask their bishops to adopt "no coalitions" policies. This does not mean that they do not work with others in the informal coalitions referred to earlier. This remains a political necessity. But it does mean that they do not engage in formal and public coalitions in some of the ways described here. They will ask to be invited to meetings and to be part of strategy and execution, but the name of the Catholic Church, state conference, or diocese does not appear publicly. One of my colleagues offers this observation:

> I tend now not to join coalitions. . . . I tell the person forming the coalition that we are supportive and we are interested, but as a policy we think it best to not form a coalition. Can you put us on the mailing list? Can we attend the meetings? We would be happy to provide any information on the issue we have. We are willing to stand with you at a press conference. We will join you at a rally. We just won't formally join the coalition and we reserve the right to publicly disagree with the coalition's position if that is necessary. They almost always agree. If they don't, I figure they really did not want the church's involvement that much. Most of the time having our involvement is important enough that they include us in everything except formal membership.

These two approaches express distinct ways of dealing with the tensions that inevitably arise from the expected compromises and ethical quandaries associated with membership in a formal and public coalition. With these variations in mind several relevant questions arise:

> Should the Catholic Church officially participate in formal and public coalitions?
>
> Should the Catholic Church only participate in formal and public coalitions that we initiate and/or control?
>
> Should the Catholic Church not be an official member of formal and public coalitions?
>
> Is the Catholic Church's identity and mission sacrificed in any way by participation in coalitions? If so, how?
>
> What is the cost of participating in formal and public coalitions?
>
> What is the cost of not participating in formal and public coalitions?

Catholic conference directors continue to debate these questions, among ourselves and with our bishops, and with current and potential partners. Other religious and secular organizations still request our involvement. However, I don't think we could say that there is any consensus on one approach to working in coalitions.

PROMISES AND POSSIBILITIES

I believe firmly that we should not abandon the practice of participating in formal and public coalitions. Of course, we should be appropriately but not overly cautious in discerning which coalitions we join. We can and should initiate the formation of coalitions around particular issues in the political arena, especially those in which Catholics have a substantial interest. These decisions about our involvement require more art than science, more intuition than analysis, and essentially more faith in the power of the Holy Spirit than the power of fear.

Decisions around full or partial participation should be informed by a clear grounding in our identity and mission—who we are and ultimately what we are trying to accomplish in the public legislative forum. In my opinion, engagement in coalitions is consistent with our identity and mission. If we are confident in our identity and trust in the Spirit, we will boldly and humbly act as we are led by God's will. This kind of faith frees us to be dynamic partners in formal and public coalitions.

The Catholic Church is fundamentally present in the public forum as an evangelist. We are there to speak God's redeeming Word to a restless and broken world. We are there to share our rich and wise Catholic vision of life rooted in right relationship with God. We are to proclaim God's love for each and all of us through Jesus the Christ, crucified and risen from the dead.

The church and its agents invest in prevailing in the competitive reality of our political order. We seek common goals with many people, and common cause with many of their associations. Through a variety of means we can and must influence those who make political decisions. We want to win, but we don't worship at the altar of politics. We expect government to play a positive role in ordering our life together, but we don't hope for government to solve all our problems.

We recognize that those who join us in political coalitions are there to win for their constituents and themselves. We can share that goal in our coalition work. The ethical framework that informs our partners' decisions may be one shared with us; it may be admirable in its own right; or it may be less than acceptable by our standards. When our partners' decisions and actions are consistent with our ethical standards we should assertively participate; when their decisions and actions are not consistent we should attempt to reform through influence; when they can't or won't choose to be consistent, we withdraw and find other means to pursue our goals, while maintaining relationships.

Our ultimate purpose for engaging in political activity is to evangelize. The Catholic Church cares deeply about protecting those persons who are vulnerable, speaking for those who are poor, promoting the common good, and seeking peace through justice. When others in society desire to join us in this agenda or ask us to join them, we should do it. Let's do it with passion for the shared cause, wisdom gained from our experience, enthusiasm for our evangelizing mission, and faith in the Spirit guiding us.

There are prophetic and practical opportunities for our involvement in formal and public coalitions. The world of politics is a gray world. But we do not need to fear the darkness because we walk in the light of Christ.

CATHOLIC HEALTH CARE AND THE CHALLENGE OF CIVIC SOCIETY

Clarke E. Cochran

> Periodically sounding its siren, a hospital ambulance made its way through a veil of snow flurries on the evening of December 20, 1954, in South Buffalo. Inside the vehicle, lying on a stretcher, was Joseph O'H., a sixty-seven-year-old retired Irish engineer. . . . After a short ride, the patient arrived . . . at the Emergency Room of Mercy Hospital . . . run by the Sisters of Mercy, an order of Irish American nuns with deep roots in the community.[1]

So begins chapter 10 of Guenter B. Risse's history of hospitals. Here he tells the story of the transformation of the American hospital during the middle of the twentieth century from a place of observation and symptomatic care to a location for curing devastating diseases and injuries. The presence of the sisters filled the halls, leading Joseph O'H. to comment that a "whole atmosphere of caring permeated the institution." Joseph O'H. had suffered a heart attack; he was given oxygen and sent to a ward for strict bed rest.

When Albert F., another man with heart attack symptoms, arrived at Mercy in 1974, it was a different place. Albert F. immediately had EKG monitoring on his way to the emergency room. CPR and other emergency resuscitation equipment was nearby. Albert F.'s medical care was incomparably better than Joseph O'H.'s, but he reported feeling alone and isolated in the hospital, his care impersonal.

What stories will be told thirty years later in 2004? Mercy's ability to cure will be light years beyond 1974, but will its Catholic identity and its relationship to its community be attenuated by market forces and medical technology?

External pressures—market forces, medical technology, and liberal culture—impinge on Catholic identity. Catholic hospitals, like most, were once freestanding institutions closely linked to their local communities. Institutions of civil society at a basic level, they formed the skeleton of civic life in many neighborhoods, towns, and cities. Medical technology and market forces changed all that. Instead of going to the closest hospital, patients now go where specific procedures are performed or where their insurance company has a contractual relationship. Community hospitals merge and affiliate, creating large non-profit and for-profit chains. Then chains break up, when the business situation dictates.

Internal pressures are also at work. Some ecclesial changes (the decline of religious orders, conflicts over doctrine, reactions to Vatican II) have profoundly affected all Catholic institutions. Others are particular to health care: the evolution of leadership from Catholic religious orders to business-trained lay executives, the shrinkage of Catholic nursing education programs, the declining ecclesial identity of Catholic physicians. The future of Catholic health care is bound up with the challenge of forming new leadership for new ecclesial, medical, and business institutions.

These external and internal challenges raise questions abut the institutional church; that is, questions of ecclesiology. They raise questions about the distinctive identity of Catholic health care and how that identity is communicated within and outside the ministry; that is, questions of sacramentality. They raise questions about the public role played by Catholic institutions; that is, questions of civil society.

Here we try first to describe more fully these challenges to Catholic ecclesiology and sacramentality in the health care field. Then we look at four recent strategies followed by Catholic hospitals. Finally, we draw some lessons for Catholic health care in the public square.

MARKETS AND BUSINESS ETHICS

Capitalist markets are simultaneously institutions and normative systems. Thus, the market dominance of American health care affects the structures and norms of institutions that participate, including Catholic institutions.[2] In the nearest Catholic hospital, for example, the CEO is most likely to be a non-Catholic layman with an MBA from a state university, instead of a Catholic nun with an MDiv from Fordham. The same hospital is no longer a freestanding institution, but a member of a major system of Catholic hospitals, long-term care, home health, and other facilities. Internally, the business practices of Catholic institutions look very much like the business practices of for-profit institutions.[3]

Market forces affect not only the institutional shell, but the ethical core.

Competing "margin/mission" mantras symbolize this: "No mission, no margin" versus "no margin, no mission." When facilities are no longer profitable, no matter how long they have been part of Catholic mission, the parent Catholic systems look for closure or for buyers, including for-profit ones.

Is health care a mission in the name of Christ or a commodity traded in the health care business? The answer, of course, is both. The tension between them can be resolved only by exiting the health care business altogether, or by the radical transformation of American medicine. Since neither is on the horizon, living with ethical and mission tension is the future of Catholic health care.

TECHNOLOGICAL IMPERATIVE

Matters would be relatively simple were the imperatives of the market the only significant challenge. Yet the modern practice of medicine itself creates dilemmas for Catholic health care. American medicine is far more aggressive than medicine in other cultures.[4] Stressing acute care, it neglects chronic conditions and preventive care. Enamored of science and technology, it seeks ever further extensions of life and victory over illness itself, symbolized by the genetic revolution's promise to unlock the secrets of disease, defect, and aging. As William Haseltine, chairman and chief executive officer of Human Genome Sciences, put it, "Death is a series of preventable diseases."[5]

Medicine shaped by this model becomes more impersonal, dominated by machines, pharmaceuticals, and computer-generated images. Yet healing modeled on Jesus is personal and incarnational. It values care more than cure, regarding death as an enemy, but by no means the most dangerous enemy. Moreover, as the American population ages and as American culture produces more human wreckage in the form of addictions, mental illness, and serious injuries, need increases for long-term care, mental health care, and recovery programs. The culture of modern medicine and the modern need for healing increasingly are at odds.

Dominated institutionally by the acute care hospital, how will Catholic health care negotiate this tension? Can Catholic health care build anew on past tradition, embrace emerging needs, and resist the technological imperative? There are signs of hope, but the challenge is profound.

CATHOLIC MEDICAL ETHICS

A deep and comprehensive bioethical theology, along with a set of practices that embody it, is a distinctive feature of Catholic identity. So is Catholic social teaching's emphasis on service to the poor, the common good, and social justice in health care. These translate into extensive participation in civil society, advocacy for expanding health insurance to all, and commitment to charity care by Catholic providers.

Yet this very ethical strength creates stress. Medical ethicists and most medical practitioners do not share the Catholic view. It is likely that most Catholics do not understand or accept most of the church's bioethical teachings. Many Catholics in health care are uncomfortable with Catholic identity and Catholic authority, a discomfort particularly acute where the issues of gender and hierarchy are concerned. Moreover, as market forces push Catholic hospitals toward mergers, Catholic ethical principles create roadblocks. When Catholic hospitals merge with non-Catholic, reproductive rights interest groups, medical societies, and state attorneys-general often object that the merger will mean loss of certain women's health services, especially emergency post-rape contraception and elective sterilization. Some mergers have faltered, and others have fallen apart over these issues.

There is now a drive in various state legislatures, and by some within the American Medical Association, to require all hospitals to offer "the full range of reproductive services." Hospitals that do not would lose accreditation or public funding. Existing state "conscience clause" laws that allow religious facilities to opt out of providing these procedures are under attack. Legislation has been introduced in California and New York that would reduce conscience claims to the most narrowly defined religious institutions. No Catholic hospital in the United States qualifies as a religious institution under these laws.

Finally, the genetic engineering and embryonic stem cell research condemned by Catholic moral theology (a condemnation not shared by most Catholics or by medicine generally) may well produce treatment modalities whose origin and application will make them difficult for Catholic hospitals to accept.

CONSEQUENCES

There is a tendency to see the current challenges to Catholic health care ministry as unprecedented, and the particular shape they take certainly is. But health care ministry has always been under pressure.[6] The reason is simple: whatever the dominant political, economic, or medical system of a given time and place, Catholic identity must always be at an ethical angle. Catholics faithful to Jesus' words and deeds are "resident aliens" in every society.

This truth, however, does not make matters easier; quite the contrary. It is very difficult for a pilgrim community to carry the baggage of multi-million dollar medical complexes. The very institutions that incarnate the sacramental identity of Catholic health care make it extraordinarily difficult to change course nimbly.

Catholic health care leaders are aware of these challenges. The Catholic Health Association (CHA) in the last five years completely reorganized and focused on Catholic identity, collaborative arrangements, leadership development, and inventing ways to bring change to the health care system. Indeed, the church brings considerable resources to responding to these challenges: institutional creativity, sacramentality, and readiness to engage civil society.

INSTITUTIONS

Catholicism refuses the American religious temptation of "God and me," which produces the belief that social change happens only through individual conversion. Instead, Catholics understand that human nature is social and that Christian faith employs the social capacities of persons to form communities of disciples. Communities, however, need structure; so Catholics build institutions, which they come to love (and hate).[7]

There is tension between maintaining a specifically Catholic calling and finding the material resources to keep the organization going (the "mission-margin" dialectic). Once one accepts that Christ founded a church, an institutional reality to continue through time, one accepts a tension between the freedom of the gospel and the strictures of organizational survival. Institutional isomorphism, Catholic institutions borrowing features of the dominant cultural institutions, is a constant possibility. Of course, there is no theoretical reason why isomorphism cannot work the other way; that is, Catholic hospitals could be so successful that other institutions would imitate them, as happened with pastoral care departments and ethics committees. Although there is considerable evidence that Catholic health care institutions did in the past serve as models, isomorphic dynamics now seem to run in the other direction.[8]

SACRAMENTALITY

In Jesus God became incarnate. God communicates love through persons, relationships, and signs. Therefore, Catholic institutions are sacramental; that is, when authentic they image grace through visible and tangible signs, symbols, and culture. Catholic sacramental theology builds on the human need to encounter divinity in the material. Because God is knowable, but always beyond comprehension, God's being is a mystery never fully transparent, but revealed and hidden in materiality.

What would be the consequences of taking quite seriously the claim that sacramentality is central to Catholic identity? If health care is to be Catholic it needs to look, feel, smell, and taste Catholic. The modality of the outward sign needs to match the inner meaning. Yet this resource is difficult to put into action. How many crucifixes and statues does it take (per bed? per floor?) to make a hospital Catholic? Does sacramentality reside primarily in the visible, or in the tangible, the touch that passes between healer and patient? Or is it in the voice, compassion embodied in words and tones?[9]

CIVIL SOCIETY

An explosion of theoretical and empirical literature on what has come to be called "civil society" in sociology and political science focuses on associations that link citizen to state, mediate between citizen and state, and defend citizen from state—organizations such as neighborhoods, unions, trade associations, churches, civic clubs, and sports associations.[10] This literature also recognizes the importance of religious or faith-based institutions as vital elements of civil society.[11] As a public religion, Catholicism should be well-placed to benefit from such renewed attention.

Institutions like Catholic health care have a unique place on the border of public and private life, having features of both. They must attend to their particular traditions and to their public responsibilities. At the same time, their public and private sides feel the force of the ideological, medical, political, and market dynamics of American society. Life on the border is uncertain and insecure. The real challenge to Catholic health care is not from business or from ethics narrowly construed, but rather it is the call to marshal institutional creativity for the common good within this field of tensions.

CASE STUDIES—STRATEGIES OF ADAPTATION

The challenge and the general response, then, are clear. What is unknown is the status on the ground. How successful have Catholic health care institutions been in transforming themselves, while remaining true to their core identity?

The following case studies illustrate four different strategies to address market, ethics, and civil society challenges: (1) aggressive expansion; (2) local alliance; (3) divestiture; and (4) hospital-community partnership for community renewal. These strategies do not exhaust the range of possible responses; nor are they mutually exclusive. However, they suggest the range of promise and difficulty facing Catholic health care today.

St. Joseph Health System

With a national excess of hospital beds and with the need for market share to facilitate contracting with managed care organizations, an attractive strategy for Catholic hospitals is to acquire other hospitals in their geographic area, as well as to build or acquire outpatient clinics, rehabilitation services, home care providers, and hospices. Increased market share allows institutions to be more economically stable and to negotiate reimbursement rates from a position of strength.

St. Joseph Health System (SJHS) appears to be a successful example of this strategy. (St. Joseph Health System is a psuedonymn, as are the other institutional names in this and the following case study; some of the information comes from informants who were promised that they and their health care systems would not be identified.) As recently as the late 1980s, SJHS existed as a single (400-plus bed) urban hospital. Established by an order of women religious nearly ninety years earlier, it had a solid reputation for medical care and Catholic identity in a largely non-Catholic environment. Near the end of the 1980s, SJHS decided that it must grow or die. Choosing the former, it opened a clinic in a low-income neighborhood and built a major hospital in a growing, middle-class area. By the late 1990s, SJHS owned or operated over twenty facilities (including community health centers, physician office buildings, a children's hospital, a home health agency, rural hospitals, clinics, and skilled nursing facilities). SJHS operates the area's only Level II trauma center, and its hospitals include the full range of typical services as well as heart and kidney transplant programs. It is now one of two major health care systems in the region it serves, and it remains a member of a national Catholic health system.

One unique feature of SJHS is its operation of the area's only public hospital. This hospital bore the brunt of services to the uninsured and Medicaid population, but was in very bad shape by the mid-1990s, after years of poor management and financial stress. Without a takeover by another entity, it was on the way to closure. SJHS was the only system that offered to lease and operate "Public," assuming complete financial risk. Public clearly needed SJHS, but SJHS also needed Public, both to expand market share and to meet its mission to serve the poor. In both these respects the agreement has been successful, and SJHS now seems widely recognized in the community for its commitment to the poor. Yet Public offered contraceptive and sterilization services before its affiliation with SJHS, and the operating agreement called for these to continue, though SJHS distanced itself by having these procedures carried out, not by its own employees, but by separately contracted providers. Ultimately, the Vatican got wind of the matter and demanded that such cooperation cease, thereby imperiling an arrangement beneficial to local government, to SJHS, and to thousands of patients. The contract had to be renegotiated at considerable expense in time, dollars, and political tension. The local government agreed to operate a separately licensed "hospital within a hospital" that will handle procedures (not including abortion) forbidden by Catholic ethical directives.

SJHS seems to have met the business challenge. Revenues have increased substantially and, despite significant subsidies each year to Public, its economic position seems firm. This success has not come at the expense of mission and Catholic identity. Informants in the homeless service community, for example, speak in praise of SJHS's service to their clients. The physical environment of the business operation also speaks symbolically of mission. The corporate headquarters section of their flagship hospital is quite modestly appointed, compared with lavish executive suites in other hospitals, witnessing commitment to service rather than perks.

Informants in the religious community testify to the respect SJHS has within and outside the Catholic community. It is perceived as very Catholic, and also as a provider of high quality care to all patients. One informant inside the system worried that SJHS presents Catholic identity to non-Catholic employees in general "humanitarian" terms, but conceded that this is probably necessary in a religiously pluralist patient and employee setting. Both Catholic and non-Catholic staff point to business success and mission to serve the poor. Results from a series of focus groups revealed the importance of mission across the ranks. Mission ("serving the poor; serving the community") emerged as one of the top three features of the environment that keep SJHS employees working there.

These features of SJHS's performance suggest that Catholic ecclesiology stimulated sound institutional creativity and adaptability to new circumstances. Moreover, Catholic sacramental witness flourishes both within and outside the institution. SJHS has a reputation for social justice and political advocacy. It received a major federal Community Access Program grant, and it has a reputation (often identified with a particular member of the founding religious community) for effective lobbying in the local community and the state capitol for policies and programs that reflect social justice and the preferential option for the poor. Public Hospital symbolizes and institutionalizes commitment to the poor, which has become SJHS's mission even more strongly than before the affiliation. SJHS is now the health care safety net for the entire region. According to one long-time employee, the affiliation "opened the eyes" of SJHS as a whole to the poor. Charity care and clinic losses increased from $21 million per year in 1997 to $44 million in 2001 (from 6.1 percent of net patient revenue to 8 percent of net patient revenue—an unusually high percentage nationally).

Yet the affiliation with Public and, in particular, the continuing adjustment of the relationship to the prohibitions in Catholic biomedical ethics has been difficult. Although all parties interviewed believe that the situation can be worked out satisfactorily, since each needs the other very much, it is a source of continuing tension within the community, breaking out again in late 2002 in a controversial SJHS decision to build a new children's hospital taken without adequate discussion with its governmental partner. According to one non-Catholic interviewee, SJHS and the local government "walked a tightrope" from the very beginning, as the affiliation evoked an "unhappy nexus" of forces—the Vatican, the U.S. bishops, medical technology, financial realities, moral principles, and the women's movement. Recognition of the extraordinary services of SJHS to women's health in other respects muted some proponents of reproductive rights, but most are quite unhappy about the likely stigma of a woman who would enter the new "hospital within a hospital" instead of the regular service of Public operated by SJHS. Two well-informed Catholic observers testified to the very creative role played by the local bishop, but one also pointed to the damage done by the Vatican's direct intervention. "When negotiations between SJHS and local government first began five years ago, opponents of the affiliation said that Public would end up being answerable to the pope; that the pope would be running the community's hospital. The events of 2001 tend to prove them correct!" The SJHS-Public affiliation, he observed, has been a double-edged sword, enhancing Catholic identity as service to the poor, but reinforcing Catholicism's least understood and least accepted principles regarding contraception and sterilization, and reinforcing suspicion of Catholic hierarchy among Catholics and non-Catholics.

Holy Family Hospital

Just as in the strategy of aggressive growth, the strategy of local alliances recognizes the need for partnerships in the new hospital environment. In this approach, however, the Catholic hospital does not seek to (or is unable to) control the new structure. It aspires rather to be an equal partner with other independent institutions. Together they hope to be more viable than they would be separately. Such a strategy may be adopted through visionary leadership that perceives it to be the most effective method of coping with the challenges and opportunities presented by the local situation. Or it may result from necessity, where an institution has fallen behind the curve and is in danger of closure. The latter seems to be the case with Holy Family Hospital (HFH).[12]

HFH is a large (500-plus bed) community hospital located in a major Southern city. Founded over 100 years ago by an order of women religious, it is now in its third location. It shares this location with a large public hospital, smaller hospitals and clinics, and a state medical school. Until the mid-1990s, HFH was an independent community hospital, though part of the national system of hospitals founded by its sponsoring order. Although its size and reputation for excellent and advanced medical care gave HFH a strong position in the community, fierce competition had also entered the picture, and there was a scramble in the local health care industry to merge and affiliate to achieve the size deemed necessary. HFH eventually joined forces with two other religious non-profit systems to form Metropolitan Health System.

By 1999, however, the honeymoon was over. Whatever the facts of the case, HFH perceived that it was being used by the other partners for their purposes and that its economic resources and good reputation in the community were being squandered. Although HFH saw the need to end the affiliation, it realized that it could not stand alone. The hospital's longtime and loyal medical staff took the lead in approaching the state medical school for affiliation. An agreement was worked out in which the medical school became the "landlord" (in reality, owner) of a new entity, "Medical School Hospital, Inc." (MSH). HFH remains a Catholic hospital, authorized by the local bishop to carry that designation, and the MSH board and officials at the medical school have committed to honor that identity.

It seems likely, though the story has just begun, that HFH will survive and possibly flourish under the new structure. Its future would have been dark without MSH partnership. There were few available partners in the region, and it clearly could not stand alone. But it is clear that the medical school will be very much the dominant player. Catholics responsible for mission and identity at HFH focus very much on the survival of Catholic identity, instead of its advance. Among rapid and unsettling changes, their energies focus inside the institution. How can HFH's historic mission, values, and religious traditions be communicated to the largely non-Catholic medical staff, faculty, and administrative staff now in control of the institution's destiny? Will economic necessities and medical school culture overwhelm Catholic mission?

There is aspiration, but no clear path for institutional creativity under Catholic auspices. Institutional creativity will lie primarily outside HFH. A great deal of energy will go toward educating medical personnel about the United States Conference of Catholic Bishop's Ethical and Religious Directives for Catholic Health Care Services. Success is impossible to gauge. A core of longtime medical staff committed to HFH's Catholic identity will help, but there are many new staff and a new administration. Although initial statements are highly respectful of HFH's history and identity, what will emerge is unclear.

One sign of hope is commitment to sacramentality among HFH's mission team. For example, a statue of the founder cannot be missed in the main entrance, and there are two chapels (one small and meditative; the other quite large) that seem to be much used by patients, family, and staff. The mission team is very much aware of how identity is communicated in signs and symbols and in attitudes and culture. Yet there also is great uncertainty about how to embody sacramentality more fully.

Most unclear is the role to be played by HFH in the larger community. The mission team is committed to the clinic for low-income persons located in the hospital and to various community programs. Although no information about charity care and community benefit directly comparable to SJHS was available, HFH will have a far lower profile and less impact than SJHS. Much of the community's charity care is done at the public hospital, with which HFH is not directly affiliated. Its on-site clinic is relatively small. The mission team's understandable focus on internal matters takes attention away from the community. HFH's principal contribution to the community likely will come in the continued provision of high quality medical care—not an insignificant matter, but not a distinctive one either. Many other hospitals in the area do as well or better.

Daughters of Charity Services of New Orleans

As the number of hospitals shrinks, inevitably some Catholic facilities will be sold or close their doors. Clearly, there are uncreative ways for Catholic sponsors to divest hospitals: Sell and use the proceeds to pay off debt or to shore up other sponsor-owned hospitals; or wait too long to sell, negotiating from a position of weakness and realizing little from the action. Holding on too long is the downside of Catholic ecclesiology.

A more promising pattern occurs when a sponsor moves completely out of the hospital business in a particular market, but uses the proceeds realized from the hospital sale to establish a new philanthropic foundation devoted to new forms of health ministry in that community. Here sponsors are far-sighted enough to let go of old institutions that no longer meet the most pressing ministry needs. With divestiture there is room for considerable ecclesial innovation, for new sacramental witness, and for a strong focus on civil society. This kind of creativity allows sponsors to maintain their historic ties to particular communities, but in new ways.

The Daughters of Charity have served New Orleans for nearly 200 years. Among their facilities was Hôtel Dieu Hospital. In 1992 the Daughters sold Hôtel Dieu to the State of Louisiana so that the state could replace its older charity hospital. Following the sale, the Daughters conducted a two-year study of the needs of the community. Ultimately, they decided to use the proceeds of the sale to establish Daughters of Charity Services of New Orleans (DCSNO), which provides grants to a variety of already established ministries and to four new ministries created in 1996: Daughters of Charity Health Center, Daughters of Charity Neighborhood Health Partnership, Seton Resource Center for Child Development, and Vincentian Ministries.[13]

The Daughters of Charity remain actively involved in DCSNO, with four of the ten positions on the Board of Directors. Moreover, DCSNO is a member of Ascension Health's Southern Division. This arrangement allows it to draw resources from a larger organization and facilitates continuation of the Daughters' historic traditions in New Orleans. Grants from the foundation have been in the annual range of $3 to $4 million. In FY2000, the four new ministries totaled 143,000 client encounters and patient visits. They project an annual growth in visits and encounters of 8 percent per year, reaching 245,000 by FY2005.

New Orleans has some of the worst health statistics in the nation, and DCSNO decided to focus on such traditional measures as improving access to basic health services, wellness and prevention programs, and school-based health. Yet the Foundation decided to go beyond these traditional services and included as central goals: a full continuum of care through an Integrated Delivery Network (IDN) for the underserved in the region; extensive mental health counseling; and working through multiple residency programs to train a new generation of health professionals in primary care, prevention, and community health for low-income persons.

DCSNO met the business challenge by avoiding it. Concerned that it could not and should not compete in the hospital business in an over-bedded community, it chose to leave behind the mission/margin dilemmas of that enterprise. It does not have to meet the same bottom line demands as hospitals, and it depends far more on volunteers and donated time. Yet it cannot rely on a continual flow of income from insurance-reimbursed services, but must depend on the Foundation's resources (in turn dependent upon investment markets), on the vagaries of grant-writing, and on sometimes fragile partnerships with other actors in the community. The kinds of leadership and technical skills needed to operate a foundation and its constituent components are quite different from those in traditional health care. Indeed, they hearken back to the institution-building and begging of the founders of religious orders.

Divestiture also avoids some of the ethical dilemmas of modern, high tech, hospital-based medicine and furnishes a clear ethical goal: meet the needs of the poor and underserved. This narrower focus resolves considerable ethical ambiguity and tension, but not all. School-based counseling and teen mentoring programs inevitably run into ethical issues: counseling a young woman headed for an abortion; whether to suggest contraceptives to sexually active young men and women; and needle exchanges for intravenous drug users. The lower visibility of such issues, however, changes the political and ecclesial dynamics. It's one thing for the Vatican to inquire about the use of surgery suites in hospital obstetric units, another to inquire about what is said in confidential counseling sessions.

The larger civil society is affected in many ways. Selling a hospital breaks up old, and perhaps staid, community relationships, requiring new ones to be formed. Yet, there is considerable tension in trying to balance being a direct service agency with being a community change agent. Such tension can be productive or destructive. Many of DCSNO's initiatives seem to respond very creatively to the new need to generate multilayered community institutions and partnerships.

For example, DCSNO participates in the Neighborhood Based Senior Care National Initiative, funded by the Retirement Research Foundation of Chicago to design approaches for church based volunteers to identify seniors who have become isolated, to assess their needs, and to connect them with social groups. These efforts require major coalition-building across the public-private border: collaboration with federal agencies, with the local Metropolitan Council on Aging, with a private research foundation from Chicago, with the local Baptist Community Ministries, with the Archdiocesan Office of Social Apostolate, and with a wide variety of church congregations.

The goal of creating an IDN to meet the continuity of care needs of marginal communities reveals an equally diverse public and private field of civil society: a private medical school, a public hospital, a public medical school, the city department of health, a federally-qualified community health center, the state department of health, Medicaid administration, primary care physicians, a HUD-funded mobile clinic for the homeless, LSU's Healthcare Network Musicians' Clinic, and a school of pharmacy, among others.

Likewise, the initiative for Preparation of the Next Generation of Physicians and Other Health Professionals requires DCSNO to work with sixteen different public and private residency training programs. Community Health Partnerships involves about fifteen different public and private entities, suggesting some of the richness and complexity of relationships in civil society.

In short, the greatest challenge of civil society today is not so much the creation of institutions of service, but the organizational and leadership skills to weave institutions into new patterns. This case study cannot assess the successes and failures of DCSNO's network building, but it does suggest the potential of Catholic health care if some institutions were reoriented from traditional hospital-based and other forms of direct service into non-traditional services and into coalitions and partnerships. Getting wholly or partly out of the hospital business might allow Catholic health care to return to pioneering, to being among the first to see a newly emerging need and to respond with institutional creativity.

Hospital-Community Partnership for Community Renewal

In this model, the Catholic hospital remains in its traditional business in the community of its origin; yet that community has fallen on hard times. The community hospital is often the only major private institution left. The kinds of public and private networks in the DCSNO case exist also in hospital-community partnerships, because the hospital can be only the lead agent for renewal. It cannot act alone, for local governments have power over zoning, water and sewer, and law enforcement. Businesses and other institutions eventually must be lured into the renewal area. Collaboration is essential. I consider two examples of these partnerships. Both are works in progress whose success is not assured.[14]

St. Clare's Hospital is the central institution in the Hunterstown neighborhood of Alton, Illinois. The neighborhood began a gradual decline a decade ago as its industries closed, businesses moved, and residential properties lost value and turned into rental units. Crime increased; schools closed. St. Clare's viability was threatened by the rise of non-paying patients, danger to employees, and the high cost of either flight to the suburbs or buying up all the properties around it to form a "moat." After one failed attempt in 1995 to encourage the city toward renewal, the hospital proposed a partnership in 1997. It would provide seed money to start renewal; the city would work on code enforcement, property condemnation, and infrastructure improvement. An extensive planning process produced a redevelopment plan now being followed by the city and the hospital. The plan's scope, however, required a new entity—a neighborhood redevelopment corporation, a not-for-profit entity, directed by a board whose membership reflects the breadth and depth of civil society: the City of Alton, St. Clare's, community business leaders, residents, and other neighborhood stakeholders. As of 2000, the effort had begun with a pilot project in the area of Hunterstown, which had the worst crime, drug, and housing problems.

Hunterstown is a neighborhood in a medium-sized city. Pembroke Township-Hopkins Park is a rural area of about 3,000 primarily African-American residents located east of Kankakee, Illinois. Unemployment is high; many homes are trailers or shanties; roads are unpaved; and family income very low. In the middle 1990s the Servants of the Holy Heart of Mary, who sponsor Provena Health in central Illinois, became interested in Hopkins Park. Together with the Kankakee Economic Development Council, the Sisters formed Pembroke Partners to pull together resources to work with the residents of Hopkins Park for the renewal of their community. The Partnership incorporates 250 organizations and individuals, including Provena Health, the Lutheran Brotherhood, the U.S. Department of Agriculture, Pembroke Township government, Catholic Charities of the Diocese of Joliet, Illinois State University, Kankakee County, the U.S. Army Reserve, and the State of Illinois.

CONCLUSIONS: CATHOLIC HEALTH CARE AND CIVIL SOCIETY

The CEO of SJHS observed that "we still don't know how much we're riding on the past." The words were about SJHS, but they are true for Catholic health care generally. The health care institutions of today are an extraordinary bequest from the past, not only buildings, but traditions and good will. Yet the challenges of 2003 are not those of 1903. Traditions can be forgotten; good will can evaporate. Traditions can be a drag on progress, as well as a resource for change. These cases are not the last word on the institutions discussed, let alone on the ministry as a whole. Nonetheless, some tentative conclusions are in order.

The Business Challenge

The jury is out regarding whether Catholic hospitals and health systems will weather the present financial storm. Managed care placed tremendous pressure on these institutions, but managed care in its present form soon will be dead. Employers, insurance companies, and government no longer possess enough incentive to accept the political consequences of strong action to restrain health care costs. The return of significant cost inflation is good news for financially strapped providers. Yet cost expansion will set off a new round of insurance loss for the working poor, and demands for charity care will increase. Medicare will continue to tinker with reimbursement rates for home health, rehabilitation, skilled nursing, inpatient, and outpatient care. The average hospital patient will be more acutely ill than in the past. But many communities will be over-bedded; consolidation and closings will persist. So the business challenge to hospitals and health systems will continue in different form.

The case of St. Joseph Health System demonstrates that some communities still need the Catholic acute care hospital and that it can be (if it expands intelligently and makes sound alliances) both financially viable and a sacramental witness of compassion and justice. Yet Holy Family Hospital demonstrates the financial and ecclesial fragility of Catholic hospitals. If HFH had sold its assets and invested them in a community foundation ten years ago, it might well be a more effective community presence now.

Non-Catholic acute-care hospitals provide outstanding medical care. Now seems to be the right time (perhaps even past the right time) for Catholic health care to reduce its acute care presence and to turn in other directions where business pressures are no less, but are different, and where the need for distinctive ecclesial and sacramental presence is greater—long-term care, the homeless, seniors isolated from social networks, decaying neighborhoods, rehabilitation, and mental health care.

The Ethical Challenge

Despite the constitutional and ethical centrality of the freedom of religious institutions to follow their consciences, Catholic health care is likely to lose the public relations battle over contraception, sterilization, assisted reproduction, and stem cell-based therapies. (At least in the short run; *sub specie aeternitatis* all bets are off.) The battle and its loss will intensify pressure on Catholic hospitals and other direct service providers. Mergers and affiliations with non-Catholic providers will draw greater scrutiny. Continued commitment to the hospital, and to aggressive expansion combined with cost-cutting, will generate more labor conflict and greater tension between Catholic social teaching's commitment to labor unions and Catholic health care's suspicion of them.

Continued (over-) commitment to the hospital could also detract attention from the battle over the uninsured and other marginal health care populations. Difficult as that battle is, it is potentially winnable. Or, if not winnable in the sense of the advent of national health insurance, at the least Catholic health care can make a clear difference when it enters more fully into the community trenches in the manner of Daughters of Charity Services of New Orleans or St. Clare's in Alton. It can make a difference in the lives of particular individuals who need help, but it can also make a difference in the intensity and direction of Catholic policy advocacy and in visible commitment to the preferential option for the poor and social justice in the healing ministry.

The Civil Society Challenge

There are still citizens and intellectuals who believe that liberal democracy demands and depends upon drawing a sharp distinction between private life and politics. For such persons, religion belongs firmly on the private side of the line. This distinction never made sense intellectually or historically. Although the private and public spheres of life are different, there is always considerable contact between them, always an important border area where most of the interesting political and social action takes place.[15] The important political challenges of the coming decades will be how governments and private organizations can manage their interactions and collaborate to solve social problems, how they can work together on the frontier, where most social problems exist. Think of the 1996 welfare reform law, which explicitly recognizes the importance of faith-based social service. In crime policy, local police forces are now far more likely to work with community institutions than they were twenty years ago. The Environmental Protection Agency does not clean up toxic waste sites; it contracts with the private sector to do so.

These examples, and the cases discussed in this chapter, emphasize the collaborative side of the public-private relationship; but they feature regular border skirmishes as well. These are endemic to any frontier. Civic engagement and civic competence sometimes require citizens to challenge government or business or non-profits. Institutions of civil society, Catholic or otherwise, not only partner with government. They also defend citizens against unjust and exploitive government and business policies; and they advocate for policy change. In short, the public-private border of the future, where Catholic health care pitches camp, will be a field of cooperative, competitive, and conflicting forces. Health care ministry within this field will call for maximum and sustained institutional creativity, for flexible and nimble leadership and institutions.

What is fascinating for a Catholic political scientist is how most political scientists (and other commentators) have ignored Catholic health care's decades-long activity on the religion and politics border. It has implemented government programs, spent billions of public dollars, and worked with hundreds of private and public organizations, all the while proudly asserting its religious identity. None of this has been without difficulties, as SJHS and HFH indicate, but this history demonstrates the possibility of creative network building and collaboration to address health care and related social issues. The examples of DCSNO, St. Clare's, and Provena Health also show how Catholic health care promotes and joins public-private partnerships that draw upon its tradition of institutional creativity. All four cases suggest, though of course they do not demonstrate, that civil society is a promising arena for Catholic ecclesial inventiveness and sacramental witness.

NOTES

1. Guenter B. Risse, *Mending Bodies, Saving Souls: A History of Hospitals* (New York: Oxford University Press, 1999).
2. "Negotiating the Health Care Market with Integrity," *Health Progress* 82, ed. Ann

Neale, (September/October 2001): 23–51. I consider these challenges in Institutional Identity; "Sacramental Potential: Catholic Health Care at Century's End," *Christian Bioethics*, 5 (April 1999): 26–43 and in "Another Identity Crisis: Catholic Hospitals Face Hard Choices," *Commonweal*, February 25, 2000: 12–16.

3. Kenneth R. White and J. W. Begun, "How Does Catholic Hospital Sponsorship Affect Services Provided?" *Inquiry* 35 (winter 1998/1999): 398–407.

4. Lynn Payer, *Medicine and Culture: Varieties of Treatment in the United States, England, West Germany, and France* (New York: Penguin, 1988).

5. Quoted in Daniel Callahan, "Death and the Research Imperative," *New England Journal of Medicine* 342 (March 2, 2000): 654–656.

6. Christopher J. Kauffman, *Ministry and Meaning: A Religious History of Catholic Health Care in the United States* (New York: Crossroad, 1995); also Kathleen M. Joyce, "Medicine, Markets, and Morals: Catholic Hospitals and the Ethics of Abortion in Early 20th-Century America," Cushwa Center for the Study of American Catholicism, University of Notre Dame, *Working Paper Series* 29, no. 2, fall 1997.

7. See Clarke E. Cochran, "Taking Ecclesiology Seriously: Religious Institutions and Health Care Policy," in *The Re-Enchantment of Political Science: Christian Scholars Engage their Discipline*, ed. Thomas W. Heilke and Ashley Woodiwiss (Lanham, Md.: Lexington Books, 2001), 169–192.

8. Kenneth R. White, "Hospitals Sponsored by the Roman Catholic Church: Separate, Equal, and Distinct?" *Milbank Quarterly*, 78 (No. 2, 2000): 213–239.

9. Cochran, "Another Identity Crisis."

10. John A. Coleman, S.J., "Deprivatizing Religion and Revitalizing Citizenship," in *Religion and Contemporary Liberalism*, ed. Paul J. Weithman (Notre Dame, Ind.: University of Notre Dame Press, 1997); *Community Works: The Revival of Civil Society in America*, ed. E. J. Dionne Jr. (Washington, D.C.: Brookings Institute, 1998).

11. "What's God Got to Do with the American Experiment?," eds. E. J. Dionne Jr. and John J. DiIulio Jr., *Essays on Religion and Politics* (Washington, D.C.: Brookings Institute, 2000).

12. "Holy Family Hospital" is a pseudonym required by the nature of the relationship to my informants. Information on this case is less complete than that for SJHS, and my interpretations are more speculative.

13. Information reported here comes from a phone interview with David J. Ward, CEO of DCSNO and from written materials supplied by Mr. Ward and from David J. Ward, "Opening New Doors: A Community Health Ministry Evolves in New Orleans," *Health Progress* 78 (November/December, 1997): 40–42. Therefore, this case is descriptive and lacks external validation.

14. Warren R. Hauff, "Reversing the Decline: Partnering with the City to Revitalize a Hospital's Declining Neighborhood," *Health Progress* 81 (May/June, 2000): 14–19, 27; and Gordon Burnside, "Leveraging Resources for a Better Life," *Health Progress* 81 (November/December, 2000): 26–29.

15. Clarke E. Cochran, *Religion in Public and Private Life* (New York: Routledge, 1990).

3

CATHOLICS IN THE PUBLIC
SQUARE: AUTOBIOGRAPHIES

How do individual Catholics, through their work or neighborhood and civic activities, bring their faith to the public square? The project asked politicians, journalists, lawyers, business executives, and labor leaders to write autobiographical essays. In the following brief reflections, they describe the influence of religion along with their family background, the neighborhood they grew up in, and their education—all of the elements that turned them to their life's work. The authors were asked the following questions by way of guiding their reflections: "Do you think that the way you pursue your work has been, or is now, shaped by your faith or by aspects of your religious background?" In inviting these essays, the project did not assume that the link between faith and work was uncomplicated or even always positive. The authors were encouraged to describe what might be called faith-based hurdles and difficulties as well as inspiration and incentives, and to think about unresolved dilemmas in relating faith and work that remain a continuing source of reflection.

PRO-LIFE, PRO-FAMILY, PRO-POOR

Mary Jo Bane

My religious and my public lives have always been intertwined, sometimes in complicated ways. I will start with brief outlines of both, and
then explore four areas where my faith and my political life have influenced
each other.

I was born to a Catholic family of Irish ancestry in Illinois. We moved
around when I was a kid, living in Catholic neighborhoods in a variety of
"garden spots": East Saint Louis, Anacostia, Chicago, Buffalo, and Detroit. I
went to parochial schools, and finished high school at the Shrine of the Little
Flower in Royal Oak, Michigan, where Father Charles Coughlin, the famous
(and by then, silenced) anti-Semitic radio priest of the Depression, was alive,
preaching, and handing out diplomas. In 1963, I graduated from the School
of Foreign Service at Georgetown, joined the Peace Corps, and left the
church.

Then ensued my dissolute and irreligious youth. The dissolute part
more or less ended with my marriage in 1975. The irreligious part ended in
1981, when I left the Carter administration, joined the faculty at the Kennedy School, and started attending Mass again. I became at that time a
"pretty good Catholic," and a somewhat desultory member of the Paulist
Center Community of borderline heretics in downtown Boston. I can't
explain this "conversion," or the one that later deepened my faith and commitment. Perhaps there really is a Holy Spirit.

In 1996, I left the Clinton administration (about which more later),
came back to the Kennedy School after trekking in Nepal, went to confession
for the first time in thirty-five years, and learned to pray. At this point I'm a
regular Mass-goer, an active member of my half-Vietnamese neighborhood

parish in Dorchester, a participant in current discussions about change in the church (see afterward) and I suppose a bit of a fanatic about it all.

I was "baptized a Catholic but born a Democrat." During my college years in Washington I became active in Young Democrats and stood in the snow for John Kennedy's inauguration. I was at the 1963 civil rights march on Washington, and then spent two years in the Peace Corps in Liberia, West Africa. I came home to go to graduate school, taught seventh and eighth grade, and marched against the Vietnam War. Teaching junior high school is really hard work, so after a few years of that, I got a doctorate and moved on to the easier life of the university, interspersed with periods of work in government.

My academic career has been mostly at Harvard, first at the School of Education and then at the Kennedy School of Government. In 1980, I spent a year in the Carter administration, in the budget and planning office of the newly formed Department of Education. From 1983 to 1986, I was the executive deputy commissioner of the New York State Department of Social Services in Albany, and returned to Albany in 1992 as commissioner. From 1993 to 1996, I was an assistant secretary at the Department of Health and Human Services (HHS) during the first Clinton term. I left that job when the president signed the 1996 welfare reform bill, and along with Peter Edelman who also opposed the law, made something of a fuss about it.

I have been back at the Kennedy School since 1996, teaching and writing on public management, social policy, and in a bit of a departure, the role of the churches. I spent a sabbatical year in 1999–2000 at the Harvard Divinity School where I learned some theology and made a start on research on how Catholic parishes and other Catholic groups participate in both service delivery and politics around social justice issues.

With that brief outline out of the way, let me turn to some of the interweavings of my faith and my public life.

The call to service. The most pervasive theme for me, both the most banal and the most important, has been the profoundly Christian call to service, which has stuck in my head and my gut through all my arguments with the church and all my failures in actually answering that call. It started with my romantic (and as I look at it now, hopelessly ill-suited) desire as a girl in the 1950s to become a nun, but led me instead to college and then to the Peace Corps. Breaking with the church was partly a reaction to what seemed at the time a tension between service and the church, which I perceived as anti-intellectual, antidemocratic, and insufficiently committed to justice and peace. As my career developed, I continued my efforts to do something useful. That has always been defined for me as trying to do something for others, as giving back some of what I have been so lavishly given. I have managed to convince myself that the research and teaching I have done, the work in government and the volunteer work I have done over the years, meet that criterion.

Now I don't want to get too carried away here. Girls who grew up in the 1950s by and large became secretaries, teachers, nurses, or nuns, and not corporate lawyers or investment bankers, because those were the roles that were open to and considered appropriate for women at that time. Women like me who discovered as adults, to our great shock, that we were ambitious for power, money, and status as well as for eternal reward found that we could actually do quite well in the helping professions and in public service. (Perhaps the abbesses of the Middle Ages made the same discovery.) I doubt that I would have made a competent or a happy stock trader, even if I had never listened to the Gospels, to my parents talking about service, or to Father Coughlin preaching (which he did, really) about social justice. But I did listen, and I listen now to the Gospels and the social teachings of the church, and I fret when I feel that what I am doing is not living up to those ideals. They are very deep within me, and although I know, from my husband and many others, that selfless service can be rooted in secular motivations, what is within me is very religious and very Catholic.

Pro-life, pro-family, pro-poor. A second pervasive theme for me has been the development, over time, of a stance toward both personal morality and public policy that I now articulate as "pro-life, pro-family, and pro-poor." The church's formulation of the consistent ethic of life is analogous, of course, but I have found the three-part rubric (which I first heard from Gene Rivers) richer and more descriptive of my own commitments. My public service and personal charity are mostly pro-poor, or at least I like to think of them that way; that stance is required, I believe, by the gospel and by obligations to one another that exist simply because of our common humanity. My writing, from my first book to more recent writing on welfare and poverty, has on occasion explored family issues. Over time, I have become more convinced of the importance of strong marriages, both from reading the social science literature and from my own marriage.

The abortion issue is a difficult one for me, as it is for many Catholic women. When asked, I identify myself as pro-life, and do so publicly, though in truth my actual positions on policy issues would surely not satisfy the orthodox Catholic thought police. Like the majority of Americans I believe that most abortions are wrong most of the time; that the law in a religiously pluralist democracy cannot and should not rigidly outlaw all abortions; that it should instead regulate and discourage.

The abortion issue has not played a particularly important role in my public life. In New York State, I had the responsibility for some eligibility and financial aspects of the Medicaid program, including paying bills for abortions. I saw that, and others saw it, as basically a ministerial responsibility, which I could preside over (as Governor Mario Cuomo did) without grave violence to my conscience and also without threatening the pro-choice political establishment. My articulated pro-life position was a bit of a problem for my appointment to the Clinton administration, but did not become a big deal.

The more interesting issue may be that of what I do and don't say in public settings. I do identify myself as pro-life, pro-family, and pro-poor and try to articulate, as best I can, the consistent ethic of life. But although I am active in social justice politics and problem solving, I don't talk about or work for what I think is desperately needed on abortion, that is, a moderate position on legislation which would, for example, severely constrain third-term abortions and discourage all abortions. I don't talk about this because there is no winning: my liberal political colleagues oppose my positions, reflecting the extent to which the issue has become polarized in elite dialogue; and my church also condemns moderate positions. We are all losing the opportunity to make important progress in limiting abortions, a dialogue in which I would be eager to participate, and, as a result, we are also losing, I think, some of our credibility on pro-family and pro-poor issues. Personally, I feel this not as an active tension or problem, but as a lingering sense of lost possibilities.

Joining and leaving the Clinton administration. A more specific example of the intersection of my religious and my public lives is provided by both my joining the Clinton administration (1993) and my leaving it (1996). In 1992, I was part of Governor Cuomo's administration in New York State as commissioner of social services, a job which I loved for its scope, complexity, and opportunity to influence social policy and practice.

I chose to leave New York and to join the Clinton administration because Donna Shalala can be very persuasive, and because, at that time, I saw in Bill Clinton echoes of the John Kennedy who had inspired me to public service in the first place. I viewed the administration as an opportunity for both designing policy for and implementing in practice a new work-oriented approach to welfare that I had been analyzing and doing research on for years with my colleague David Ellwood, who also joined the administration. We believed, and thought the president did also, in work, family, and mutual responsibility; in local administration with federal protections; in support for work; and in guarantees of job opportunities along with requirements for participation. David and I had taught and discussed the U.S. Catholic bishops' 1988 letter on the economy. We saw our commitments as consistent with theirs (or perhaps, with typical Harvard arrogance, vice versa). I articulated mine, at least to myself, explicitly in the biblical and ethical concepts of social justice used by the bishops. The first two years of the Clinton administration were heady and exciting. Many of us, including myself, felt we were both doing the Lord's work and having one heck of a good time.

Much changed after the 1994 congressional elections, when the Republicans took over the Congress and the agenda. The politics of welfare became much more contentious and conservative, and for the administration much more reactive. Because the HHS office I headed, the Administration for Children and Families (ACF), had responsibility for granting waivers to the states for welfare reform experiments, I continually found myself in arguments both within the administration and with the external groups that I considered the good guys. On the policy side, my HHS colleagues and I were most concerned about important protections for poor families, such as exceptions to time limits and assistance to children even when parents broke the rules. We were convinced that the president should veto the welfare bill that the Congress passed in the summer of 1996, and made the strongest moral, policy, and political arguments that we could think of. We lost that battle for a variety of good and bad reasons.

My decision to resign in response to the president's signing the bill was a difficult one, made after considerable thought, discussion, and prayer. Some of my considerations were clearly utilitarian: Could I do more good by staying where I was and trying to implement the bill well? Could I get out of my apartment lease? Some were issues of loyalty: to Donna, to the president, most importantly to the ACF staff I had worked with and grown attached to over the three and one-half years. The decision finally came down to a gut-level insight: I tried to imagine myself staying in the job, implementing a law I thought was harmful, and defending it in congressional hearings and public speeches, which I would have had to do; and I realized I simply couldn't do it. I'm not sure where that certainty came from, though I suspect it, like so much else in my life, was rooted in my early and continuing conviction that God expected generosity and integrity from us and gave us the guidance and strength to live those virtues.

Again, I don't want to go too far with this. Men and women of good will could and did disagree about welfare policy and the relative dangers and potentials of the bill the president signed; the jury is still out on its actual effects. And men and women of courage and integrity made different decisions than I. But my own faith and prayer took me where they did, both in joining the administration and in leaving it. I wish things had come out differently, but I regret neither decision.

Faith and academic life. Finally, let me note something about my current life and work, in which my faith plays a much larger role. I have more time now for prayer (which I should never have seen as a luxury), volunteer work, and research directly related to important public issues and to the role of religion in public life. The freedom I have is, in part, externally imposed (leaving Washington the way I did burns bridges), in part the fruit of economic good fortune and a preference for a relatively simple lifestyle, and, in part, the result of a willingness to take advantage of the privileges of tenure. I am determined to preserve that freedom: Harvard pays me for three-quarters time for nine months, and I have become quite fierce about what I do and don't agree to do both for Harvard and for others. Daily prayer and Mass, continuing study of Scripture and theology, time with my mother, volunteer work in my parish, work retreats in Haiti, pro bono board service, and speaking and consulting for various do-gooder groups are all important parts of my life.

For the last few years, I have been participating in a seminar at Harvard on religion and public life, which began with a conversation about the role of religious organizations in the politics and service provision aspects of welfare reform, and recently has been looking more broadly at the intersection of faith and civic life. As part of this, I have been doing research on what Catholic teachings say, what Catholic parishes actually do, and why there seems to be such a large gap between the two. My interest in this topic was generated partly by my observations of the political activity of the Catholic lobbying groups, Catholic Charities USA and the National Conference of Catholic Bishops about the 1996 welfare reform bill: they were professional and respected, but much less effective than one might have expected of an institution with 60 million members, many of whom vote. There are lots of reasons for this, but it does seem clear that there is a significant gap between the institutional response and the grass roots.

Understanding this is important, both for the church and for the wider polity, as we work though issues of religion and public life in new ways. The work provides an opportunity for me to engage as a Catholic with the wider intellectual community of theologians, social scientists, and policy analysts who are confronting these issues. We can, I hope, contribute both to understanding and to practice, to discipleship and to citizenship.

As I work through the empirical and theological facts and arguments, I find myself hypothesizing a tension between the internal structures and authority patterns of the church and its ability to teach and practice social justice. I have been trying to analyze and lay out these important arguments as a loving critic.

As I hope is at least implicit in the above, both my religious life and my public life have been quite an adventure: hardly ever boring, mostly fun, increasingly joyful in that very deep sense of a life developing in understanding and lived in love. I sometimes think I would like a slightly more mundane life, and maybe it will be so in my next decades. But in another sense I hope I can continue to learn and work and love with all the challenge and excitement that I have had thus far.

Postscript, Spring 2003. The two years since I wrote this piece for the Pew Forum have been, to say the least, challenging for the Catholic Church, especially in Boston. The winter 2002 revelations of clergy sexual abuse and cover-up by the hierarchy shocked all Catholics. Like so many, I read the news stories obsessively, anguished for my church, and struggled with the question of what I personally should do. My professional experience with management and politics influenced my analysis of the situation: that the very human power-holders in the church had been behaving like human power-holders in non-accountable, non-transparent hierarchical institutions over the centuries. I read extensively in ecclesiology and (even) canon law, and tried to develop for myself a way of thinking about the church both as a human institution and as a community called and shaped by God. I wrote a couple of pieces laying out some of my analyses, and joined the continuing conversation about structural change in the church. I am convinced that greater accountability, transparency and participation is necessary if the church is to remain true to its mission. Clearly this will be a long and difficult process.

My own commitment to this often frustrating process is rooted in my love for the church and my absolute certainty that the church is called to "bring good news to the poor, to proclaim release to the captives, and recovery of sight to the blind, to let the oppressed go free" (Luke 4:18, NRSV). That mission of salvation and liberation is too important to be compromised through the loss of credibility of those who speak for the church. We must regain our voice as a church of honesty, integrity and compassion. In trying to do my part in this, I have obviously once again passed up an opportunity for a boring life. Luckily, there is still time.

STATE HOUSE POLITICIAN

David Carlin

I was born April 1938, in the middle of the FDR administration, in an Irish-Catholic working-class family, in a city (Pawtucket, Rhode Island) whose people were overwhelmingly blue-collar and Catholic. City Hall was controlled by an Irish Democratic political machine. My parents were not politicians, yet they were friendly with some of the local politicians, and they taught me to be a Democrat. I still vividly remember two things my father told me when I was a small boy. One, that the Democrats were the party of poor people, like us, while the Republicans were the party of the rich. The other, that Al Smith was defeated for president in 1928 because of anti-Catholic prejudice. This early political indoctrination took. Today, more than a half-century later, I still believe it is "natural" for Catholics to be Democrats and for Democrats to be the champions of the disadvantaged and marginalized. I also believe that today's Democrats are behaving in "unnatural" ways: they grow increasingly indifferent to the marginalized, and they are driving Catholics away from the party.

Back to my boyhood. The local Democratic machine, while largely made up of Catholics, was corrupt. Despite the corruption, and despite what seems to have been a general public awareness of it, the machine remained in power for about twenty years, from the early 1930s to the early 1950s. It was not that the good Catholic voters of Pawtucket approved of corruption. But what could they do? The alternative was to vote Republican—but that was unthinkable. Besides, years before, the Republicans, who were largely Protestant, had run the city, and they had a machine, and they were corrupt too. If we must have crooks, better our crooks than theirs.

154

Given the social circumstances of my early life, how could I be anything but a Democrat?

But what about Catholic theology? How did that affect my political views? To begin with, it reinforced my anti-Communism, the anti-Communism that dominated American life in the late 1940s and early 1950s. I remember (this was in the late 1940s) one of our parish priests, Father Fountain, delivering a strongly emotional sermon denouncing the then ongoing trial of Cardinal Mindszenty in communist Hungary. And of course I remember, a few years later, Bishop Fulton J. Sheen, who could be seen every Sunday afternoon on our first television set. More than a few of his talks developed the idea that communism is essentially atheistic, and that, since atheism leads logically to immorality, this explains why communists had a long record of great wickedness. This lesson must have sunk deeply in, since I still believe that atheism leads to immorality, although I now think the connection between the two is somewhat less direct and immediate than I used to think in the days when I was a Bishop Sheen devotee.

In my Christian Brothers high school we had a civics course; but it wasn't called "Civics," it was called "Christian Principles of Democracy." It was American democracy justified on Catholic grounds. I think it was also the New Deal justified on Catholic grounds. I don't remember the details of the course, but it introduced me to the idea that there could be such a thing as a specifically Catholic theory of society and politics. It was in that course that I first remember coming across the name of Jacques Maritain, whose writing I was to encounter at great length a few years later. Also in high school I read—at the recommendation of a Christian Brother who happened to be the most remarkable teacher it was ever my good luck to have—Arthur Schlesinger's *The Age of Jackson*, then a relatively new book. As a result I learned something about the Jacksonian era, but I learned a good deal more about the values of the Franklin Roosevelt era; for Schlesinger presented Old Hickory as a proto–New Dealer. This book solidified my New Deal convictions, convictions I retain to this day. That I am a New Deal Democrat explains in large measure why I am so profoundly unhappy with today's national Democratic Party, which, it seems to me, has drifted far away from its New Deal moorings.

And speaking of drifting: During my twenties (a time that fell in the 1960s), despite—or perhaps *because of*—being in a Catholic academic milieu (first a Catholic undergraduate school, Providence College, then three years of graduate school in philosophy at Notre Dame, then a few years of teaching at a small Catholic women's college in Boston), I tended to drift away, though not very far away, from the Catholicism of my boyhood. But if I was less of a believer, I became more of a moralist. In fact I came to see morality as the essence of religion; I came pretty much to agree with Matthew Arnold's definition of religion as "morality touched with emotion." I now regard this as a foolish notion, a serious misunderstanding of the nature of religion and of morality; but it is a notion that has proven attractive to many people who, having had a strong religious upbringing, decide as adults that they would like to renounce their religion without really renouncing it.

I do not remember exactly when I began my retreat from this mistaken notion of religion and morality, but I think it was when the United States Supreme Court handed down its 1973 *Roe* v. *Wade* decision. I thought then and I still think now that you do not have to be a religious believer to know that abortion is wrong, terribly wrong. Perhaps an arguable case can be made for the rightness of abortion when done for grave reasons early in the pregnancy; but in all other cases—that is, in 99 percent of the cases when abortion is actually performed—its wrongness, it seems to me, should be quite obvious to a morally rational person. Yet even if you don't have to be a religious believer to see this, the empirical fact is that only religious believers, and strong believers at that, actually do see it. Reflecting on this fact eventually led me to the conclusion that morality cannot stand on its own; it needs a religious foundation. In other words, it led me back to the idea Bishop Sheen had been preaching years before.

In the years after I left South Bend and began teaching, I worked on a dissertation having to do with the political philosophy of Maritain. I wrote a long first draft but never completed the dissertation because I became involved in other things, political things. But before abandoning Maritain I had pretty thoroughly absorbed his political thought. What I got from Maritain were three main ideas.

First, that Catholicism was reconcilable with liberal democracy; and not just in the weak sense that it did not contradict liberal democracy, but in the strong sense that it could provide a theoretical basis for it.

Second, the idea of the primacy of culture, especially the "beliefs" aspect of culture. Maritain held, in effect, that ideas govern the world. He was the very opposite of a Marxist, who would hold that ideas are nothing but a reflection of economic and social forces. For Maritain the Cartesian revolution was more important to society than the Industrial Revolution.

Third, the idea of natural law and the role it should play in a modern pluralistic democracy. Modern society, according to Maritain, is incorrigibly pluralistic in religion and philosophy. Thus there is no returning to the "thick" cultural consensus of medieval Christendom. Since modern society is made up of people having many different worldviews, it cannot demand a religious and theological consensus. But we have to agree on something, don't we? If we cannot agree on religion, we can at least agree on morality. Why? Because of natural law, which is the same for all human beings and it is knowable by all. Thanks to natural law, Catholics and Protestants and Jews and atheists can all agree on the fundamental principles of right and wrong, of good and bad. Now I approved of this natural-law-consensus theory of Maritain's until abortion became a big issue in America, and then I realized that believers and unbelievers, though they may be in agreement as to the wrongness of bank robbery and race prejudice, are in radical disagreement as to the wrongness of abortion. If natural law theory is true, how could this happen?

In 1968—the year of assassinations in America, of abortive revolutions in France and Czechoslovakia, and of an ongoing and increasingly unpopular war in Southeast Asia—I finally got involved in actual politics, first by working on Eugene McCarthy's presidential campaign. I had been a big fan of Lyndon Johnson. His plans for the Great Society seemed to me just right. It was a revival of the spirit of the New Deal, and from the point of view of an old-school Catholic Democrat like myself, nothing could possibly be better than the New Deal. Yet it was my Catholic mentality that later turned me against Johnson. Vietnam, it seemed to me, did not pass the "just war" test. From the U.S. point of view, I agreed, it would be better if South Vietnam did not go communist. But the price that would have to be paid to assure an American victory—the price in both American and Vietnamese lives—didn't seem to me proportionate to the good that would be obtained or the evil averted.

By now I was back in my hometown of Pawtucket, and I decided to run for office. In the September 1968 Democratic primary, I challenged a long-time incumbent Democrat for the state senate. I was politically naive; I didn't appreciate that I had taken on a nearly impossible electoral task. I lost by a margin of 1,500 votes to 1,000. Not close, but local political veterans considered it a respectable showing, and it was expected I would try again in two years. And so I did, this time against a different long-time incumbent Democrat, this one from the state House of Representatives. By now I had the entire Democratic Party in Pawtucket united against me. I lost again, but this time more narrowly: about 800 votes to 750.

I was married by now, and after a couple of years my wife and I left Pawtucket to move about thirty miles away to Newport (where we still live), where I had taken a job at a small Catholic college as a sociology teacher.

(Along the way, motivated by my political concerns, I had picked up a master's degree in sociology, temporarily abandoning my philosophical interests.) I soon became involved in Newport politics, and after a few more tries I finally got elected to the Rhode Island Senate in 1980.

My career in the state Senate lasted twelve years, and included two years as majority leader (the top post in the Senate). As I look back I can find some things in my Senate career, but not many, that were influenced by my Catholicism. Mostly I attended to the routine business of Senate work, business that would be carried on pretty much the same way by persons of any other faith or no faith. I was not corrupt, a point perhaps worth noting in a state rather famous for its political corruption. Would somebody like to attribute that non-corruption to my Catholicism? Just keep in mind that Rhode Island in recent decades has had more than its fair share of corrupt politicians, and every one of them, to the best of my knowledge, has been a Catholic (including a governor who served a year in state prison and a mayor of Providence who is now serving a five-year term at a federal prison).

But not everything in the Senate was a matter of routine business, and some things I worked on were inspired, at least indirectly, by my Catholic mentality. For one, a friend of mine, a Sister of Mercy named Liz Morancy, was a member of the Rhode Island House. For several years she had attempted to win passage of a bill that would outlaw housing rental discrimination against families with young children. Not surprisingly, the real estate lobby objected, and her bill had not become law. Finally she got it passed in the House, and when it came over to the Senate I went to bat for it, and it passed. Without my aid I doubt it would have become law.

For another, I took the lead on child-support enforcement legislation. It was my natural-law convictions that made me embrace this cause, and embrace it with something like a passion. We were now (by the 1980s) living in a society in which much of our traditional moral consensus had broken down, abortion being a case in point. But surely, I felt, there are *some* things we can agree on; there are some rights and wrongs that are so obvious that no one has an excuse for not recognizing them. Support for one's children was one of those things. Who could deny that parents have no right to walk out on their children? Yet during the 1970s and early 1980s, millions of fathers—some divorced, some never married—were doing precisely that. American society had come to tolerate easy divorce. We had come to tolerate out-of-wedlock births. And as a byproduct of these two, we had learned to look the other way when fathers abandoned their children. By now it was a deeply rooted cultural evil, one that government, all by itself, didn't have the power to correct. But government could at least do *something*. By strict enforcement of child support payments, government could address part of the problem, and it could set an example for society as a whole.

I think it was in 1982 that I introduced a bill requiring Rhode Island to divest itself of South African investments. At the time, Massachusetts was the only state to have enacted such a law. Rhode Island's general treasurer opposed my bill, and it didn't become law until 1985, after he had left office. But it finally did become law.

My career in electoral office ended in 1992, when I ran for the United States House of Representatives, figuring that this would lead to one of two things: if I won (a long shot), an interesting adventure in Washington; if I lost (a more likely outcome), more time to spend with my wife and my books. I won the Democratic primary, but I lost decisively to the Republican incumbent, who outspent me five or six to one. Since 1992 I have read a lot of books, and my wife and I have seen a lot of movies and eaten in a lot of restaurants.

The most explicitly Catholic motivation for any political action on my part came after my retirement from political office. Beginning in 1993 I became an unofficial (and unpaid) adviser to the woman who ran the Respect Life office of the Diocese of Providence, Maria Parker. Pressing at the State House for pro-life legislation and resisting pro-choice legislation was one of her responsibilities, and she proved to be an exceptionally talented lobbyist. I advised her on the personalities and prejudices of key legislators, recommending strategy and tactics.

The most useful advice I gave Maria was that she should create a Catholic network of pro-life voters who would promise, at a signal from her, to call their legislators and request that they vote Yes or No on this or that bill. She created the network with the help of many pastors and of the diocesan newspaper. Eventually she signed up about four or five thousand volunteers for LifeNet, a name I recommended for the volunteer network.

The logic behind this was simple. Rhode Island has a population of only about 1 million. Legislative districts have very few voters, and candidates can ring the doorbells of a large percentage of their voters. In such districts campaign money does not matter very much; a few thousand dollars will do. Thus no candidate is likely to do what candidates with large constituencies often do: disregard the wishes of a significant number of voters in order to please a much smaller number of generous contributors. Thus if LifeNet could get fifty to a hundred voters in a district to call their legislator and ask him or her to vote Yes or No on a particular bill, it was very likely that the legislator would comply.

But couldn't the pro-choice people match this by organizing a "Choice-Net"? No, because pro-choice sentiment was strong in only a small number of high-income legislative districts; for the right-to-abortion ideology, we often forget, is a value characteristic of upper-middle-class secularists or quasi-secularists. In 80 to 90 percent of the state's House and Senate districts, prolife true believers easily outnumbered prochoice true believers. At the grassroots level we could beat them—provided we were organized. Maria Parker supplied something that had never existed before: effective leadership at organizing Catholic pro-life voters.

Another essential ingredient in the strategy was a good working relationship between Parker and the late Anna Sullivan, the woman who at the time headed the Rhode Island Right to Life Committee. In the middle 1990s this alliance between LifeNet and the Right to Life Committee produced a series of pro-life victories. First, a "Woman's Right to Know" bill passed the Senate, despite strong opposition from the Senate majority leader; it failed, however, in the House, and has not passed until this day. Second, a bill outlawing physician-assisted suicide became law. Third, a partial-birth abortion ban became law, although the federal district court subsequently overturned it.

Perhaps most important, in the early 1990s the conventional wisdom among Rhode Island Democrats was that the people of the state were pro-choice and that it was, consequently, politically suicidal for a politician to run as a pro-life candidate for higher office. (My own lopsided defeat by a pro-choice incumbent in running for Congress contributed to that perception.) Pro-life successes at the State House altered that perception, and since then we have seen two pro-life Democrats elected to the U.S. House. This is doubly significant in that Rhode Island is a state located in the Northeast, the heartland of American prochoice sentiment.

Eventually Maria Parker left her Rhode Island work and moved on to do similar work for the Massachusetts Catholic Conference. When she left, my prolife volunteer work came to an end.

Today I remain a Democrat, though an unhappy one, one who disagrees with a very great deal of what the national Democratic Party now stands for. I am the chairman of my local Democratic Party in Newport, and I am on the governing board of a national organization of pro-life Democrats, Democrats for Life of America.

ON THE BEAT IN THE SOUTH BRONX AND CENTRAL AMERICA

David Gonzalez

It would be nice to say that all my years of Catholic education in the Bronx culminated in my choosing journalism as a noble profession in defense of the poor.

But it didn't—at least not at first.

I went into this business in my mid-twenties for reasons I never quite understood, except that I was really into "Lou Grant" and could not imagine myself working in an office, wearing a suit, getting a haircut, or otherwise growing up and behaving myself. In graduate school, my adviser, Penn Kimball, insisted I go back to the Bronx and write about the poor. Years later, working for the *New York Times*, I found myself drawn yet again to the streets of Hunts Point, Crotona, and Mott Haven where I found much more than I ever imagined.

In this twisty, seemingly random journey, my profession brought me back to my faith. What started out as professional curiosity about how the South Bronx (or Bushwick, Red Hook, or East New York, for that matter) had transformed itself from a burned-out wasteland led to a much more personal change. It came not from some touchy-feely magic moment of generalized spirituality among the long-suffering poor. I found it in meeting people like the Reverend John Flynn in Crotona, he of the quixotic mission to exchange crucifixes for guns; the Reverend Luis Barrios in Mott Haven, who put a drawing of Christ laughing heartily on his church's steeple; or several dozen residents of West Harlem who ended their Good Friday procession by stopping and praying in front of the crack dealers who had overwhelmed their neighborhood.

There was no sudden revelation. Somewhere along the line, I saw how the faith that I had rejected as a teenager for being preachy, abstract, and depressing, was real, passionate, and joyful. Rather than wonder about some invisible force and whether or not it existed (and judged me in the process), I saw how faith in action made a difference in the lives of those people who now lived in the neighborhoods where I was raised. In turn, it has helped me to become, I hope, a more sensitive journalist, one who now understands the old journalistic counsel, "Comfort the afflicted and afflict the comfortable," in a whole new light.

Although the priests at Cardinal Hayes Memorial High School for Boys on the Grand Concourse did their best, the lessons they gave me in religion didn't stick. Or so I thought in those years right after graduation when I went off to Yale. But in retrospect, they planted a seed in me that would slowly tremble back to life years later. We Hayesmen were a motley crew of Irish, Italian, Latino, and black teenagers from working class families. Some of us were poor, living in housing projects with only one parent. Others, like me, had both parents around; though they were too busy working and making ends meet in order to send us to Catholic school while trying to stay one step ahead of the arson that was devastating the South Bronx in the 1960s and 1970s.

We had a common bond as working-class kids who wanted to get ahead, and it was there that the priests made their first impression on us. Rather than look down on us or pity us for being Latino, poor, or living in the South Bronx, they challenged us to excel. They gave of themselves, asking only that we push ourselves to our fullest.

Years later, as a *Times* reporter covering the South Bronx, I began to notice how the same church that I had attended as a child had become a force in the community. In much the same way that the priests at Hayes had pushed us, the priests and nuns at St. Martin of Tours supported, prodded, and encouraged their parishioners to organize themselves. I remember one conversation with Father Flynn, who explained his sense of mission: "What I am supposed to do?" he asked. "Baptize them, marry them, and then give them a nice Catholic burial when they die too young?"

In his view, the church had to be there not just for the spiritual sustenance of the flock, but for their daily needs in a community that was trying to survive with dignity in the face of official neglect from the outside and criminal chaos from within. That was why Father Flynn, a lanky Irishman who grew up comfortably in Yonkers, ended up in the South Bronx where he sometimes took to the streets offering teenagers a crucifix in exchange for a gun.

Yet, why bother to believe when all you see around you seems so daunting and hopeless? That became a question that gnawed at me. It also became a main reason why in the mid-1990s I asked to cover religion for the paper, trying to find those instances where faith and action converged. In time, I found myself writing about why people prayed, missionaries in the South Bronx, grottos in Staten Island, and little acts of faith that often go unnoticed in the city.

Why believe? Just look around.

There was nothing abstract about this. It was visceral and as real as the streets that I walked. It connected me to something greater, something that I saw actually changed neighborhoods and people. So, somewhere along the line, I found myself praying again, this time not reciting some words by rote as I clung with white knuckles to hope. Prayer became a conversation, a word of thanks and even a journalistic credo. More than once I have sat down to write uttering the simple words: "Use me."

Before you get the wrong impression, I consider myself a practicing Catholic in the sense that I have a lot of practicing to do. I attend church more often while on assignment than when I am at home in Miami. Yet my connection to the church—tenuous as it is at times—is one that plays itself out on several levels.

These days, I cover Central America and the Caribbean, traveling outside of the country at least twice a month. It is, at times, stressful and disorienting. But it is also a chance to connect. Recently, I was at El Mozote, the site of an infamous massacre of 800 men, women, and children during El Salvador's civil war. In the early morning hours, I walked through the church where the caskets containing the exhumed remains of several dozen victims were laid out on pews. I really didn't interview people as just walk around, watch and feel. In front of the church, the walls had been decorated with Christmas ribbons and Nativity scenes.

Later that night, a priest said Mass in the plaza outside the church. All around me, people sang and children ran about. The music was a familiar echo of the Spanish songs I had heard years before in the Bronx. Later, the coffins were put gently into the ground by a monument. I noticed a child, cradled in his mother's arms and reaching out to touch a casket as it passed by. All these scenes stirred something within me, and they went into the piece that I wrote.

Looking back on it, that article, which contrasted the pain of the past with the promise of Advent, wrote itself. As journalists, we are trained to use our senses, though sometimes we overlook one of the most powerful of all, our hearts. We are not automatons, and we do a disservice to our profession if we shut out one of our most powerful tools—our feelings at witnessing something of great power. What I witnessed, in every sense of that word, at El Mozote moved me to tears, and I tried to harness that emotion to the service of my writing, not in some sentimental way, but in an attempt to give the reader a sense of what had happened.

It is hard to travel in Central America and not think about the role of faith: whether it is the lives of the Jesuit martyrs, the villages named after saints, or even the buses whose windshields declare "*Gracias a Dios.*" When reporting on the drought in Central America, most interviews began with an impoverished peasant saying that he would make it through hard times because God would provide. There is also a darker side, which I saw after the earthquakes in El Salvador, when some villagers insisted that the disaster was divine punishment.

Being Catholic has made me sensitive to these cues, sometimes giving the stories an added texture or insight. It is also one way to paint a broader picture of the church, one that goes beyond some currents in mainstream media, where Catholicism is often seen only in relation to conflict among lay people or only through the lens of sex, abortion, or homosexuality.

An awareness of the role of religion in the life of people has been crucial to understanding some groups. I have always felt, for example, that you cannot tell the story of the South Bronx in the later twentieth century, without telling the story of the Catholic Church and how it organized entire communities. To overlook that relationship or to fail to understand its true impact and reach—as some have done in attempting to relate that history—results in either an incomplete portrait, or an exercise in spiritual sentimentality.

Just as I do now, when I travel to rural villages and seek out the local priest, knowing New York's various priests and parishes has been as important to getting some stories as knowing the local police. Among New York's growing Mexican population, for example, one of the few institutions trusted by undocumented workers is the church. When a Mexican migrant was stabbed to death in Central Park in 1998, the police first reported that he was homeless. There was no great follow up on the story, even though assaults in Central Park are routinely covered as serious events when they involve tourists or upper middle class residents.

A few days after the killing, one paper ran a tiny item that said the deceased lived on East 106th Street in El Barrio—an area that I knew was home to many Mexicans. A quick call to the local church (Saint Cecilia's) got me the assistant pastor who, as it turned out, knew the family and was willing to take me over there. As I left their home, I noticed a mural of St. Sebastian on a wall down the street, with an inscription about how people move though life ignoring each other and committing little acts of violence. I used that as an inspiration, writing a column about the life and death of a man who was only anonymous to those who lived below 96th Street. The resulting column wound up triggering more than $35,000 in donations from readers.

On a personal level, it is almost impossible to walk among these communities here and in Central America and not have it affect your own faith. In some ways, these experiences have centered me in the midst of difficult work. Whether it is in after-work conversations with clergy I have met in my travels, or at Mass in the Haitian Village of Gros Morne (where Sister Pat Dillon, formerly of St. Martin's, now lives) there are reminders that I am part of something larger, a community that extends far and wide. There is something reassuring about being at Mass in a convent in Guatemala City, where my friend Dennis Leder celebrates the Eucharist for a group of Franciscan Scholastics. I look around the tiny chapel and see young women from Mayan villages that are worlds removed culturally from the South Bronx of my youth or the Miami of my adulthood.

Still, in that same moment, I look around and know we are, in a very deep way, one and the same.

POLITICS AND POLLING

Dotty Lynch

For me, political journalism is a cop-out: an enjoyable profession, which has given me financial stability, intellectual satisfaction, and some very good times, but not the type of service that I believe defines a truly good life.

GROWING UP AND FINDING POLITICS

I grew up in Flatbush, the much-loved only child of a couple who waited ten years to have children. They were devout Catholics who had no guilt about practicing birth control in the 1930s and 1940s. The depression, family obligations, and World War II were good enough reasons for them to postpone having children—and my mother bragged about being forthright in confession about this. I thought growing up an Irish Catholic Democrat in Brooklyn in the 1950s was about the best thing anyone could be, and I treasured each one of those labels. I was way more Irish than my parents, third generation types who had only a faint glimmer of "where we were from." I was enthusiastic about my parochial school, St. Brendan's and the young nuns who taught classes of '69 and '71 in split sessions and was a Democratic Party groupie who loved to watch Congressional hearings on TV (we were strongly anti-McCarthy and Frank Costello and pro-Kefauver and John McClellan) almost as much as Howdy Doody and Hopalong Cassidy. The big heroes in our family were my four cousins who had become Jesuit priests, and their ordinations and first Masses were the biggest celebrations I can remember.

In 1960 I got my chance to find out what politics was really all about.

166

My schoolmate's dad and family friend, Hugh Carey, decided to run for Congress and recruited us to be "Carey-Kennedy girls," dressed in red, white, and blue uniforms. He sent us through the district in a matching Cadillac convertible equipped with a sound system to chant and sing and give "visibility" to the campaign. We were the advance team for him at events, modeled our outfits for Rose Kennedy at a tea, and shook our white-gloved hands with JFK when he came to Brooklyn. And we won. Kennedy carried the district handily and Carey upset an incumbent Republican, Frank Dorn by 761 votes.

My paternal grandfather grew up on the Lower East Side of Manhattan with Al Smith and was his New York City Labor chairman in the 1928 Presidential campaign. I was raised with stories of political discrimination against Catholics, and the election of Kennedy was a moral and well as political victory for me. It also gave me faith in the American political system and whetted an already huge appetite for politics.

My next campaign was not such a positive experience. In 1961 the "Carey girls" were recruited to campaign for Arthur Levitt, the regular Democrat who was who challenging incumbent Mayor Robert Wagner who had become a reformer (only in New York City could a two-term incumbent become the reformer.) After our "visibility" at his Manhattan announcement, we were sent to a "backroom" and given postcards and phone books and told to pick out names and address them to WPIX which was conducting a poll for the mayoral contest. After three or four postcards I decided I couldn't participate in anything so shockingly corrupt (!) and marched my little group out of the room and back on the BMT to Brooklyn. I remember hearing my father on the phone screaming at Hugh Carey that this was a terrible thing to do to idealistic kids. As a young teenager, I had become wise to the tricks of the trade and to the uses and abuses of polls!

John Kennedy's death was one of the worst days of my life. Kennedy was for me a teenage crush as well as a political icon. I was so identified with him that on November 22, 1963, friends and relatives called my parents to check on my condition. In 1964 I was a Kennedy girl again—this time for Bobby, running for the U.S. Senate—and once again we won.

COLLEGE AND ACTIVIST YEARS

By Kennedy II, I was at Marymount Manhattan College, and Vietnam was heating up. I wound up majoring in sociology rather than political science

because of the strength of the sociology department, but I did all my special-
izing in methodology and political behavior. I became news editor of the college paper and starting polling the student body on everything from the "real
cause" of the 1966 blackout to attitudes toward Vietnam and the Berkeley
free speech movement. The school had an interesting mix—a rather conservative student body, a liberal faculty, and a radical administration. The president of the college, Mother Jogues Egan brought Jesuit Daniel Berrigan in to
teach (much to the distress of some traditional Dominicans in the theology
department), and she was subsequently charged as an un-indicted co-conspir-
ator in the draft board raid at Harrisburg.

Vatican II killed any need I had to rebel from traditional Catholicism.
As with the Kennedy election and the U.S. political system, Vatican II reaf-
firmed my faith in the institution of the church and made me believe that it,
too, would change with the times. My liberal politics melded completely with
the spirit of Catholic action I found at Marymount and later in graduate
school at Fordham. I became involved in small, home liturgies with the Jesuit
seminarians at Fordham, in antiwar activities (the non-violent ones), soup
kitchens and other activities with the poor in New York and Baltimore. As I
pondered a career, a line from the musical *Hair* and a sermon by Fordham
sociologist Joe Fitzpatrick, S.J. had profound impacts on my thinking. "People who care about strangers / Who care about evil and social injustice, / Do
you only care about the bleeding crowd? / How about a needy friend?" rang
in my head and argued for some direct action. Fitzpatrick, however, suggested that those who can operate through complex institutions to affect
change could serve in that way. I dismissed religious life—in part because I
couldn't be a Jesuit and a convent seemed a lesser life—but mostly because
in the late 1960s a life of chastity and obedience didn't have much appeal.

JOURNALISM—THE FIRST TIME

I landed at NBC News in a job totally right for my secular interests: political
researcher in their election unit. I continued my antiwar and social action
activities on the side, and worked with TV reporters and producers who were
generally in synch with my point of view. But by 1972 I felt too removed.
My friends were dying in Vietnam, sweating out the draft, or getting arrested
in demonstrations, while I was wining and dining in fancy restaurants and
posh hotels. The movie *Medium Cool*, whose climactic scene has a photo-
journalist trying to decide whether to help a man in a car crash or take his

picture, crystallized things for me. I made friends with the leaders of the McGovern campaign and at the Democratic convention in Miami, resigned from NBC, and headed off to Washington to work in the campaign as a polling analyst and to try to have a more direct role in ending the war.

POLITICAL YEARS

From 1972 until 1985 I worked in politics as a pollster for Democratic candidates and liberal causes. Most of the candidates, most notably presidential contenders George McGovern, Jimmy Carter, Ted Kennedy and Gary Hart, were simpatico with my liberal values, and I felt somewhat fulfilled in working through them to build a better society. I had become a very ardent feminist and concentrated on exploring the political attitudes of women voters, developing the concept of the gender gap. In 1984, I was very involved with the effort to get a woman on the Democratic ticket for vice-president and in the particular decision to pick Geraldine Ferraro, another graduate of Marymount Manhattan College. During those years I continued to be a churchgoing Catholic. While not doctrinaire on the abortion issue (that was to change later) I was uncomfortable enough to opt out of working on pro-choice issue campaigns that came our way. I did however work on strategies for Democratic candidates on how to "handle" the issue suggesting hiding behind the mantra that "it's the choice of the woman, her clergyman and her doctor and not the role of government." I was in and out of a series of relationships and never had much trouble reconciling the disparities between the Church's teaching on sex and the role of women in the church with my own personal behavior and attitudes. Probably my parents' dissent on birth control in the 1930s and 1940s steered me away from thinking that absolute adherence was necessary to be a good Catholic. Much of my volunteer activity had stopped due to the busyness of life and the changing times, but prayer and the sacraments became important pillars of my emotional comfort and stability.

BACK TO JOURNALISM

By 1985 I was burned out on politics—or at least burned out trying to make a living through politics; I no longer felt that my work was advancing my values—in fact many of the political candidates I was lining up as clients weren't ones I was even sure I'd vote for. I took an offer from CBS News to return to television as their political editor. The chance of going back to journalism, gaining some financial stability, and continuing my polling and political research in an institutional environment was very appealing.

While I'm known inside CBS as a practicing Catholic (especially by other Catholics), I think it has affected my work only in a peripheral way. My beat is domestic campaigns and elections, but I tend to get asked to help on religion stories, and I worked a bit on the pedophile priest stories that were rampant in the 1990s. Probably the proudest moment I had came when the allegations surfaced against Cardinal Bernardin in 1993. I argued strongly that these seemed totally out of line with anything we knew about the cardinal, and I persuaded CBS not to air the story until the cardinal himself responded.

The one issue which has "marked" me as a religious Catholic has been abortion. As I wavered over the years about my position on legalized abortion, I refused to work on pro-choice causes, but helped some friends who were looking for doctors to perform safe abortions. At Easter 1986, I had a personal epiphany on the issue. Five years earlier I had suggested to a relative who was pregnant out of wedlock that abortion was one of the options open to her. Instead, she decided to have the child and raise her. At my home that Easter Sunday, I realized that this darling child would not be alive if my relative had followed my counsel and the issue of the taking of human life ceased to be an abstraction or a moral possibility for me.

In the late 1980s the polling group at CBS and the *New York Times* happened to include a small band of Catholics who were personally uncomfortable about the abortion issue. We embarked on a groundbreaking poll, an in-depth testing of attitudes on abortion that got beneath the surface of the interest group formulations. It showed that Americans had great ambivalence on the issue (as we had a hunch it would) and found significant support for a great many restrictions. This went against the liberal orthodoxy but, to its credit, the *New York Times* put the story on the front page. Though the lens of that one issue I've been able to see the liberal bias, which the right accuses us of, quite clearly. Many of my close friends in journalism and politics have never met anyone who is pro-life, much less liked them. Their only interpretation has been that I must have been brainwashed by the church. On the other hand, my pro-life position has allowed me to make common cause with some conservatives and get beyond some of the mistrust that has built up over the years. (The surprise and delight with which conservatives greeted a column I wrote recently on embryonic stem cell research was a reminder of the chasm that still exists between religious conservatives and the "media." Perhaps even more meaningful to me was that one of my Jesuit cousins saw it on the Web and cited it in his parish bulletin—one of the greatest kudos I've ever received.)

As I said at the start of this paper, I've viewed my work in journalism as a bit of a cop-out and don't see my Catholicism, per se, reflected heavily in my work. I believe my faith is related more to my personal life than my professional career, more influential in my dealings with others and in my view of the world than in my coverage of politics. Unlike other colleagues in the media, I am not hostile to religion and tend to be supportive of organized religions and their members. The values I developed through my Catholic upbringing, education, and practice have, no doubt, come into play in the workplace. But while I remain very fond of the Catholic Church and am not embarrassed about being known as a religious Catholic, the notion of "a Catholic presence in the workplace" is somewhat disturbing. It seems exclusive or self-aggrandizing. (Possibly the fact that I've started to attend an Episcopal Church in Washington with the divorced Catholic man in my life—who *does* have issues with the Catholic Church—has made me more prickly about this.) I find my faith in God a great source of joy and comfort, and the values which I received have served me well. But, the "big *C*" Catholic is not necessarily something I want to define me in the workplace. Maybe this colloquium will cause me to think more fully about this—and even to open my eyes to ways my Catholicism has been reflected in my work.

A JOURNALIST'S CALLING

Don Wycliff

I can as easily imagine myself not Catholic as I can imagine myself not black. Which is to say that I cannot imagine it at all.

I can't imagine *not* getting up on Sunday morning, going to my parish church and sharing with my friends and neighbors there in the celebration of the Eucharist.

I can't imagine *not* having that mystical sense of connectedness with other Catholics all over the globe through the prayers and rituals and tradition and teaching of the church.

I can't imagine *not* thinking of life in terms of sin and grace and sacrifice and the cross and the resurrection.

I can't imagine *not* thinking of the pope as the head of my church, the vicar of Christ, the principal teacher and shepherd of the faithful.

Along with my race, my Catholicism has always been a pillar of my identity in this life, in this society. These two facets of my identity account for the way I think about, feel about and react to almost everything that I experience and observe. And both were part of my upbringing from birth.

There is a room in my parents' house in Texas that I humorously took to calling several years ago "the colored museum." It is a veritable Wycliff family gallery. Photos cover almost every inch of wall space. The oldest picture, taken not many years after the Civil War, is of a woman ancestor three generations before my parents'. The newest picture also is of a female, a member of the third generation after my parents'.

It says something important about our family that, right along with the graduation photos and baby pictures and wedding and prom poses, my parents have hung the First Communion class pictures of eight of their nine

172

children, me and my seven younger siblings. The only one missing is my older brother Francois's, and that's because, as best I can determine, it never existed. No picture was taken of him and his small class of First Communicants at St. Joseph the Worker Church in Dayton, Texas.

The presence of those photos bespeaks the importance to my parents of their Catholic faith, and of our education and upbringing in it. But one particular aspect of those pictures makes that point with special force.

Take my picture, for example. It was shot on a sunny spring day in 1955, on the front steps of Holy Family Church in Ashland, Kentucky. There must have been at least fifty children in the class, girls and boys. But scan the faces and you'll see only one dark face among the First Communicants: mine. The only other dark face in the photo is that of Francois, who, dressed in the cassock and surplice of an acolyte, stands to one side of the pastor, Monsignor Declan Carroll.

The other pictures show pretty much the same racial pattern, although there is at least a sprinkling of other African Americans in the classes of the youngest siblings. But when we washed up in Ashland, on the banks of the Ohio River east of Cincinnati, in autumn 1954, the Wycliffs were the only black family in the parish and we children were the only black kids in the school.

You'd have had a hard time convincing me of it at first, but we were blessed to be there. Holy Family, I later realized, was for us an ark, a refuge. My father, who now is eighty-four, related to me a few years ago how we came to be on that ark. In one respect the story was very common to black people of that time; in another respect it was utterly uncommon.

Mother and Daddy both were born and raised in Dayton, a farming community in East Texas, almost exactly halfway between Houston and Beaumont on U.S. Highway 90. Daddy was an only child; Mother was the second oldest of ten. Daddy's mother, my grandmother, was a Baptist; his father, my grandfather, was a Catholic. Daddy was raised "basically Baptist" and converted to Catholicism after he and Mother were married. Mother's parents both were Catholics, with roots in those Creole communities of southern Louisiana.

(It has always baffled me to hear and see black Catholics referred to as unusual, because in my earliest years I was surrounded by black Catholics in Dayton and the other nearby communities. A great grandfather, Sylvester Wickliff, donated the land for Our Mother of Mercy Church in the nearby hamlet of Ames. One of mother's aunts was a nun in the Sisters of the Holy Family, a black order in New Orleans. We were always ambivalent when Sister Ambrose came for one of her extended visits. On one hand, it meant that Mother would kill the fatted calf and we would eat exceptionally well. On the other, it meant our already overcrowded house would be even more crowded, as we made room for Sister Ambrose and whichever other nun accompanied her.)

My parents, Wilbert and Emily, were married on June 2, 1942, in Bisbee, Arizona, where Daddy, an Army lieutenant, was stationed at the time. Francois was born ten months later in March 1943. Daddy shipped out for Italy with the all-black 92nd Division not long afterwards.

After the war Daddy came home and, using his GI benefit, went part-time to the Texas State University for Negroes (now Texas Southern University) in Houston while working at various jobs to support his family. He earned his degree in industrial education in 1950. For his trouble he got a series of jobs that gave him inadequate pay and even less dignity. It would never be otherwise in the segregated South, he realized, and so he resolved to leave.

His ticket out was a civil service exam that brought an offer of a job as an instructor of industrial arts at the Federal Correctional Institution—a federal prison—in Ashland, Kentucky. He went there alone in June 1954, to see whether he and the job and the people in charge would all find one another agreeable. They did, and in August 1954 the family packed up and moved north to join him. By then, he and Mother had five children—Francois, Don, Karen, Christopher, Ida—and a sixth, Joy, on the way.

Ashland was not exactly the racial Promised Land. In some respects it was worse than Dayton. We could not, for example, go to the downtown movie theaters at all in Ashland; we at least had been able to sit in the balcony in Dayton.

In one crucial respect, however, Ashland was an improvement: It had an alternative to the segregated black public school in the form of Holy Family School. Or at least it was a theoretical alternative, because to that date no black child had ever gone to the Catholic school.

Daddy recalled to me how he visited the black public school, Booker T. Washington, saw the decrepit building and equipment and was heartsick at the thought of sending his children there. Part of the purpose of moving had been to get away from that sort of Jim Crow education.

It was his immediate supervisor at work, Walter Graybeal—a lapsed Catholic from Lafayette, Indiana; a white man who, Daddy swears, sacrificed his career advancement by routinely going to bat on Daddy's behalf—who first broached the idea of Holy Family as an alternative.

"You're a Catholic, aren't you, Wyc?" Graybeal asked. "Well, why shouldn't your kids go to the Catholic school?"

Why not? Daddy went to the parish and talked with Father Carroll. As he related it to me, the priest told him, "Well, Mr. Wycliff, I don't see why your children can't go to school here. But let me ask the bishop."

A day or so later, Daddy got a call at work. It was Father Carroll. "The bishop said the Catholic schools are for *all* Catholic children," Father Carroll said. "Your children will be welcome here."

But that wasn't all of it. Father Carroll went the extra mile. On the Sunday before school was to start, he mounted the pulpit at Mass and laid down the law. One of Daddy's co-workers at the prison, Charles Eckenrode, who later became my confirmation sponsor, told him about it later. According to Eckenrode, Father Carroll announced that, starting that fall, there were going to be "colored children in our school. I want them treated properly. And anyone who doesn't will have to answer to me."

In those days, such words carried weight, coming from the Irish Catholic pastor of a largely Irish Catholic parish.

We were treated more than properly. I think it is fair to say that we were embraced as part of the Holy Family Parish family. To be sure, there was some nervousness at first. Mother tells of her anxiety in taking us to school on the first day—this was, after all, just months after the Supreme Court had overturned "separate but equal" public schooling in its now-celebrated *Brown* decision and the South, of which Kentucky was definitely a part, was full of talk of "massive resistance."

But there was no such resistance at Holy Family. There was, Mother says, a moment's hesitation and then another mother smiled, walked over to her and introduced herself and her daughter, who was the same age and had the same name as my sister Karen. The ice was broken. "You'll never know what a smile can mean to a person," Mother says as she recalls that day.

I did not plan to be a journalist. I was going to be a teacher—a professor of political science. I graduated in June 1969 from the University of Notre Dame and was admitted to graduate study at the University of Chicago and given a fellowship to finance it.

It took me only a few weeks to realize that I did not want to be there. The University of Chicago was about as thoroughly disconnected from the neighborhood, the city and the social ferment surrounding it as if it had been on the moon. And the lively engagement with people and ideas and social movements that I had enjoyed at Notre Dame was absent in the intense, isolated atmosphere of graduate school at Chicago.

Still, while I didn't want to be doing what I was where I was, I had no idea what else I might want or be able to do. Then came December 4, 1969.

I awoke just before 7 A.M. in my studio apartment at 47th St. and Drexel Blvd. and flipped on the radio next to my bed. The all-news station crackled with word of a "shootout" overnight between units of the Chicago police assigned to the Cook County State's Attorney's office and members of the Black Panther Party on the city's West Side. Two Panther leaders, Fred Hampton and Marc Clark, had been killed in the exchange.

I had no relationship to the Black Panthers. I knew of Fred Hampton only what I had seen of him during brief television interviews in the weeks preceding his death. But his words and his manner in those TV appearances suggested to me that this was no mere street thug. Indeed, I saw something of myself in Hampton: We were both young black men full of passion to see our people's lot improved. He was trying to do it one way; I was trying another. His got him killed—unjustly, I was convinced.

In the days and weeks following the "shootout," the Panther story consumed me. I would get up in the morning, buy every newspaper I could find and devour the latest news. I watched every TV new show I could. And I listened to the radio constantly for news.

Gradually, the Chicago news media unearthed and exposed the truth. There had been no *shootout*; it had been a *shoot-in* by the police. Hampton and Clark had been deliberately targeted and slain.

As I watched the Chicago media do their splendid work, I began to feel myself attracted to that work as a socially relevant and useful way to spend a life. It was in every sense of the word a *calling*, a *vocation*.

It took until the end of the spring quarter at the University of Chicago for me to get up the gumption to strike out in a new direction. I packed up my books and my meager other belongings and headed home to Texas, to Houston. I hoped to get into TV news, but—no surprise, really—had no luck at the stations there.

I finally made my way to the spanking new offices of the *Houston Post* and filled out a job application, telling the lady in the personnel office that I wanted to be a reporter. I should have been surprised when they agreed to give me an interview—nobody walks into a big-city newspaper off the street and gets an interview, much less a job. But I suppose the educational pedigree helped. So also did the fact that, at that time, there was all of one black reporter in the *Post* newsroom and there was unease in the city over a Black Panther-type group that called itself Peoples Party II.

Anyway, I was interviewed and hired. The passion for justice and righteousness cultivated by my parents and teachers had led me to my profession.

I am blessed to have had a career of more than thirty years in the news industry. The last seventeen of those have been in the most rarefied part of the industry: opinion writing. I wrote editorials for more than five years at the *New York Times.* I did the same for ten years at the *Chicago Tribune,* and for nine of those years I served as editorial page editor. For the last two years, I have written a column of personal opinion, mainly about issues of media process and ethics, but often about other matters as well.

The stock in trade of opinion writers is ideas—ideas that challenge, provoke, clarify. The Catholic Church, with possibly the oldest and richest intellectual history in the Western world, ought to be a powerful contender for the time and attention of columnists and editorial writers at the nation's newspapers. In my experience, however, it is not. The reasons are complex.

There is an enormous amount of anti-Catholic sentiment in newsrooms, as there is in the society at large. Some of it is plain old lowbrow bigotry—I've heard Catholics referred to on more than one occasion as "mackerel-snappers." Some is more sophisticated, holding the pope responsible for famine and starvation because of the church's official opposition to artificial birth control and abortion. And some is rooted in the conviction, not entirely unjustified, that the church has over the centuries fostered or tolerated anti-Semitism and assorted other kinds of bigotry and intolerance, and therefore is not to be trusted.

But the antagonistic attitudes of others are as nothing compared to the wounds the church has inflicted upon itself. It will be decades before the anguish and anger generated by the clergy sex abuse scandals dissipate, before innocent mentions of priestly concern and caring don't provoke snickering, before the church enjoys the sort of regard it once took for granted. And this is a totally self-inflicted injury.

On top of this, Catholicism suffers from the same things in attempting to influence the news media as it suffers from in its pulpits on Sunday mornings: bad preaching. The church simply does not have many spokesmen—any spokesmen?—who can speak its message in ways that make it relevant and understandable to modern men and women of a secularist bent. Add to this the fact that the church's message is fundamentally a countercultural one, and thus a demanding one, and the problem of making the message understood is compounded.

Additionally—and this will not be much appreciated by Catholic liberals—the Catholic Church in America has become a Tower of Babel.

Non-Catholics—and many Catholics as well—have become confused because there is no Catholic trademark to distinguish one so-called Catholic opinion from another. The brand name "Catholic" has been devalued in the marketplace through confusion. Catholics for a Free Choice is the same as any other Catholic group or opinion—or at least that's what that Catholic professor on CNN or ABC or in the *New York Times* said.

For a Catholic like me, attempting to bring what little I know of that distinguished Catholic intellectual tradition to bear on deliberations in the newsroom or the editorial boardroom, this causes fits. Not only am I unable to speak authoritatively about Catholic positions, I am unable any longer to *feel* authoritatively.

So what do I do? I try to go with the basics. I read a lot of scripture and try to apply what I read to the situations that present themselves in the news. Interestingly, the older I get the more I find myself attracted to the passages about forgiveness and reconciliation. I suspect that's not coincidental.

But always, always, the most powerful passage of all is about Judgment Day, Matthew 25:31–46. Especially, Verse 40: "I assure you, as often as you did it for one of my least brother, you did it for me."

LOOK FOR THE REAL STORY

Paul Moses

During the years I served as city editor of *Newsday*'s New York City edition, I often began the work day with a phone call from Jimmy Breslin, one of his many stops on the way to finding his next column. He had pegged me as the office Catholic, so when I wasn't called on to explain the sins of the editors, I was handling his complaints about the sins of the church's leadership. I was aware that more than a few times, Breslin had been assailed as anti-Catholic because of his scathing attacks on the church hierarchy and the anger his columns have displayed toward the Irish-Catholic culture from which he sprang. But the more we spoke, the more I realized that he is a religious man, a churchgoer who takes Catholic teachings to heart—accusations he would no doubt deny. I saw that Catholicism shaped his outlook as a writer. Breslin's best columns and novels are stories with a strong sense of human dignity; as Pope John Paul II wrote in *Redemptor hominis,* his first encyclical, Christianity can be defined as "deep amazement at man's worth and dignity." (Breslin would ask, "What about the women?") I saw, too, that a sense of outrage—his keen sense of right and wrong, good versus evil—was very much a part of his Catholic upbringing.

I see those tendencies—reporter as storyteller; reporter as righter of wrongs—in my work, similarly rooted in a Catholic outlook. The difference, though, is that I've never been at war with my Catholicism; it has always been a comfortable fit. For the most part, I have been involved in some form of church ministry since I was a teenager.

I have no difficulty stepping back and, with a journalist's eye, writing about the very human problems that beset the church. At various times, these have included the autocratic style of certain leaders; the counterproductive

179

wars between liberal and conservative factions; and the sex and financial scandals. At the same time, none of this has shaken my belief that the church is divine as well as human, and in the long run, guided by the Spirit. I've tried to use whatever ability I have to write not only about the church's weaknesses but also of its spiritual mission, doing articles on such topics as centering prayer, healing Masses, *cursillo*, iconography, Catholic evangelization, and Christian Base Communities. And I broke through the objectivity that newspaper writing requires to mix spiritual reflection with journalistic observation in a book about Pope John Paul II's pilgrimage to the Holy Land. Fellow *Newsday* writer Bob Keeler and I wrote *Days of Intense Emotion* (Catholic Book Publishing, 2001) because we were moved to retell the story through eyes of faith.

Of course, for the loudest critics, it doesn't matter how many so-called positive stories you do if you write one that is supposedly negative. At least, that was my experience when I wrote a story summarizing new books about the historical Jesus; it ran in *Newsday* on the week before Christmas some years ago. There was a torrent of angry phone calls, many of them accusing me of being anti-Catholic. Some callers, noting my last name, had a distinctly anti-Semitic edge. The newspaper published a letter that said I wrote like an atheist.

The truth is that I was hooked on Catholicism at an early age, thanks to the stories Sister Maris Stella told my first-grade class at Mary Queen of Heaven School in the Flatlands section of Brooklyn. Each one seemed better than the next: Adam, Eve, and the talking serpent; Noah's ark; the escape through the Red Sea; no room at the inn; and later, in other grades, the lives of the saints. As a journalist, I gradually learned that one person's story could tell you everything about a subject. It wasn't always necessary to have statistics and experts and leaked documents and graphics. The truth could be found in one person's tale if it was well told and verified.

Some of the most compelling stories in Scripture are about people struggling to be truly human, which is to be like God. It took me a long time to realize this, but the same could be said about the best stories in the newspaper.

Another columnist with whom I've worked, the late Murray Kempton, once held a criminal complaint in his hands and gave me the following advice: "Look for the names in small letters, for those are the ones whose souls have been put to the test." In criminal charges, the defendants' names are in capital letters. In the sometimes novelistic charges federal prosecutors wrote up in the big organized crime cases Kempton loved to cover, the names of unindicted conspirators were in lower case. Often enough, they were FBI informants. To Kempton, this was the place to look for the real story, a story of the soul—of frightened individuals pushed to betrayal as a means of securing freedom. His columns exhibited a Graham Greene–like insight into human weakness and hope for redemption. While Kempton was not Catholic (he was an Episcopalian who knew more about the Catholic faith than the vast majority of Catholics.), I learned a lot from him about what it meant to be Catholic and a journalist. It meant telling the stories of people struggling against the odds toward human dignity.

But my Catholic schooling also dwelt on the battle of good against evil. I can recall a second-grade teacher, a laywoman, who sweepingly predicted that the Third World War would be fought over religion and that it would be the bloodiest war. At our Confirmation, we exited to a song proclaiming ourselves "an army of youth." We were sent forth to battle the dark forces.

I started my career in daily journalism in 1978 and quickly sought a role as righter of wrongs. When I began as a reporter at the since closed *Dispatch* in Hudson County, New Jersey, I was assigned to cover Union City. Within its forty-eight-block length, it held these ongoing stories: (1) It was the New Jersey headquarters of the Teamsters Union, run by mob bosses suspect in the disappearance of Jimmy Hoffa. (2) It was the focus of investigations into Omega 7, an anti-Castro terrorist group that committed twenty-five bombings and two murders, one of the victims being a local man I knew quite well. (3) It had a mayor, a school board president, and other key officials who would go to jail for taking hundreds of thousands of dollars in bribes from a construction company controlled by a reputed mob hit man.

I wasn't particularly interested in compelling human stories—I wanted to root out corruption. I saw things pretty much in black-and-white, and dug up information that helped lead to a federal investigation of the mayor, who was New Jersey's senior legislator, and his top aides.

It was jarring to watch these men I knew get convicted of racketeering before their wailing families. In a strange twist, I was the one who delivered news of the verdict to the wives and friends. As the verdict was being delivered, the judge had cleared the courtroom because of the relatives' emotional outbursts. The reporters were allowed to stay, and when I left the courtroom, the relatives surrounded me to find out what had happened to their loved ones. I blurted out, "guilty on all counts," and fled the scene, their cries echoing in the corridor. I steeled myself and moved on.

I don't think it's an accident that many investigative reporters are Catholics. The same can be said for the most determined criminal investigators, people like Rudolph Giuliani in his days as U.S. attorney in Manhattan or former FBI Director Louis Freeh. I've heard federal prosecutors speak with only a touch of irony of being "on the side of the angels"; former prosecutors who become defense lawyers have "gone over to the dark side."

This business of punishing wrongdoers figured prominently in the first decade or so of my career, as I went from covering one scandal to the next: Abscam; mob involvement in the New Jersey toxic waste industry; the New York City Parking Violations Bureau scandal in the mid-1980s; insider trading; the Wedtech bribery scandal, to mention a few.

Somewhere along the line, though, I tired of seeing people sent to jail. I became concerned about prosecutors' excesses and started writing about defendants more favorably. I wanted to write *stories* about people rather than simply collect facts pointing toward corruption.

So near the end of 1990, I got myself assigned to the religion beat at *New York Newsday*.

Societal views of the role of religion have changed so much since then that I need to explain what a backwater beat this was considered. Many newspapers have started religion sections and hired religion writers; large papers may have two, three, or even four. Back then, fellow reporters asked me if I was being punished.

As I started the beat, my view was that the Catholic Church was being covered mostly where it intersected with the liberal social agenda, that is, when it opposed a new sex education curriculum, or women in the priesthood, or gay and lesbian rights legislation. These were all worthy topics for news coverage, but it was a little like covering schools only when there was a dispute about handing out condoms; no one would ever find out if the students were learning to read.

The Catholic Church took some pretty tough hits in the media through the 1980s and into the 1990s. This was not always the media's fault; church leaders insisted on speaking out loudly on controversial issues, which was bound to draw a negative reaction from those on the other side of any divisive issue. But there was also a prevalent view in the news media that religion in general (and, I think, the Catholic Church in particular) did not have a valid role in the public square. Religion was supposed to be kept private.

My solution was to be sure that in addition to covering the controversies, the paper also ran stories on how religious faith played out in everyday life. In coverage of the Catholic Church, I tried to take the focus off the hierarchy and write more about what was happening in parishes.

The situation was much different when I returned to the religion beat early in 2001 after serving as City Hall bureau chief and city editor. The cutting-edge story was that religion was becoming part of public life in many arenas. Academic sociologists were delving into it as never before; medical researchers were studying it, too. Business people were meeting in prayer or meditation groups, or reading about Jesus as CEO. Science was exploring it on many fronts. News magazines kept putting it on the cover, even telling us that religion is wired into our brains. Television aired specials about Jesus, and about Islam. Major publishers started seeing it as an avenue to profits. Newspapers joined in, providing more complete coverage of religion. (I'm not sure if the same can be said for television news, with the exception of the excellent PBS show *Religion and Ethics Newsweekly.*)

In the process, the Catholic Church got much more favorable coverage, at least for a while. The PBS affiliate in New York, WNET, offers a case study. In the past, many Catholics were angry at the station over what they saw as a biased report on a dispute between the church and radical AIDS activists. Now, as I returned to the religion beat, I wrote about how the bishops and the station were partners in a beautiful production called *The Face of Jesus*, a religiously tinged film on Jesus in art.

I think it should be added that during this period, newspapers seemed more reluctant to offend Catholic readers. Church officials in some parts of the country became more aggressive about pressuring their local newspapers. And it could well be that with a much heavier emphasis in the newspaper industry on increasing corporate profits, this pressure discouraged negative coverage of the country's largest church.

That didn't serve the truth, either. The church's credibility is undercut when its spokespersons are hypersensitive or counter just criticism with the threat of economic retaliation.

In September 2001, I left my job as *Newsday* religion writer to join the faculty of Brooklyn College of the City University of New York, where I teach journalism. So I was largely on the sidelines when the systematic cover-up of clergy sex abuse was exposed. The disclosures made me realize that I should have been more probing in my coverage of the chancery. Documents that became public showed part of the problem was that church leaders had been willing to go to incredible lengths to avoid bad publicity.

For what it is worth, I can report that I once told the bishops to be honest with the media on this subject (albeit many years too late). In 1998, I was on a panel at a closed session of the National Conference of Catholic Bishops; the topic was clergy sex abuse and the news media. I warned the assembled bishops that any cover-up would be a bigger story than the individual cases of abuse. Any journalist would know that; so would the bishops' own communication directors. Various bishops said they were not getting credit for reforms they had enacted earlier. Some were testy, asserting that cases involving Catholic priests got more media play than cases involving ministers from other faiths. I left with a vague sense that it hadn't gone well.

The Catechism of the Catholic Church offers good advice: "By the very nature of their profession, journalists have an obligation to serve the truth and not offend against charity in disseminating information." The gospel message is a difficult one for people in all walks of life; journalists are no different. It is not an easy matter to tell the truth with charity, since the truth will often hurt. But it is possible to treat those on the receiving end of some unfavorable report with fairness and dignity—that's the balance I look for. Charity "does not rejoice at wrong," Paul says, but neither should it flinch at the truth.

Those who are both journalists and active Catholics play a special role in the newsroom when it comes to reporting on the church; other reporters and editors will seek their advice. We should walk between the extremes of those who are prejudiced against the church and those frightened to criticize an influential institution—we should tell the truth with charity.

This is all a sticky business because, as a journalist, I am committed to objectivity. But objectivity does not mean checking all my values at the newsroom door. Catholic values have made me more interested in writing about poverty and giving the poor and immigrants a voice in the paper, for example. Catholic Charities officials have been an important source of information on these stories by arranging interviews with their clients.

One of the best journalism lessons I ever got came in a course I took on the way to getting a "training for ministry" certificate from the Pastoral Institute of the Diocese of Brooklyn. In a class called "Spirituality for Social Justice," the instructor spoke about the importance of asking the right question. At so many news conferences I attended during my years as a reporter in City Hall, I've seen journalists ask the wrong questions. The "right questions" are aimed at discerning how public policy will affect people's lives, particularly the disadvantaged. To me, that's good journalism. It's also the "preferential option for the poor."

As an editor, I felt that choosing where to concentrate resources was in part a moral decision. I chose, for example, to invest the staff's time in writing about such topics as the crisis in housing immigrants. Often, the decisions about what to cover are made in moments. Send a reporter to wait the day for a murder victim's family to come home? Let the reporter work on an in-depth piece that might matter more in the long run? The editor's values will help guide the decision.

There was a line in *Humbolt's Gift,* a novel Saul Bellow wrote in the 1970s, that I've never forgotten. His narrator, Charles Citrine, had written a play that ran successfully on Broadway for eight months. He lamented: "I had the attention of the public for nearly a year, and I taught it nothing."

Those who have the ear of the public, even if for five minutes over the morning cup of coffee, have a duty to teach it something.

FAMILY, FAITH, AND UNION

Kirk Adams

My personal roots lie in a broader Trinity than that laid out in my catechism. Three pillars—family, faith, and union—were and probably
still are the source of my worldview. Admittedly, those three values sometimes exist in tension with one another.

My Catholic faith came to me in the context of an Irish Catholic family,
and in growing up in an Irish Catholic neighborhood in Springfield, Massachusetts. I learned my catechism from priests and nuns who not only supplied
religious teachings and doctrine, but also were the source of education,
healthcare, and, for a young Catholic boy, all the sports he could possibly
play in one twenty-four hour day.

I saw Catholicism not from an intellectual perspective or through some
inner reflection; rather it was an organic part of my everyday universe. I
played sports in the CYO programs because that was where you played. I
went to Mass not so much as an expression of faith but because my mother
said I must, and because, as an altar boy, I had a job to do. I didn't think of
Catholicism in terms of my immortal soul; I thought of Catholicism in terms
of cheering for Notre Dame and JFK.

But somehow, somewhere, some way, certain Catholic values took root.
(It is hard to determine the precise source of these beliefs: they are certainly
Catholic but they are also union values and the values of my parents.) I came
to believe in the importance of one's involvement in and commitment to a
larger community and its common good. What should bind people together
is not that they were all alike but that they all have a responsibility to each
other's well being. The Catholic Church's contribution to my developing this
sense and commitment to a community was probably driven by both Satur-

day morning catechism class and Saturday afternoon CYO coaching—in both cases articulated by the same priests and nuns.

Finally, and again from all three sources, there came a simple dictum: honor work. My father and mother essentially worked a twenty-four hour day, he as a milkman and janitor, she as a postal worker on the graveyard shift. My mother was a union steward; at a very early age my education on the nature of work extended to countless union meetings about wages and benefits, dignity, respect, and solidarity.

I don't recall any formal lessons on class, discrimination, or economic justice. But somewhere between Catholic teachings and union rhetoric (and simply watching my father work so hard), I developed a yearning to be part of that historical march towards social and economic justice and a common good. As a young boy, I certainly had no idea how to be part of that march, but it seemed like the right thing to do.

Much later, when I actually did some personal reflection, I identified one source of this belief. Whether it was my family, my neighborhood church, or the union talk that crossed our dining room table, all three emphasized the Beatitudes a lot more than the Ten Commandments. To this day, with or without the weekly refresher course called the Mass, it is probably the only part of the New Testament that I can recite.

It was with these somewhat unformed beliefs that I left my boyhood neighborhood of family, faith and union to see a much larger, complicated world.

AN EXPANDING WORLD

My world and my worldview expanded rapidly in the late sixties when I was awarded a scholarship to study in England in 1968. I spent as little time as possible at the English public school to which I was assigned, and as much time as possible in Ireland and France during that turbulent year. That year and the subsequent four at Wesleyan University in Connecticut saw me lose touch with the church as an institution. However, I don't think I lost touch with those basic beliefs from my early years. While I stopped going to Mass, I held on to a fondness for the church like a boyhood friend you leave behind in the old neighborhood. I never developed, unlike many of my contemporaries, strong negative views about the church.

On the other hand, while I got involved in both the demonstrations in

Europe and the Vietnam War protests, I never could relate these struggles back to my core beliefs.

In the mid-seventies, I set off to look for the right struggle. I went to Tanzania to experience "African Socialism" but immediately saw a much stronger force for social and economic justice: the Catholic Church. By chance and good fortune, I became involved with priests, nuns, and lay Catholics who by providing training on agriculture techniques and targeting financial grants, were making a real difference in the lives of individual families and whole villages. This was a Church I liked! It was a Church that seemed absolutely committed to helping a community reach a common good for people's everyday lives. At the same time, it did not neglect the care and feeding of the soul. Some have criticized this particular version of the Church because it did not dot the "i's" and cross the "t's" of orthodoxy. While there probably were some wavering lines in terms of Church doctrine and ritual, it seemed as close to living the New Testament as any place I've ever seen. It truly was about community and caring for the least of us. I had found what I was looking for in terms of my core beliefs, but it was too far from home, in so many ways, for me.

THE LABOR MOVEMENT
AND THE CHURCH

By the beginning of the eighties, my own thinking, experiences, and roots had convinced me that organizing in the workplace was the best means to the variety of ends I was seeking. The practical solutions of the issues raised in the Beatitudes—healthcare for the sick, retirement security for the old, a living wage for the working poor and time together for working families— seemed to be achievable for low-wage workers not through government action or the wonders of a free market economy, but rather through workers organizing in such a way that the system honors and rewards their work! The decision that this was the march for me was not easy. The Labor Movement, then and now, is not a pretty thing. Like the Church, it is an institution that suffers from all of the weaknesses and frustrations inherent in large institutions. But on the one hand, given where I came from and what I had experienced, it was an easy task to complement my labor organizing work with my Catholic faith. On the other hand, it has not always been easy to live in the same house with these two institutions. As a self-defense mechanism, I make the distinction between the Catholic Church, that is, the institution, and the

Catholic faith all the time. I do so in this chapter. I also make this distinction for a particular union's bureaucracy and the Labor Movement. With respect to the Church, making this distinction may be invalid but, as they say, it works for me.

THE CHURCH IN THE PUBLIC SQUARE

What is the role of the Church and the Catholic faith in the "Public Square"? I start by encouraging the Church to enter the Public Square. I *do not* support "the liberal argument that the public square should remain scrupulously neutral on ultimate questions." However, much of my frustration with the Church revolves around how it has injected itself into the Public Square. There seems to be an imbalance and selectivity in the level and degree of intensity in the Church's public pronouncements on reproductive issues, as compared to its public pronouncement in support of other Church teachings on social and economic justice.

Over the last twenty years, a substantial portion of the Church hierarchy seems to have focused all its firepower on the abortion issue and other reproductive questions, at the expense of issues like the rights of immigrants, access to healthcare, and poverty in general. This is not to say that the Church does not speak out on these issues. It does so in very strong language. However, Church actions on these two sets of issues are uneven. These are all life and death issues. If one set of issues can be made into a litmus test in the public square by the Church, others can and *should* be also. On the Sunday before Election Day, the sermon should not mention abortion alone in providing Catholic congregations instructions on how to vote. How various candidates have addressed Catholic teachings on healthcare, immigration, and poverty should also be part of that sermon.

THE CHURCH AS AN EMPLOYER

Given my work, I have not always agreed with how Church institutions have reconciled Church teachings on the worker's right to organize, and a particular institution's response to its own workers' desires for organization. I must say that at a variety of levels, there has been a serious effort to bring into alignment Catholic teachings on the rights of workers and the response of Catholic Health Care employers. In this particular sector, the tension for

Catholic employers comes from two sources: a fear that workers' desire for a union will divert the institution from its mission and, secondly, the pressures from health care market forces that can push Catholic Health Care managers down a road that equates competitiveness, and thus viability, with maintaining a "union-free environment."

Recent discussions and relationship-building between Catholic Health Care leaders and union leadership, in a number of markets, have shown that there is another road to go down. These discussions have led to the recognition that the real threats to the achievement of the Catholic Health Care mission are market forces and funding issues. This new road requires management and the union to look at new approaches. This road promotes and enhances the institution's viability in a health care market based on a partnership between Catholic health care employers and the workers' organization. This partnership in fact increases the ability of the Catholic institution to fulfill its mission in areas like access to quality health care, indigent care, and health care in immigrant communities. An alliance of Catholic Health Care and a union like the Service Employees International Union (SEIU) can be a powerful force in the Public Square in promoting what are jointly held missions in the world of healthcare.

THE NEW PUBLIC SQUARE

In the forties, fifties, and sixties, in the world of my childhood, the Church *was* the "public square" in many communities. The changes in America over the last forty years, socioeconomic and demographic, now present that sort of opportunity for the Church only in Latino immigrant communities. If the Church seeks a role and a voice in the new Public Square of the twenty-first century, it needs to reflect on what its goals are there, and the risks involved in seeking that role and that voice. The values and teachings of the Catholic faith can be a powerful force in shaping public debate. I believe that this powerful force needs to be directed at a larger vision of social justice vision than one issue. Further, it should go beyond simply articulating this vision. The Church and its natural allies can not only have a voice about this larger vision, but have the potential to energize shared constituencies into a movement that can drive an approach to public policy that seriously looks at the issues of the sick, the old, the poor, and the rights of immigrants.

I know that I cannot return to the Church of my youth. However, I now have three children. Perhaps in a different way, definitely in a different neighborhood, they will find in the Catholic faith the same values I found in my youth, values which have sustained me in my life and work.

THE WORKER'S WORKER

John J. Sweeney

In my adult life, I've been blessed to know many members of the hierarchy in the American Church. I've also been blessed, as have countless others, by the courage and the sacrifices of the worker priests and social justice fighters in the Church. From Monsignor John A. Ryan to Monsignor John Egan to labor's chaplain for the past fifty years, the late Monsignor George Higgins, so many have inspired and fortified us by their faith, grace, and persistence.

The recent exposé of the shameless and terrible abuse of youngsters by a small number of our clergy have led me to this reflection: how sad it is that the champions of the reign of God on earth are being asked to shoulder yet another burden in trying to lead the faithful to a richer life of grace.

Cardinal Theodore McCarrick, my current archbishop, has brought his humble and superbly engaging pastoral leadership to the Washington, D.C. area, following in the footsteps of his predecessor, Cardinal Hickey. One of the key messages that the truly tireless Cardinal McCarrick shares in his incessant rounds of the archdiocese is that what we are comes back to the foundation of faith. His 2002 Holy Week homilies at St. Matthews Cathedral stressed, time and again, the centrality of faith.

My participation in the life of the Church is typical for my generation: begun in Baptism, "made official" in confirmation, and rooted, week in and week out, in the Eucharist. Along with my wife Maureen and our two children, Trish and John, I have been blessed with rich opportunities for participation in both the sacramental and the public life of the Church. Throughout all the years, my faith sustained me—not without question and, at times, not without doubt—as a constant sign of the forgiveness and the love of God and as a redemptive force. Faith has been the key to it all.

191

I have received a great gift from God in being able to pursue a life dedicated to justice, and have received daily nourishment in my career from working families struggling to make ends meet, fighting for dignity and respect as human persons. Today, I experience these blessings as the president of the AFL-CIO. I can't tell you how refreshing are my daily encounters with working women and men as I travel the country. While I genuinely relish my work in Washington, the influence of money and the dominance of special interests cast a pall on our nation's capitol as a place of the people's business. A day with immigrant workers in Chicago, Los Angeles, or New York; a few hours with workers hurt by repetitive stress injuries but fighting to protect their coworkers; or a session with ex-Enron employees who want to warn others about blind faith in their company stock—this restores the energy I can lose from repeated encounters with partisans in Washington.

I grew up in the Bronx, a child of working class immigrants from County Leitrim, Ireland. James, my father, was a bus driver, active in the Transport Workers Union. Agnes, my mother, was a domestic worker in the employ of a well-to-do Fifth Avenue household. In my upbringing, the family was the source of unfailing love and support, the union the source of a living wage and inspiring social justice work, and the Church the path to redemption. Almost as regular as attending Mass with my parents was the experience of going to union meetings and picket lines with my father. The Transport Workers Union was then headed by the legendary Mike Quill. I remember one of my father's pet phrases, "Thank God for Mike," when the latest union contract meant more food for the family, an extra's day's vacation on the beaches of New York, or more time with us, because the work week shrank from forty-eighty to forty hours (after a tough strike).

My family upbringing was augmented by Catholic grade school (St. Barnabas in the Bronx), secondary school (Cardinal Hayes High School), and Iona College. My first union job after college was with the International Ladies Garment Workers Union (now merged with the former Amalgamated Clothing Workers Union and called UNITE!). In 1960, I went to work for the janitors union, a branch of the Service Employees International Union I belonged to because I was a laborer in a Catholic cemetery, which was my work ticket through Iona.

As a young officer of the janitors union in New York City, I led the organizing and contract bargaining for service workers at the World Trade Center. How often have the cold days of December 1976, when workers picketed in stiff winter winds, come back to me as I visited that site since September 11, 2001, when 633 members of New York union families lost their lives? Those workers, and the many more who were left without jobs, were the contemporaries of those working families and of my family and my neighbors—immigrants to the new world, all in search of a better way of life for themselves and the generations to follow. For them, as much as for us, faith was the rock, and belief in the ultimate triumph of God's reign the beacon, in a harsh and often troubling world.

For all of us, participation in the life of the Church was anchored in the Eucharist and extended to all the Sacraments. But it also extended into more social dimensions of Church life, the parish community and the mission of the Church in the wider world.

Our work life is prominent within this latter range of participation. Work takes up a large amount of our waking hours. It includes a significant portion of our social interactions—indeed, the overwhelming part, for many today. Given the steady rise in families with two, three, or more wage earners, total work-time dwarfs other categories of activity in many families.

In its spiritual and ethical dimensions, work offers a rich path of participation in the kingdom of God outside the Church proper. Whatever else our jobs may be, our work provides the opportunity for spiritual participation in God's ongoing act of creation. Through our own creativity, ingenuity, diligence, commitment to service, solidarity with coworkers, and stewardship of resources, we are given the chance to emulate God's love for us all, thereby honoring the Creator as we fulfill the mission of the Church in the world.

Does the Church (we) represent Christ in the world of work? This is the mission question we all face in our daily work lives.

Participation at work takes many forms. First, work itself is a form of participation in the life of Christ, since all creative effort stems from and reflects God's love. Second, the manner in which work is done—how skillfully, diligently, honestly, effectively, responsibly—reflects ethical values. Third, the social dimensions of work—service to family and community, faithfulness to the work enterprise, collegiality and solidarity with coworkers of all stripes—mark degrees of participation in the mission of the Church in the world.

The social dimensions involve both rights and responsibilities. Workers are entitled to participate fully in the decisions that affect their work lives and their work organizations. They have a concomitant responsibility to participate fully, and to do so with deep respect for the rights of coworkers to participate as well, and with the need for effective work organization—for example, the division of labor and decision-making among coworkers, whether peers, supervisors, or subordinates.

In practical terms, workers' primary responsibility is to provide quality products and services to the public they serve—the "customers," in today's parlance. A closely allied responsibility is captured in the old phrase "a fair day's work for a fair day's pay"—that is, an equitable relationship with the owners of the enterprise in which they work. All workers have a stewardship responsibility for the time, material, equipment, and reputation of the enterprise, as well as an obligation to work cooperatively with superiors.

Owners need to live up to their end of the bargain and provide fair pay and benefits, consistent with industry and area standards, and a healthful and discrimination-free workplace. They also have a responsibility, to whatever extent possible, to encourage the human development of their workforce through skill development. Lastly, they have the responsibility to provide avenues of participation for workers and to respect their freedom to choose their own voice at work without interference.

While genuine participation can exist in various types of workplaces, under different management styles and work culture, a traditional form of participation is through worker self-organization, or unions. While workplaces do not need unions to have fair policies, non-discriminatory practices, decent wages and benefits, there are many practical reasons why workers turn toward unions. The most common is a perceived lack of respect and fairness. Another is that the scope of the business enterprise may require collective action across many workplaces. But even in individual workplaces and in relatively respectful work relationships, workers may choose a union to help them establish a voice at work independent from management, with access to skills in collective action and resources to support their interests.

Today, unionization efforts among American workers range across different industries and different skill levels, from airline pilots and aerospace engineers to nurses, hotel staff, poultry-processing workers, janitors, and home health aides. The common denominator among these groups is that belief in collective action (solidarity) overcomes both the deep individualism of American culture and the common fear of reprisal.

Unions in the United States have developed a strong democracy/strong leadership model of organization, beginning with organization at the work site through elected bargaining committees and shop stewards, and continuing with elected leaders at all levels of the union movement. Unions work best on behalf of their members when there is extensive involvement in the process of negotiating contracts, developing health and pension benefit plans, and representing worker interests in the public issue debates of the day.

In one sense, union organization brings a "worker culture" and worker participation to enterprises that are often strongly hierarchical, with little accountability to the bulk of the people who produce the goods and the wealth. What workers realize from unions in a material sense is well-documented: additional dollars per hour, largely employer-paid family health benefits, traditional pension plans with guaranteed benefits, safer workplaces, and additional opportunities for skill development.

These kinds of gains take time and the hard work involved in bargaining for contracts that give a greater share of the economic benefits to workers. But what workers gain more immediately is the sense of self-respect and dignity that comes from acts of solidarity and empowerment.

FAMILY, GOOD FORTUNE, AND STEWARDSHIP

Thomas J. Donnelly

The invitation to participate in the Pew Charitable Trusts study of the place of American Catholics in the Public Square is a welcome opportunity to review an imperfect record and pass on a few constructive thoughts to future generations.

When I was asked to assess how my faith has shaped my working life, the concept of stewardship immediately came to mind. In December 1992 the bishops of the United States published an elaborate statement on stewardship. It was highly theological in content and received some initial criticism for its lack of emphasis on the financial aspects of church operations. For my purposes, the concept of stewardship can be phrased in very simple terms, which date back to Old Testament days. Broadly speaking, it can be described as sharing of time, talent and treasure for the benefit of others.

I was born in Pittsburgh, Pennsylvania, seventy-seven years ago, the oldest of three children. When I was three both my parents died within several months of each other. My father's maiden sister, a young woman of twenty-eight, stepped forward to raise the three of us. She was truly a great lady. Over the years I have come to regard her heroic act as my first experience of stewardship, a unique calling by the Lord. Aunt Mary died some thirty-two years ago and we honor her memory by the activities of our family foundation, the Mary J. Donnelly Foundation.

I had the good fortune of receiving a splendid elementary education from the Sisters of Mercy and my secondary education at Central Catholic High from the Christian Brothers. Good fortune continued as I graduated from high school in the summer of 1943 and was admitted to a Navy program designed to educate and train naval officers. The educational phase was eight full semesters, leading to a bachelor's degree at the rate of three semesters per year. In the spring of 1944, at the end of two semesters at MIT, I was shipped by the Navy to the University of Michigan. That was the beginning of some happy times—rare during the difficult war years of 1942 through 1945. The Catholic Newman Center at St. Mary Student Parish played a large part in my life on that campus. This was the beginning of my intense lifetime interest in campus ministry.

A tragic event marred the happiness of those times. In November 1944 I was called from class and told that my brother Bill had been killed instantly in an automobile accident at an intersection only a few blocks away from the main campus of the University of Pittsburgh. Returning to Michigan after the funeral services, St. Mary Student Parish became my oasis—a source of spiritual consolation and strength. I became deeply involved with Newman activities, and for about one and a half years at the end of my undergraduate days I served as President of the Newman Club at St. Mary.

With a degree in electrical engineering, in 1947 I entered the student engineer program at Westinghouse Electric Corporation in Pittsburgh and quickly determined that this was not where I intended to spend the rest of my working life. In the fall of 1947, after the war I returned to law school at Michigan—again, a series of happy times and wonderful associations.

Following graduation from law school in 1950, I settled into practice in Pittsburgh with a small family firm. One of my first clients was a high school friend, Jack Donahue, a West Point graduate who had achieved a sterling record in the Strategic Air Force—a major achievement in those Cold War days. By sheer coincidence Jack had resigned from the Air Force a few weeks before the outbreak of the Korean War in June of 1950, had begun what turned out to be a very large family, and was making a living by selling mutual funds.

In 1955 Jack joined Dick Fisher (another Central Catholic alum) and me, as the Pittsburgh lawyer, and several outside partners (who left the operation after a few years), to form a company known as Federated Investors, Inc. The first few years of operation were precarious. The greatest assets were the quality of the people and their common spiritual values. To fast-forward, Federated Investors, Inc. today is one of the top ten mutual fund companies in the United States. Since 1998 Federated stock has been listed on the New York Stock Exchange. The forty some years of Federated's successful development were a time of great growth in the mutual fund industry. But Federated's outstanding performance is based on strong leadership and a pervasive atmosphere of creativity in product design, investment management, administration and sales. Exchange funds, amortized cost pricing of money market funds and computerized service to banks and their trust departments are a few examples of Federated's creative product design.

Beginning in the 1970s, a number of companies in the industry attempted cooperative ventures with insurance companies to use their sales forces to sell mutual fund products. Most were failures. Federated (dominated in the eyes of many by the Central Catholic High School team) joined Lutheran Brotherhood, one of the largest fraternal insurance companies in the United States. For a period of fifteen years, Federated organized and operated a series of mutual funds, which were sold exclusively to Lutherans by the Lutheran Brotherhood sales force. Ecumenism in the financial world!

From its beginning until 1998, when the stock was listed on the Exchange, I served as a director as well as counsel to the Company. In 1966 a legal department was formed within the company; it now employs seventeen lawyers, all under the competent direction of John McGonigle, another Central Catholic graduate, who now is the executive vice president of the company. I hired him in 1966 when he was a young lawyer with the SEC, on a tip from one of his relatives, a Pittsburgh judge—by sheer coincidence I had chatted with him one day on the way back from daily Mass.

As it grew Federated became a major player and employer in the expanding financial services sector of Pittsburgh. It is interesting to reflect on the tremendous change that has occurred in the profile of business leadership in Pittsburgh, which is also largely representative of what has occurred within the country during the period from the end of World War II to the present. During my 1947 Westinghouse year I can recall periodic conversations with my close friend, Clif Brown (also a Central Catholic graduate). We reflected on the fact that the highest-ranked Catholic in the Pittsburgh business community was the head of the accounting department at one of the major banks. Today more than 50 percent of the CEOs and top officers of the major Pittsburgh companies are Catholic. Have their spiritual values been reflected in discharging their stewardship obligations to the community? In my view they have, as a group, earned high marks in providing leadership to organizations and initiatives addressing the civic and charitable needs of the area.

With regard to questions of stewardship, by way of comparison and contrast with Federated, I also served on the board of the Pabst Brewing Company for some 26 years. This began in 1958 with a rather vigorous proxy fight. As part of the incumbent group, we won by a margin of fifty-four to forty-six. In stark contrast to the Federated situation, the brewing of malt beverages was a no-growth industry. Annual industry statistics reflected at best a 1 percent increase—more often a 1 percent decrease—in aggregate sales of all companies. This made for extreme competition in a field that was dominated by one major player, Anheuser-Busch, which by the early 1980s had approximately 40 percent of the total market. Pabst's attempt to create a viable competitor through a merger with Heilman at that time was struck down by the federal courts as a violation of the antitrust laws, and precipitated the eventual sale of the company shortly thereafter. Determining the stewardship responsibilities to shareholders, employees and community were much more complex and vexed than at Federated.

Beginning in the 1970s, the financial progress of Federated and the establishment and growth of its inside legal staff afforded me a greater opportunity to pursue stewardship obligations to the larger community and the institutional Church. On the civic level I have been able to work in some depth with the United Way and its distribution committees, and to participate as a member of the board of the Pittsburgh Symphony Society. On a national level my activities have favored those organizations which have addressed the legal dimension of critical societal problems. In the pro-life arena I have served for more than ten years as a director of Americans United for Life. This is the legal arm of the pro-life movement; we are engaged in trial and appellate activity, developing policy and educating state legislators on the appropriate and successful techniques of combating abortion and euthanasia, and addressing the new and increasingly pressing questions of cloning and stem-cell research. For the past decade or more, I have served as a director of Morality in Media, Inc., the legal arm of the anti-obscenity movement. The range of their activities is much like those of Americans United for Life. Addressing the legal aspects of the obscenity problem presents an even more difficult assignment, especially with the evolution of the Internet and the problems of placing legal restraints on the pornography so universally distributed by this new medium. These are both challenging endeavors.

During the late 1980s and early 1990s I served on the board of Bread for the World, a multi-denominational organization engaged in lobbying Congress and pursuing broad-based educational activities addressing the problems of world hunger.

For the past twelve years I have served on the Maryknoll Advisory Board, a group of dedicated and seasoned business persons offering their talents to aid the Maryknoll Fathers and Brothers and the Maryknoll Mission Association of the Faithful (lay missioners) in handling their property management, investments and associated financial issues. The invitations to this activity and Bread for the World were inspired by our daughter, Betty Anne, whose first job was as an intern for Bread for the World, and who along with her husband, Phil, served in South America as Maryknoll lay missioners.

Relating to activities of the Church I find myself focusing on the broader subject of the religious education of college-age Catholics, rather than Catholic higher education alone. I served on the Board of the Catholic University of America for twelve years, including eight years as Vice Chairman, and I'm still designated as "Emeritus." For twenty years I served as chairman of the board of Carlow College, a women's Catholic college in Pittsburgh, and I am currently a board member of the Weston Jesuit School of Theology in Cambridge. All of these relationships have been rewarding and have provided valuable insights into the operation, maintenance and prosperity of Catholic higher education institutions. Nevertheless when one considers the total spectrum of young college-age Catholics (some 5 million in number) and the fact that nearly 90 percent are in institutions other than Catholic colleges and universities, it is clear that campus ministry should be a priority. In my case I know that this is a calling, a vocation.

I mentioned my brother's death in an auto accident some fifty-eight years ago. Ten years ago I found my vocation confirmed. Several years before, to facilitate the high school religious education of our two youngest children, we became involved with a CCD program conducted by the Oratorian Fathers. Some thirty years ago the Oratorians were given the assignment by the late Cardinal Wright, then Bishop of Pittsburgh, to provide campus ministry at the University of Pittsburgh, Carnegie Mellon University, and Chatham College. The Oratorians performed beautifully in this assignment but like many of their peers were operating from inadequate facilities. I was on the planning committee looking for a new residence for the Fathers, one that would meet a condition of their rule (which had never been fulfilled) that would allow them to have a church building dedicated to their liturgical activities. The committee had exhausted the possibilities of nearby existing structures, and was looking for land on which the required facility could be built. I still have vivid memories of the committee meeting in which it was reported that there was one lot some blocks away from the University of Pittsburgh campus available for purchase from an evangelical Christian association. They had hoped to build on the spot but had not been able to raise the money to do so. That site was at the very intersection of the streets where my brother was killed in the auto accident some fifty-eight years ago. This was certainly no coincidence.

Every day it becomes clearer to me that this was confirmation of my calling to this particular vocation of campus ministry. The land was purchased and a $5 million campaign undertaken. The campaign has been successful. A beautiful structure was erected to provide offices, meeting space, residence facilities for ten priests, and a 100-seat chapel named to commemorate my brother, the Donnelly Chapel of St. Philip Neri. The building is called the Ryan Catholic Newman Center, named in honor of the John T. Ryan Family who generously provided over 50 percent of the funds necessary for its construction and maintenance.

During the past decade and a half I have also been able to devote time to fundraising campaigns at St. Mary Student Parish at the University of Michigan. Over that period of time nearly $6 million has been raised, providing badly needed brick and mortar improvements, as well as endowment and programmatic needs.

During the past four years, the national "umbrella" organization, the Catholic Campus Ministry Association (CCMA), acquired a new executive director who has applied fresh energy stimulation to CCMA. Three companion organizations—CCMA, the national Catholic Student Coalition, and the National Association of Diocesan Directors of Campus Ministry—have moved forward. Last summer they published a paper entitled "The Missionary Challenge of Campus Ministry," which called attention to the serious problem of insufficient personnel and financial resources in many campus ministry operations. The paper was distributed to all of the Bishops and campus ministry facilities throughout the United States. Important changes have occurred in the structure at the National Council of Catholic Bishops (NCCB), due to the strong support and interest of Cardinal George of Chicago and Bishop Wuerl who chairs the NCCB's Education Committee. Campus ministry is now handled in a permanent subcommittee of the Education Committee and not, as previously, on an ad hoc basis.

There is a virtually unanimous consensus of campus ministers throughout the country that, while young students have an ever-growing interest in liturgical activities and to such outreach efforts as Habitat For Humanity, visits to Appalachia, and running soup kitchens, the "profound gap," as best described by Father Bryan Hehir, lies in the low level of their theological literacy. This gap must be remedied if they are to become effective members and leaders after their college years. I currently chair the Advancement Council of CCMA.

Looking back on what I have written, the obvious question is, what was the motivation—the decision-making process in all of this? Certainly it wasn't a master plan concocted some sixty years ago. Several factors immediately come to mind.

PRAYER

At some point in my elementary or secondary education—I can't actually recall when—the Sisters of Mercy or the Christian Brothers introduced me to the morning offering: "O Jesus, through the Immaculate Heart of Mary, I offer my prayers, works and sufferings of this day for all of the intentions of your Sacred Heart in union with the Holy Sacrifice of the Mass throughout the world and in particular for (specific persons, etc.)." To this I have for most of my life added a request for guidance: "lead me in the right direction Lord—tell me what to do."

FAMILY

Nineteen fifty-five was indeed a banner year. The foundation of Federated Investors was important, but was not the really big event in my life. It was my marriage to Marilyn Kohl, a beautiful, talented young woman who has been the greatest source of happiness in my life for the past forty-seven years. We have been blessed with seven wonderful children, their six fine spouses and, at this point, thirteen delightful grandchildren. Without exception their own sense of stewardship is well demonstrated in their daily lives. They have been a source of true inspiration for me. Without the full story of each of their lives (which would consume another essay), in the interest of full disclosure we are proud of the fact that our second eldest daughter, Daria, is the associate editor of *Commonweal.*

FRIENDS AND ORGANIZATIONS

The associations developed through business, civic, religious, and educational activities have introduced me to many new friends and colleagues who have provided extremely valuable guidance in many areas.

For nearly thirty years I have enjoyed a strong friendship with Father William J. Byron, S.J. I met him at the funeral of my friend Clif Brown. As president of the Catholic University of America, Bill invited me to serve on that board, which brought me into contact with some very fine lay people, priests, and members of the American hierarchy. He has been a close family friend. He officiated at the marriages of five of our seven children and has provided valuable academic and career guidance to a number of them. As a respected theologian and economist his books and our conversations have provided valuable assistance in shaping my life.

For the past fifteen years, our small foundation, the Mary J. Donnelly Foundation, has been a member of Foundations and Donors Interested in Catholic Activities (FADICA). It is a unique organization of some fifty individual donors and foundations ranging in size from small "mom-and-pop" organizations like ours to older and more heavily endowed entities, such as the Raskob and Humanitas Foundations. FADICA's symposia addressing cutting-edge challenges of the Church, and the warm friendships our family has made with other members, have been valuable resources in determining our foundation's grant making priorities.

I count among my greatest blessings a ten-year friendship with Cardinal Joseph Bernardin. It began with service on the Board of CUA (he was then serving as chairman), and deepened as I was privileged to work with him in the four years preceding his public announcement of the Catholic Common Ground Initiative. In his vision, the Initiative was to address the disturbing polarity within the Church through a process of civil dialogue. Following his death in November 1996, the work of Common Ground has been carried on by a committee representing the views of left, right, and center, under the competent tutelage of Monsignor Phillip J. Murnion of the National Pastoral Life Center.

Cardinal Bernardin's generosity of self, his availability to every echelon of society, demonstrated his sensitivity and Christ-like concern for all. Nonetheless he was subject to unjust criticism and an outrageous allegation—later withdrawn—of sexual abuse. His sufferings were obvious to us all, yet he bore his crosses with great dignity and courage. His greatest legacy was teaching us how to die. In his last days we observed a deepening of his personal spirituality and, in his own words, he "made a friend of death." His example is indelibly etched in my mind, with the hope and prayer that I can embrace God's grace in the same fashion when I am called.

GOD DEALS WITH ME
THROUGH MY CLIENTS

W. Shepherdson Abell

I begin with some hesitation. Do I consider that my Catholicism has had a powerful impact on my work? I do, and yet I have no confidence that I can trace the exact connections. Perhaps no one can trace them for himself. In any event, I can say something about what I have believed, and I can say something about what I have done. I'm not sure I can connect the dots.

Life began with a ridiculously happy childhood near Washington, D.C. A very clever therapist might be able to uncover deeply repressed problems, but all my recollections are of adoring my parents, two fascinating and witty people, and not so incidentally, extremely devout Catholics. We said the Rosary before dinner every night, and the meal itself was often accompanied by dialogue on racial and economic justice, the evils of McCarthyism, and the obligations of the more affluent to the poor. It was Catholic schools for me all the way, including Jesuit high school, college, and law school.

This must sound increasingly boring, but I do not recall my faith being much troubled by doubt. It was, and is, a naïve sort of faith, not much concerned with esoteric theological issues, focused (perhaps in a Protestant sort of way) primarily on the person of Jesus. I went readily to Sunday Mass every week and sometimes weekdays as well.

I should round out this sketch of my Catholic background with three additional influences. At twenty-five, I married a woman who has turned out to be an incredibly solid pillar of my own faith, someone whose instinctive living out of the Gospel virtues of generosity and steady love for others has taught me something every day of my married life. A few years later, I encountered a group of men who were seriously seeking to apply their faith to their daily lives. *Commonweal* readers may shudder when I identify them as members of Opus Dei. The movement itself never had much appeal for me, but I attended retreats and evenings of recollection—I used to tell my Opus Dei friends that I liked to use the facilities but didn't care to join the club—and learned something of what it means to carry faith into daily life.

Later still, I was invested in the Order of Malta, a group that I had suspected was a fat-cat organization whose members did little more than write the occasional charitable check, if they did that much. This perception was dead wrong. The Order of Malta, a lay religious order, has introduced me to an entirely new spirituality—one fashioned for men and women seeking a deeper spiritual life while remaining active in the world. It has led me, among other things, to accompany sick and disabled pilgrims to Lourdes twelve times, an experience which has taught me to be less hasty in judging who is "sick" and who is "healthy" in the ways that count most.

What effect did all that Catholicism have on my working life? Early on, I had conceived a great ambition to go into politics. I worked on Capitol Hill during law school and fancied myself in high electoral office someday. Was my motive to advance the common good I had heard so much about from the Jesuits? Or was it just the ambition I shared with thousands of other young people looking to make their mark? I cannot say.

My hoped-for march to the Maryland legislature was interrupted by a draft notice; I believe that I was the first law student in the country drafted during the Vietnam War. Since I was bitterly opposed to the war on moral grounds, my Catholicism might well have put me into crisis—but in the event, I was assigned to an intelligence job at the National Security Agency. My distance from the front lines seemed to numb any qualms I might have had, and perhaps *should* have had, over indirect participation in the war. In any event, after about three years, I was able to finish law school and accept a job working for the Lieutenant Governor of Maryland, whose portfolio included a wide range of health and welfare issues. I threw myself into these with enthusiasm, while working with legislators and political leaders. During the last part of my government service I served, briefly, as secretary of the cabinet department which ran Maryland's social services. I was the Democratic precinct chairman in my suburban neighborhood. I thought I was on my way.

How I ended up with a quieter and more private life as a lawyer is something I cannot fully explain to this day. But the same Catholicism that has drawn many fine people into political careers might have actually prodded me away from politics.

Now, there is no special reason to believe I would have been successful as a politician. I had no particular charisma, and didn't enjoy plunging into a room of strangers. But even assuming I might have overcome some natural shyness and somehow might have persuaded voters that I was what they wanted, this was the early 1970s, when the poison of abortion politics was seeping into the Democratic Party. There were a handful of prolife Democratic legislators who hung on for a couple of elections, including Maryland State Senator Peggy Schweinhaut, a wonderful woman who served almost until her ninetieth birthday. But in retrospect, I think that it would have been impossible for me, as a prolifer, to be elected as a Democrat—at least in my part of Maryland. Since other fiercely held beliefs, or perhaps they were family prejudices, would not have allowed me to be a Republican, politics became a distinctly unpromising career.

More factors were at play, but it's not easy to sort them out. The prospect of an endless string of evenings at precinct meetings and civic dinners was not as appealing as quiet evenings at home with the family, and the chance to read some good books. But it also seemed to me that politics, like many lines of work, could bring out either the best or the worst in a person. We are blessed with many politicians of fine character, who coexist easily, but virtuously, with the demands of getting elected. Thanks be to God for that. But I had the intuition that politics would draw on my worst impulses and character traits: the instinct to plan ahead carefully and the ability to sense what people want to hear could, in my case, slide pretty readily into manipulation and deceptiveness. I had a sense of what my exploration of politics was doing to me, and I didn't like it very much.

Or so it seems in retrospect. Perhaps, in reality, it was more a matter of inertia and the selfish wish for quiet evenings at home by the fire, reading books, or perhaps *Commonweal.* Be that as it may, I joined two friends to form a law practice.

A few words about the legal profession: Today there are 900,000 lawyers in this country; there were many fewer in 1975. An increasing number work in one of the large firms that have grown today to be huge firms, some with more than a thousand attorneys. Television focuses all eyes on the litigators, though most attorneys have an office practice and rarely see the courtroom. I was originally on track to be a litigator in a Washington firm, which has since developed into quite a large firm; instead, I ended up planning trusts and wills in a very small suburban practice. As Robert Frost said, taking that path has made all the difference.

Big firms demand an incredible time commitment of their attorneys:

fifty- to sixty-hour weeks, or even longer. And if you are in litigation, you may be constantly on the road. Your schedule is at the mercy of judges and other lawyers. The work is obviously confrontational in nature, which I am not, and every year it seems that more and more aggressiveness and incivility intrudes into litigation. And big-firm life is increasingly driven by the bottom line. I have good friends who are litigators or in large firms, or both. Most are excellent lawyers and wonderful people. But that kind of legal career does exact a toll.

In a small firm, on the other hand, if you are with like-minded individuals the pace can be slower. I have also found my little corner of the law to be a more constructive, less confrontational, kind of practice. It has, in addition, allowed me much more control over my time than some other kinds of lawyering.

I would never have expected to feel at home in the dry world of trusts and wills. But to my surprise, I readily settled in. I was dealing constantly, not with corporations or financial instruments, but with human beings. Much of the work is, of course, repetitive, but I have found that the intersection of death, family, and property can be pretty interesting.

Even better, I was blessed with wonderful law partners. The firm grew slowly; it now has seventeen lawyers, tiny by comparison with the largest firms, but a nice scale for daily life. The nature of the practice—and the acquiescence of my partners—has allowed me to do a reasonable amount of pro bono work, and to take on many outside activities: law school teaching, serving on boards of directors of nonprofit groups, working with the U.S. Bishops Conference, and volunteer work of different kinds. I have also been able to do some small public service jobs—state study commissions on welfare, hereditary disorders, and the like—and a modest amount of writing on public issues, mostly for local newspapers. And a piece of exceptional financial good fortune has given me a large measure of security. I have been able to arrange my schedule to make time for reflection, retreats, and good works. To have this kind of flexibility in my professional and personal life has been a tremendous grace; few people in our society are granted such freedom over their work. Nor are most of them paid as well as I am for what, as Bob Dole famously said about the vice presidency, is indoor work, with no heavy lifting. I consider myself blessed. In the words of the Psalmist, "The lines have fallen for me in pleasant places."

As I said, it's not clear to me exactly whether, or how, my Catholicism led me to this particular kind of legal career. But once I arrived here, has my faith influenced my work?

The *substance* of what I have been doing each day for the past twenty-seven years is not so easy to connect to my faith. Much of what I do is related to money—helping people make and keep more of it—and I don't think it comes as near to the Kingdom of God as, for example, representing impoverished immigrants.

But it does have its moments. When I can help parents with a disabled child, for instance, whose constant, overriding fear is that their child will not be taken care of after they have died, I can feel some sense of having fulfilled Gospel values. I make it a point always to suggest to clients that they consider leaving something to charity. Some respond with great generosity, and it is very satisfying to be able to assist them in their philanthropy. Another example: a widow wanted to leave her estate to three of her four children, stating flatly that she was estranged from the fourth child and would leave her nothing. In a situation like this, as a lawyer, you have two choices. You can honor the dominant principle of client autonomy—the client is always right, the lawyer merely a paid scrivener—or you can take the risk of probing the client a bit more. In this case, further discussion revealed that the client really didn't want to give up on her daughter, and didn't want the final written expression of her feelings to be a statement of disinheritance. Our discussion led her to something of a reconciliation.

Legal life has not been all wills and trusts, either. An increasing part of my practice has been the representation of non-profit organizations, most of them Catholic, including the Archdiocese of Washington and a local Catholic hospital. I do think that this work helps to create and preserve an environment in which the Church's social teachings can be implemented. But for every hour spent assisting Catholic Charities or lending support to an anxious widow, there are entire days of routine projects without such redeeming significance. It would be hard for me to pretend that most of *what* I do each day as a lawyer is, in substance, the Lord's work. If the Lord enters in, it mostly has to be in *how* I do my work.

I am not talking about "legal ethics." That is a subject I taught several times at Georgetown Law Center, usually to a sleepy group of graduating seniors who did not want to be there, but who were unable to figure out a way to avoid this required course. Most of contemporary "legal ethics" has come down to a dreary recital of ways in which lawyers can operate just barely within the disciplinary rules. Even the more interesting issues revolve around what has been called "quandary ethics"—if I am representing a murder defendant, may I put him on the stand if I think he will lie? My view is that the heart of true legal ethics involves the day-to-day practice of simple virtues:

the dignity with which a lawyer treats her clients and staff, her commitment to tell the truth in matters large and small, an attorney's willingness to subordinate his own interests to those of the client. I have tried to incorporate those aspects in my teaching.

If Catholicism means respect for the dignity of the individual, then for a trusts and estates lawyer it would mean special efforts to make sure that the client understands what a complicated set of documents means for him and his family—an understanding the tax laws are carefully drafted to thwart. It might sometimes involve calling the client to be their best self. To live that faith consistently, an attorney would have to remember that, as Thomas Shaffer of Notre Dame Law School once wrote, "My client was sent to me by God; God proposes to deal with me through my client."

Now *that* is a tall order. The crush of daily work, the pressures of the legal profession, and—yes—the behavior of some clients all make it difficult to see the client as sent by God. Some clients seem to have been sent by the Devil. Few of us lawyers can consistently measure up to Professor Shaffer's standard.

When I have succeeded in doing so, I might have been aided by the fact that my small firm and our employees seem to have evolved into a true community. Perhaps Father Andrew Greeley is right when he says that an important characteristic of Catholicism is the impulse to community. I don't want to romanticize it, but it does seem to me that the people in our office do have a sense of responsibility for one another. That affects a lot of what goes on in the workplace: how we interact, how we treat clients, supporting one another in times of sorrow, even how we go about disciplining or (as a last resort) firing those employees who simply cannot cope with the work.

Do not assume that I consult a well-thumbed copy of the bishops' pastoral letter on the economy at the beginning of each management committee meeting. But I like to think that some of the principles in that letter flow into the management of our small business. (I would not be too quick to credit *Catholic* teaching with creating a humane law firm, however. Many of the actions of which I'm proudest originated with my two fellow committee members, a Jew and a Presbyterian elder.)

The reader will note a thread running through this essay—an emphasis on little, everyday things. Is this related to the particular brand of Catholicism I seem to have absorbed over the years? I think of the Catholic writers to whom I turn again and again, like Dorothy Day, Charles de Foucauld, Jean Vanier, Sheila Cassidy. All of them emphasized the smaller virtues, the hidden life. My comfortable life is about as far removed from their asceticism and untiring service as could be imagined; it must be their stress on little things which draws me back to them. Perhaps this has led me away from the public square—or it may be to a more private corner of the public square.

I left school intent on an active, engaged public life. Over the years, my goal seems to have evolved into engagement in more private arenas, in some of those "mediating institutions" about which so much has been written. Most likely that is all that is possible for most American Catholics. Ultimately, it may have a more pervasive influence on society than the more public engagements.

Was this evolution driven by my faith, or has the faith only served to rationalize decisions I made, or drifted into, for other reasons? I cannot say. But I do not look back with regret. In 1965, Thomas Merton wrote in his journal that he had lived "a flawed and inconsequential life, believing in God's love." At twenty-one, I would have thought that a sorry epitaph. Now that I am fifty-eight, it doesn't sound bad at all.

4

CATHOLICS IN THE
VOTING BOOTH

The American Catholics in the Public Square project commissioned two wide-ranging surveys of *how* Catholics vote. This work was carried out in election year 2000 by CARA (Center for Applied Research in the Apostolate), based at Georgetown University; the survey is posted on their Web site. The poll focused not so much on whom American Catholics vote for, but how they think about voting. This focus was meant to assess the impact on Catholic voters of the Catholic social tradition, of sermons, of parish community and sacramental life, and of papal and episcopal statements. David Leege uses that and other polling data to examine whether there is a Catholic vote. This issue receives further analysis from Kate O'Beirne and E. J. Dionne Jr. William Bole's essay offers an interpretive analysis of the CARA survey.

HOW CATHOLIC IS THE CATHOLIC VOTE?

David C. Leege and Paul D. Mueller

CATHOLICS—A UNITARY FORCE?

Ethnic parish histories show similarities, whether located in a small rust belt city or the Lower East Side of Manhattan. Not far from the downtown of one modest-sized rust belt city sits Immaculate Conception church (a pseudonym), and not fifty yards from its Mary chapel sits Saint Thaddeus church. For the better part of a century it would have seemed odd for well-off Irish Catholics and Polish factory workers to pray together at the same church. The next thing you know one of the Polish ward heelers would want to be slated for mayor!

Not far away sits Saint Cyril's. In the 1960s it celebrated three Hungarian Masses and one English Mass on a Sunday. Now it celebrates two Spanish, one English, and one Hungarian Mass on a weekend. Priests from a nearby Catholic religious community often celebrate the Spanish Masses, since the diocese was not ready for the new migrations. Three congregations share one church, but the parishioners do not interact much socially across the congregational divides. Careful studies of the church as a political context have shown that such interaction is necessary to inculcate values and mobilize in elections.[1]

A bit farther out sits St. Philip's, which celebrates African-American Catholic Masses. At a wedding banquet not long ago, the senior author asked a Saint Thaddeus's lay leader if he had ever gone to church at Saint Augustine's. His response: "Why would I? I am a Catholic."

And yet politicians and pundits speak of the *Catholic vote*, treating Democratic identification, economic liberalism, and cultural conservatism as normative for Catholics. More recently they have noted, and Republicans celebrated, the erosion of Democratic loyalties. Despite a veritable cottage industry of scholars who have studied religion and politics among American Catholics, a single theory that explains the dynamics of Catholic political behavior has eluded their grasp. And well it should.

Catholics constitute 25 to 30 percent of the U.S. adult population. They are a mosaic difficult to capture, composed of diverse ethnic groups with varied histories of separatism, persecution or acceptance, and assimilation. Often they do not like each other; for example, the dominance of Italian, nominally Catholic men in the leadership of Eastern Republican party machines has its roots a century ago in disdain for the Irish priests who told devout Italian women that Catholics should be Democrats. Catholic groups occupy different rungs on the economic and social status ladders, and sometimes those have shifted radically over a short span of three generations.

Given the greatly decentralized structure of the Roman Catholic Church in the United States, even well after Vatican II into the 1980s, the laity were led by shepherds who shared the central faith but had rather different perspectives on its implications for life. As the Jadot generation of bishops has retired or died, some church-watchers mourn the passing of diversity and local autonomy. Yet if U.S. church history is any guide, decentralized control will reassert itself as changes occur in the Vatican. But regardless of what happens in ecclesiastical politics, the diverse collectivity of Catholic Americans will follow their own individual consciences, sometimes informed by Church social teaching, sometimes not.

Finally, approximately 30 percent of those who call themselves "Catholic" on surveys have only a tenuous historical relationship to the Church. Contrary to the arguments of some scholars, as we will see later, their political behavior and attitudes have more in common with seculars than with Catholics.

This essay argues that Catholics are not a unitary or even a unique group in American political history, but respond, sometimes similarly, sometimes differently, to the social, economic, political, and cultural forces that impact other religious groups. This includes important changes in patterns of religiosity that affect political solidarity. Perhaps the principal contribution of this paper is its examination of the strategies political elite have used to contest for Catholic voters during the post–New Deal period, and analysis of the issue and group themes to which Catholics responded in partisan ways. Because politicians maintained the myth of *the* Catholic vote, they expended considerable effort targeting politically vulnerable sectors of the Catholic electorate.

Still, the story of the last two decades of American politics is not its "Catholicization" but its "evangelical Protestantization" and "secularization."

CHANGING PATTERNS OF CATHOLICS
IN PARTISAN COALITIONS

Little attention was paid to the politics of Catholics until the heavy Irish and German migrations in the 1830s, 1840s, and 1850s. Alexis de Tocqueville, writing in the 1830s, was skeptical that Catholic communitarian and egalitarian values would fit well into a democracy based on freedom and individualism. As usual, however, the precipitating events for a religious group's organized involvement in politics would be the deep sense of persecution and social injustices faced by its adherents. For Catholics in New England and Middle Atlantic cities in the two decades following 1830, not only were jobs foreclosed, but church institutions were pillaged. First the American Protestant Association and then the Know Nothing party organized mass bigotry and gave political representation to anti-Catholic sentiments.[2] In like manner, Irish politicians rose to prominence in the big-city machines; they advised solidarity with the Democratic party, an antigovernment party which showed greater respect for minority rights and traditionalistic social organizations. Since nativists (that is, anti-Catholics) were anchored in the Know-Nothing party and the established Protestant elites dominated the Whigs, this decision made good sense. It ignored the historical fact that both the Federalists and Whigs had included prominent Catholics in public office.[3]

Still, Catholics were growing as a proportion of the electorate in the cities of the important electoral college states. In 1852, according to Prendergast, the Whig Party made conscious appeals to Catholic voters across the country, charging their Democratic opponent with nativism.[4] Once elected, however, the victorious Democratic President Franklin Pierce selected James Campbell, a Catholic from Pennsylvania, to his cabinet as postmaster general. The willingness of the fledgling Republican Party to incorporate nativist voters into the party and its subtle and more blatant uses of anti-Catholic appeals continued to convince Catholic politicians and journalists that they should remain in the Democratic Party.

By the turn of the century, it was another matter. The tide of immigration was disproportionately Catholic. While many became economically established along the eastern seaboard, earlier generations also had pushed west to the growing cities rimming the Great Lakes and, the German Catholics especially, to the rich farmlands. Catholics were increasingly thrust into conflict with the core leadership of the Democratic party from the South and West. By the 1890s, the two parties have been described as "political churches" with a partisan cleavage "that arrayed pietist against anti-pietist religious group."[5] Each side sought the power of the state to impose its position on prohibition, Sunday-closing, foreign-language instruction, and parochial schools. The religious war within the Democratic Party reached explosive proportions in the first run of pietist orator William Jennings Bryan for the Presidency in 1896.[6] Mark Hanna, the Republican leader, and William McKinley, his candidate, saw great opportunity among Catholics, especially in the cities. Their version of corporate capitalism with government as the engine of economic progress gave respect to workers and embraced the bread-and-butter interests of organized labor, reeling after the economic downturn of 1893. Their denunciation of the American Protective Association said that nativism was no longer welcome in the Republican Party.

Archbishop John Ireland, a Republican loyalist with considerable political involvement, publicly denounced the Democratic convention and its ascendant coalition. A substantial electoral realignment followed these events, with many urban Catholics embracing the Republican Party of their corporate managers. Simultaneous to this realignment, Progressive reforms had taken away the franchise from the most recent immigrants and crippled the patronage bases of many urban Democratic machines.[7] Electoral participation, particularly by Catholic immigrants, plummeted. Save for the schism in the Republican Party that led to Woodrow Wilson's two terms (1912–1920), a period of Republican normalcy ensued. Even rural and small-town German and Irish Catholics were driven into the Republican camp by the anti-German and pro-British bigotry spawned through "Wilson's war on the side of the British," and the resurgence of the Ku Klux Klan in the upper Midwest—with some ties to the Democratic Party. Realignment, defection, and depressed turnout among Catholics were characteristic of the early twentieth century.

Change once again bubbled up from state and local sources. New York Governor Al Smith, a product of the tenements, urban wage slavery, anti-Prohibition, anti-Catholic persecution, and Tammany Hall, collected the aspirations of Catholics in the Eastern cities. In his run for Albany, he had shown that he could mobilize dormant Catholics.[8] His nomination for president on the Democratic ticket symbolized for Catholics which party really cared about them, no matter his disastrous defeat by Hoover. The largest and second most reliable (after Jews) component of the New Deal coalition was in place for Franklin Delano Roosevelt; parts of the coalition have lasted to this day. In gripping ways, Samuel Freedman captures the meaning of this homecoming for urban and unionized Catholic poor.[9] Through depression and war, this was to be the party of Catholic aspirations, incorporating group respect, economic justice and security as rewards for hard work, and firm challenges to totalitarian states that threatened the homeland, Catholicism, and American interests. No one could again challenge their loyalty as their sons fought and some died for this kind of a country, and their daughters kept the economic recovery alive.

When the sons returned home, they went to college on the GI Bill, left the ethnic ghetto, populated the new suburbs, and voted their supreme commander into the White House. It was just a short rift; no one knew whether Ike was a Democrat or Republican, or really cared. He wasn't a silk stocking egghead.

The coronation of this generation of Catholics came when one of its own, John F. Kennedy, was elected to the Presidency in 1960. While many are inclined to point to the reception of Vatican II as the source of great change in the American church, we prefer to attribute much of it to the war, to the GI bill and its consequences for personal autonomy and for economic and family life, and the Kennedy election. These actions changed forever the strategies of the two parties.[10] Democrats would have to fight to retain the loyalties of autonomous Catholics, and Republicans would find no electoral advantage in anti-Catholic nativist appeals. In fact, one Republican president, Ronald Reagan, could appoint more Catholics to his cabinet than had any Democratic Administration before or since.

Most analysts point to the fact that Kennedy received the votes of over 80 percent of Catholics who cast a ballot, despite the fact that barely 60 percent of the Catholic electorate identified as Democrats during the late Eisenhower years. Also interesting to note are the Catholics who voted Democratic in 1960. Phillip Converse has shown that regular Mass attendance was a weaker predictor of Republican defections to Kennedy than was a sense of "closeness" to other Catholics.[11] Furthermore, Irish Catholic Republicans were more likely to defect to the Democrats than Catholics of other ethnic backgrounds. Thus, even when this remarkable opportunity to affirm the social worth of Catholics presented itself, party loyalty and ethnic differences loomed larger to many Catholics.

The primary purpose of this short history is to suggest that the "vibrant imaginative worlds" of Catholic ethnic subcultures did not yield solidarity in a single party coalition. It left bases in both political parties, with different expectations about the treatment of newer ethnic groups and the poor, with different designs for the role of government, conflicting feelings about each other, and perhaps most important, each wanting to claim the church for its own positions. Joan Fee has traced enduring political alignments to how each American Catholic ethnic group formed and its degree of assimilation.[12] On a continuum from black Catholics and more recent ethnic concentrations such as Latinos, to Polish, Italian, Irish, to other Eastern European and German, finally to Scandinavian, Canadian and British Catholics, Leege and Welch have shown that the degree of assimilation not only powerfully affected party preference, but political ideology (conservatism/liberalism), and a whole host of political attitudes and issue positions.[13] In short, a recipe for culture wars among Catholics can be found in early ethnic assimilation patterns. Regional and local ethnic histories were compounded within these patterns. Few other predictor variables—including current social class—could match the power of ethnic assimilation among Catholics.

The other reason for this short history is to provide a baseline for interpreting the political behavior of Catholics in the post–New Deal period. Even William Prendergast, a former director of research for the Republican National Committee, has pulled back from the optimistic future of Catholics in the Republican Party, based on trend data from the 1970s and 1980s.[14] The 1980s did indeed show Catholic alignment and realignment advantaging the Republican Party, but the 1990s showed a contrary movement to the Democratic party, along with uncharacteristic disloyalty by Catholic Republicans.

CATHOLIC PARTISANSHIP IN THE POST–NEW DEAL PERIOD

For purposes of this analysis, we are going to follow white non-Latino Catholics through four decades of recent political history.[15]

First, there has not been a general realignment of Catholics to the Republican Party. With the exclusion of the early 1960s, white non-Latino Catholics and Protestants have followed similar paths in the party they advantaged, but Catholics have always been about eight to twelve points more Democratic than have Protestants. The partisan advantage measure we use for our analysis differs from a straight party identification measure or a partisan vote-choice measure in that it includes turnout. We call it a politician's calculus of the vote because not only the direction of the vote but the size of the vote determines the outcome.[16] The measure will be described in detail later when we present table 20.1. In only one instance, 1988, both choice and turnout-level among Catholics slipped enough to advantage the Republicans. Even half a century after the New Deal and two decades after the administration of the highly popular "apostate Irish Catholic politician" Reagan, white non-Latino Catholics are still delivering for the Democrats, and similar Protestants are delivering for the Republicans. But, like God, the real story is in the details.

Table 20.1 is filled with the details that show changing party loyalties, turnout failures, and defections. These are the important products of political campaigns. When refined even further to certain target groups in the Catholic population, they tell us where the movement is occurring. They also permit us to isolate precisely which kinds of campaign themes have resonated with Catholic targets. In short, by the time we are done, we will know whether "faithful" or "unfaithful" Catholics have moved about politically, whether Catholics are attracted by political positions consistent with church teaching or whether they ignore these inducements.[17]

The measure of party loyalty in table 20.1 and succeeding analyses compounds three pieces of information—party identification, turnout, and the party of presidential-candidate choice. The product of the percentage identifying with a party and party loyalty generates what we have called a measure of partisan yield. This is a politician's calculus of the vote. It matters not a great deal to the campaigner what proportion of the population or of a given group identifies as a Democrat or Republican. The campaigner needs to know through time what proportion identifies with the party, goes to the polls, and actually votes for that party's candidate. Furthermore, with partisan yield measures for both Democrats and Republicans, we can calculate a measure of partisan advantage, by subtracting one from the other. This measure allows us to see at what point in time the relative measures of partisan yield shift to the advantage of one or another party. It is not uncommon for a group—for example, white Southern Democrats—to shift their basic party identification through time to the Republican side. Assuming high party loyalty to the new party, the partisan advantage measure will now favor the Republicans. Also not uncommon is that a group—for example, white non-Latino Catholics—may maintain Democratic identification but either fail to vote or to vote, but to defect to the Republican candidate. The measure of partisan advantage may show a similar outcome in each case, but the underlying reasons are different.

Thus, table 20.1 is the map of Catholic voting behavior from 1952 to 1996 and includes the following measures:

Democratic Party Identification—the summed proportion of the group reporting strong Democrat, not so strong Democrat, and Independent leaning Democrat.

Proportion Loyal to Democratic Party—the proportion of non-Latino, Catholic, white Democrats who turnout and select the Democratic candidate for President.

Proportion not voting—the proportion of these Democrats who fail to vote for President.

Proportion defecting to opposition candidates(s)—the proportion of these Democrats who turnout and select the Republican or other candidate.

Democratic partisan yield—the proportion of non-Latino, white Catholics that is both Democratic and loyal to the party, i.e., Democrats who turned out and voted Democratic.

(The following are the same sets of measures for Republicans)

Democratic Partisan Advantage—the difference between the Democratic partisan yield and the Republican partisan yield. (A positive number favors Democrats, negative Republicans.)

"True" Independent—the proportion of the group who claim to be Independents and lean to neither party.

Apolitical—the proportion of the group who claim not to be Democrats, Republicans, or Independents.

The utility of this set of measures is that it allows us to take any designated group in the electorate such as Catholics and (1) see its basic patterns of partisanship and loyalty, (2) measure precisely when it stays stable and when it shifts, and (3) diagnose whether the shift is the result of low turnout, defection, or a change in the group's party loyalties. Such information will yield clues as to when a campaign appeal is operating on the group. Furthermore, by breaking all non-Latino, white Catholics into political generations for our later analyses—(1) pre–New Deal, entering the electorate before 1932; (2) New Deal, entering the electorate between 1932 and 1964; (3) older post–New Deal, (the original Baby Boom generation), entering the electorate between 1968 and 1976; and (4) the John Paul II generation of young Catholics, entering the electorate in 1980 or thereafter—we are able to see whether changing patterns of basic partisanship in the group are the

Table 20.1. Partisan Patterns of White, Non-Latino Catholics, 1952–1996 (Source: NES Cumulative File)

Political Characteristics	1952	1956	1960	1964	1968	1972	1976	1980	1984	1988	1992	1996
Democratic Party Identification (a)	68	59	73	69	63	62	61	54	52	45	53	52
Proportion Loyal to Dem. Party (b)	61	57	87	79	61	39	58	45	60	67	64	65
Proportion not voting	15	18	6	14	19	19	22	24	17	17	14	20
Proportion defecting to opposition candidate(s)	24	25	6	7	20	42	21	31	23	16	23	15
Democratic Partisan Yield (c)	41	34	64	55	39	24	35	25	31	30	33	33
Republican Party Identification	25	27	19	22	25	25	26	31	36	45	36	41
Proportion Loyal to Rep. Party	83	83	60	65	72	77	66	68	83	73	60	67
Proportion not voting	12	14	13	9	10	11	22	19	13	19	11	11
Proportion defecting to opposition candidate(s)	5	3	28	26	18	12	12	13	4	8	29	23
Republican Partisan Yield	21	22	11	14	18	19	17	21	30	33	22	27
Democratic Partisan Advantage (d)	20	11	53	40	21	5	18	4	1	–3	12	6
"True" Independent (e)	7	11	8	9	11	12	12	15	11	10	11	7
Apolitical	0	3	1	0	1	1	1	1	1	1	0	1
Number in Sample	376	360	215	333	313	595	494	316	428	343	432	330

[a] Includes percent strong Democrat, not so strong Democrat, and Independent leaning Democrat.
[b] Proportion of Democrats who turn out and select the Democratic candidate for President.
[c] Product of Democratic party identification and reported vote for Democratic candidate.
[d] Subtract Republican partisan yield from Democratic partisan yield to calculate partisan advantage.
[e] Respondents who claim to be Independents but do not lean to either party.

result of the entry and exit of generations (the stork and the grim reaper), or are the result of actual partisan realignment by individuals.[18]

In 1952 and more so in 1956, Catholics found Eisenhower quite attractive, resulting in depressed Democratic partisan advantages when contrasted with the next decade. It was not until the disastrous McGovern race in 1972 and the Reagan-Bush-Clinton years that the Democratic partisan yield figures dropped even below the level of the Eisenhower reelection. Already by 1968, however, the warning signs were clear: Catholics would not be permanently anchored in the Democratic Party after the Kennedy election. This pattern seems to repeat what historians told us had happened about a decade after Al Smith had mobilized so many Catholics as Democrats in 1928.

In 1960 with two cold warriors contesting the White House at the peak of the cold war consensus, Catholic voters selected the Catholic candidate by an enormous margin. The Democratic Party identification figure is impressive but what is astounding are the huge turnout (94 percent) and low defection figures (6 percent) among Catholic Democrats and the high turnout (87 percent) and high defection (28 percent) rates for Catholic Republicans. There was gradual decay during the Johnson and Humphrey elections on all measures—modestly dropping Democratic Party identification, lower turnout, increasing defection, and a modest rise in Republican Party identification. By 1968 already the turnout and defection figures signaled trouble for the Democrats. But defections by Catholics in both parties were nearly equal (20 percent and 18 percent), and favored third-party candidate George Wallace. With Wallace out of the picture in 1972, the bottom dropped out among Catholic Democrats. Faced with the opportunity to embrace the McGovern antiwar, socially liberal party, 42 percent of all Catholic Democrats crossed over to vote for Nixon and 19 percent failed to vote. The gap between Democratic Party identification (62 percent) and vote yield (24 percent) was the greatest of any election in the time series. Our later analyses will show whether these voters were casting their ballots on cold war issues, race, gender, class values, or religiously based cultural differences. What is clear is that they had not yet realigned because of the Nixon cultural strategy. Democratic and Republican identifications remained basically stable through 1976, and Carter cut the backdoor losses in half.

In the first Reagan race of 1980, realignment of Catholic voters was finally evident. Democratic identification dropped by 7 percent and Republican identification grew by 5 percent. But now it continued to be accompanied by low turnout among Catholic Democrats, 24 percent reporting not voting, and 31 percent defecting to Reagan. Thus an initial Democratic advantage of 23 points in party identification was reduced to 4 points in vote yield. The realignment—and alignment—of Catholics continued throughout the Reagan-Bush era. By 1988, Democratic identification dropped to a new low of 45 percent and Republican identification grew another 14 points since 1980 to reach 45 percent, virtually even in a group that had begun the era heavily Democratic. Alignment of younger generations with the Republican Party is indicated by the decline in the percent Independent.

This latter point suggests that the real story among Catholics is in the generations. We have also noted increasingly greater differences between the sexes. Younger Catholics differ from older Catholics, and younger women differ even more from younger men. It is possible to map the changing partisanship of pre–New Deal (before 1932), New Deal (1932–1964), Baby Boomer (1968–1976), and the John Paul II generation (after 1980) of Catholics.

In tables not shown here, but available from the authors, pre–New Deal Catholic men, unlike other age/gender groups grew increasingly more Democratic and less Republican with age; so that by the Carter-Ford election 80 percent of them were Democratic and only 8 percent were Republican. On the other hand, pre–New Deal Catholic women declined from 76 percent Democratic at the time of Kennedy to 48 percent at the time of Carter; their Republican identification grew from 17 percent to 44 percent. After 1976, mortality renders this generation an inconsequential force in the electorate. We cannot say whether these changing figures represent realignment in divergent directions for this older Catholic cohort. It may be simply a matter of Democratic men and Republican women surviving longer.

The New Deal generation of Catholics is the only one we can follow throughout the period. Both sexes enter the Kennedy election with virtually identical levels of Democratic partisanship (74 percent to 73 percent) while the women have slightly higher levels of Republican partisanship (19 percent to 13 percent). From there, the men plummet quickly to 54 percent Democratic and rise as rapidly to 23 percent Republican by 1968 (Nixon-Humphrey-Wallace). In the remainder of the time series, the men fluctuate within a range of 5 to 6 points, never dropping below 50 percent Democratic (1988 and 1996). In these same two elections, their Republican identification rises to 41 percent, but usually it is in the low 30s. New Deal–generation Catholic women, on the other hand, hardly decline in Democratic partisanship until 1972 (8 points in that year) and then stay steady in a range around the lower 60s until 1996, when the bottom drops out for the Democrats at 47 percent. Republican Party identification ascends slowly until it reaches the low 30s in the Reagan years and climbs steeply to 42 percent after four years of Clinton. Obviously Catholic men and women who came of age during the Depression and Second World War responded differently to the forces operating on the electorate. The men became disillusioned with the Democrats already by the time of Nixon, but still over half of them remained with the party. The women simply never lost their Democratic partisanship until the end of the period. Nevertheless as we shall see, when turnout and defection are included in the equation, the men still gave the Republicans a net partisan advantage in 1972 (7 points), while the women gave the Republicans a slight advantage in 1980 (1 point) and 1996 (3 points).

The next generation of Catholics was the Baby Boomers. Although they entered the electorate in 1968, not enough men were available for analysis until 1972. The men entered the Nixon-McGovern election with virtually the same Democratic partisanship as their fathers' generation, and with slightly depressed Republican identification. However, the Reagan phenomenon altered their partisanship from there on. In one quadrennium (1976–1980) Democratic partisanship dropped twenty points and Republican identification gained ten. Democratic identification recovered slightly to the low 40s, but Republican identification grew to the mid- and high 40s, with the exception of 1992. Baby Boom–Catholic males, then, realigned during the Reagan years; one of the reasons Clinton had two terms in the White House is that Catholic-Republican-Boomer males failed to support their party in the 1990s, with Republican defection rates of 52 percent and 31 percent. We should note that many Boomer men were middle managers who experienced the economic effects of corporate downsizing late in the 1980s. Boomer females were even more Democratic and less Republican than their mothers' generation in 1976. From there they declined swiftly in their Democratic partisanship, while their mothers' decline was slow. By the Bush-Dukakis election of 1988, the Boomer women shifted wildly (only 29 percent Democratic and an amazing 57 percent Republican). But just as suddenly they shifted back to previous patterns; by 1996 they joined the John Paul II generation of young Catholic women as the most Democratic group, 63 percent, versus 29 percent Republican. What explains the volatility of this generation of women in 1988 is hard to say; Governor Michael Dukakis, dubbed the "Ice Man" had done poorly with the hypothetical question about rape in the debate, and never registered well with younger women.[19] We can see a vast gulf widening between Catholic men and women of the Boomer generation throughout the 1990s, with the gap in party identification being fully 20 points.

The same gender difference among Catholics is repeated in the youngest generation. By 1984 when there are enough men in the sample to permit reliable generalizations, this cohort enters the electorate strongly with Reagan's party (55 percent Republican to 35 percent Democratic), and they continue within 6 points of that level. Only in 1996 is there a spurt of Democratic strength (45 percent). The youngest Catholic women are just the opposite. There partisanship starts with volatility, shifting from 46 percent Democratic in 1984 to 56 percent Republican in the disastrous Dukakis year. Then, like the next closest generation of Catholic women, they shift abruptly to the Democratic side, where nearly two-thirds held Democratic partisanship in Clinton's reelection. Furthermore, in data not shown, these young Catholic women reversed their earlier apathy of the 1980s and were more likely to vote in the 1990s. The upshot is that the sharpest cleavage in the Catholic electorate is now between the young women who have grown enormously as part of the Democratic coalition and the young men who have remained fairly reliably in the Republican camp. In data not shown here, the steady decline in the number of Catholic women as homemakers, the remarkable increase in those completing higher education, and the equally large growth of young women in business and professional occupations has created a sea change in political behavior. Each succeeding generation of men has grown more Republican, but each succeeding generation of women has grown more Democratic after the Reagan flirtation. After standing stolidly Democratic while the men moved the other direction, only the oldest Catholic women have moved toward the Republican Party in the 1990s.

Partisanship is only part of the story. It is also possible to map the differences in partisan *advantage*, which is the measure that accounts for turnout failures and defections, in addition to party identification. It captures the net product of each political campaign. Our figures, not presented here, show that Catholic men from the New Deal generation moved out of the Democratic camp only in 1972. Otherwise, both they and the oldest generation of Catholic men always remained voting Democrats. The Republican strength came from the two younger generations; only in 1972, 1992, and 1996 did the Boomer males visit the Democratic camp. The youngest Catholic men, however, have always advantaged the Republican Party. The gaps between generations of males are wide. The gaps among the generations of females are quite constrained, growing slightly wider in the1970s, but becoming even larger than the male gaps in 1988. Although there is a trend toward the Republicans, the oldest generation of Catholic women never leaves the Democratic camp, and the New Deal generation tiptoes into it only in 1980 and

1996. The Boomers start the time series somewhat similar to their elders, then plunge deeply into Republican territory in 1988, and return solidly to Democratic advantage in the 1990s. Finally, the youngest generation of Catholic women is almost a carbon copy of the Boomers, except that they are slightly more Democratic in their vote yield in the last three elections. This period of American electoral history ends with the generations and sexes as almost mirror opposites: younger women solidly Democratic and older women trending Republican, while the youngest men are solidly Republican and their elders, who had shifted slightly Democratic, again are moving in a Republican direction.

With these baselines established, we can now turn to the political forces that moved Catholics from one camp to another. That is largely a story of Republican campaign strategies designed to disable the majority Democratic Party's winning coalition. Since Catholics were a major part of that coalition well into the 1960s, they became the target of a wide variety of Republican campaign themes.

THE ISSUES AND GROUP BASES
FOR POLITICAL CHANGE

The customary story for the increased appearance of Catholics in the Republican Party emphasizes cultural politics, particularly concerns over human sexuality and abortion. A subtheme is that Catholics, as cultural conservatives in a male-dominated hierarchical church, would be slow to accept change in gender roles, equality of opportunity for women, and the resultant restructuring of the family. The story often stresses *realignment*—that individual Catholics actually *moved* permanently from one party to another. The data we have already presented minimize the last point. The data we are about to present will revise our understanding of the former, so that we will see that concerns about race dominated negative feelings toward the government and the contemporary party of government, the Democrats.

First, there was not a great deal of realignment among white, non-Latino Catholics, although it was more pronounced among men. There was substantial defection among the New Deal generation, especially the men, but most of the defectors remained Democrats. Most of the lasting realignment actually occurred among the Baby Boom men during the Reagan years. In this respect, the "Reagan Democrat" was misnamed all along; these were "Nixon Democrats." By the time Reagan arrived, a new generation had crowded into the electorate and they had become Republican. The most pronounced instance of Republicanism is not the result of realignment but alignment of the youngest Catholic men as they enter the electorate in the mid-1980s and 1990s. The older women never moved very far in the Republican direction although they too had momentary problems with the McGovern party. The younger women initially thought they belonged with the Republicans in the 1980s but quickly made a wholesale shift to the Democrats in the 1990s. There is too much volatility in their electoral history to call this a lasting realignment to the Democratic Party.

Was the movement based primarily on cultural conservatism? Was it informed by Church social teaching, particularly on the human life agenda and the preferential *option for the poor*? We have conducted complex analyses to understand these issues.[20]

The evidence is very compelling that what moved Catholics most from their political moorings from 1968 to 1992 were negative feelings on race and the role of government as an engine for change and equality. In 1960, few Catholic Democrats defected to Nixon; the primary reason for defection, however, was the feeling that the government should not be doing so much for social welfare. In 1964, defections were also limited, but the Goldwater party gave coherence to feelings that the government should be less active in assuring equality of opportunity, that government could not be trusted, that conservatives and Republicans were more attractive than Democrats, and that the United States was declining as a military power in a world imperiled by the communist threat. By 1968, negative feelings about African Americans were added to this bundle, and this comprehensive factor became far and away the primary reason why Catholic Democrats would come to embrace Republican presidential candidates for the next two decades.

Race-based, party ideology generally includes lukewarm feelings toward African Americans (although people generally deny that they are racists), later poor people and welfare recipients are added to the list, negative feelings toward several welfare state programs that are perceived to benefit blacks, and opposition toward various regulatory initiatives intended to equalize opportunities for blacks and whites. These become attached in the voters' minds with positive feelings toward Republicans and even more so with negative feelings toward the Democratic Party. In election year after election year from 1968 to 1992, this cluster of feelings best explains why Catholic Democrats defected to the Republicans. In the 1980s another factor first surfaces as a possible explanation for partisan defection—*moral restorationism*. This factor includes opposition to the availability of abortion, hesitance about changing roles for women, and negative feelings toward assurances of civil rights for homosexuals. Contrary to arguments by Steven Wagner, moral restorationism never becomes a statistically significant factor accounting for defections by Catholic Democrats until 1996.[21] In 1992 it had begun to take on a party base, so that Catholic Democrats who defected for reasons of cultural threat felt positive about Republicans, conservatives, and the police, and negative about Democrats, liberals, and labor. Curiously, in 1996 this factor grew even more to pick up negative feelings toward government programs that help anyone who is less well-off. Lukewarm feelings toward racial minorities, however, became a separate factor in that election.

Untangling what exactly was in Catholics' minds in these post–New Deal elections is a tricky business. Campaign appeals may articulate a quite principled theme. Voters may react according to these principles. At the same time, some voters may be responding to less principled subthemes articulated by politicians to take advantage of fear and racial or gender stereotypes. For example, Senator Goldwater's appeal to "states' rights" could mean democratic responsiveness from a unit of government closer to the people; yet, for some whites in the 1960s, it could mean that no federal court order would force my child to go to a predominantly black school. Currently "local control of schools" carries both principled and opportunistic content. For the many who felt that the growth of big government threatened America's unique blend of democracy and republicanism, the reduction of taxes was the way to reduce government programs, but to others it was the way to keep my hard-earned money from undeserving black hands.[22] The reduction of regulations might mean both less paperwork that stifles economic growth and greater freedom from the long reach of government, but it might also entail less civil rights enforcement and a diminished role for liberal intellectuals, many of whom were perceived to be Eastern establishment Jews. Affirmative action might be a way to open opportunity to minorities seeking to support themselves through work, but to some it sounded too much like reparations for the racial sins of the distant past. Harsh penalties on criminals might be a wise idea to reduce crime, yet to some this was a way of removing black criminals, who typically received harsher penalties, from the streets longer.[23] Abolishing "welfare as we know it" was a principled way of reducing intergenerational dependence on government, but in the perceptions of most it was removing a financial incentive for black mothers to have babies out of wedlock.[24] In short, negative stereotyping and racially charged appeals did not need to be as blatant as the Willie Horton advertisement in 1988. A system of racial code words sufficed.[25]

Catholics have generally been more compassionate toward the poor and the "other," and to have been more accepting (than other religious groups) of government action to assure equal opportunity for minorities.[26] Yet, the jeering and violent mobs of whites in heavily Catholic Gage Park (Chicago) and Cicero, Illinois during Martin Luther King's northern marches suggest some Catholics were not immune to racial antagonisms. The fascinating study *Canarsie*[27] indicates a long history of Catholic racial ambivalence going back to the New York draft riots following the Emancipation Proclamation. Freedman's gripping intergenerational narrative of three Catholic families indicates that, while the first and second generations loved what the New Deal did to create economic opportunities and social acceptance for ethnic white Catholics, the second and third generations resented Great Society programs and federal intervention to assure equal opportunities for African Americans.[28] The second generation defected or stayed at home, but the third generation entered the local leadership of the Republican party. In particular Kevin Phillips' "Southern strategy" for Republican victory was also directed to urban and inner-rim suburban Catholic men who feared big government and resented tax transfers and racial/gender favoritism. Phillips thought the big issues—civil rights backlash, taxation, ERA and the women's movement—could dissemble Catholic men from the Democratic Party.[29]

The data presented above suggest that there is some reason to believe that Phillips was right. While Catholics as a group may be more compassionate toward the poor and blacks, those white Catholic Democrats who were mobilized to defect to the Republican Party showed less warmth toward blacks and black political activity, disliked government programs that were intended to increase opportunity for blacks, reacted negatively to the directions their party had taken and responded positively to the Republicans. In elections from 1972 to 1984, this constellation of racial factors also modestly depressed turnout, but heavily depressed it in 1972. Generally, however, Catholic Democrats upset over race actually voted for the Republican candidate. While race receded in salience by 1996—moral restorationism replaced it—no other cultural factor had the same staying power throughout the post–New Deal.

It is difficult to discern whether white Catholic Democrats were hearing principled appeals or were reacting from visceral dislikes or a sense of relative deprivation. Certainly those ethnic Catholics who were at the lower to middle rungs of the employment ladder were in competition with African Americans for some of the same jobs, homes, and neighborhoods. Whatever the reason, Republican campaigners were more successful among Catholics with the racial symbols and code words than they were with the patriotic and moral restorationist packages.

CATHOLIC INFLUENCES ON
POLITICAL VALUES

Some may argue that this evidence about the attitudinal sources for Catholic partisan mobility does not give proper due to the role of the church in forming Catholics' political outlooks. The Catholic Church had offered its people a century of social encyclicals that culminated in the Pueblo and Medallin conferences, where the preferential option for the poor was articulated. In the United States in the 1970s and 1980s, the National Conference of Catholic Bishops promulgated a series of pastoral letters on human life, race relations, economic justice, and war and peace. There is little question that Catholics see the world through more communitarian lenses than do Protestants.

Therefore, we have selected a variety of political issues from ANES 1988, 1992, and 1996. These are issues where one might expect the Church's teaching on social justice, human dignity and minority relations, and the sanctity of human life to condition the laity's attitudes. Then we have selected a variety of predictor variables: generational cohort, sex, education, income, region (South, non-South), political party affiliation, and four types of religious variables: (1) frequency of Mass attendance, (2) importance of religion in one's daily life, (3) feeling close to other Catholics, and (4) the interaction of church attendance and the importance of religion. The third is an attempt to tap the Catholic communal dimension, which scholars have claimed is so important in shaping Catholic social and political outlooks.[30] The fourth is an attempt to isolate Catholics who not only receive regular cues about faith and life in church, but consider it important to apply those values in daily life.[31] Republican Party affiliation is included because the current maxim states that the higher the level of religiosity—regardless of denomination—the more likely that a voter will be Republican and espouse religiously formed political values.[32] If Catholic religiosity is shaping political values, we should expect that one or more of these "religious" measures should show statistically significant relationships with each attitudinal variable.[33]

From the perspectives of a church committed to social teaching, some positives are evident in table 20.2. The principal religiosity variables appear with some regularity on the human life issues. In 1988 the strongest combination—regular attendance, with its concomitant exposure to religious

Table 20.2. Predictors of Social and Political Attitudes among White Catholics, 1988–1996

Outcome Variable	1988	1992	1996**
Warmth Blacks	Warmth Catholics (.287) (Neg.) Republican (−.144)	Warmth Catholics (.390) Education (.162)	(Neg.) Education (−.187) (Neg.) Republican (−.176) (Neg.) Generation (−.152)
Warmth Chicanos	Warmth Catholics (.222) (Neg.) Republican (−.174)	Education (.209) Warmth Catholics (.203)	None
Warmth Poor People	Warmth Catholics (.416) (Neg.) Education (−.180) Generation (.122)	Warmth Catholics (.315) Generation (.198) (Neg.) Republican (−.179)	None
Warmth Welfare Recipients	Generation (.165) (Neg.) Republican (−.193)	Warmth Catholics (.222) Generation (.177) (Neg.) Republican (−.175) Education (.164)	(Neg.) Republican (−.272) Generation (.168)
Warmth Women	Warmth Catholics (.394)* (Neg.) Generation (−.169)	*	

Issue			
Abortion (+ oppose)	Attendance & Guidance (.563) Warmth Catholics (.160)	Attendance (.226) (Neg.) Education (−.147) Republican (.134) (Neg.) Sex (Female) (−.123)	None
Death penalty (+ oppose)	(Neg.) Republican (−.161) Education (.180)	Attendance (.440) Region (South) (.316)	Attendance & Guidance (.556) (Neg.) Republican (−.167)
Military spending (+ decrease)	(Neg.) Religious guidance (−.427) Attendance & guidance (.532) (Neg.) Republican (−.277) Education (.147)	Education (.180)	(Neg.) Republican (−.297)
Govt. role/equal opportunity (+ active)	(Neg.) Republican (−.282) (Neg.) Income (−.189) Sex (Female) (.142)	(Neg.) Republican (−.314) Sex (Female) (.213)	(Neg.) Republican (−.440)
Govt. Health Insurance (+ support)	(Neg.) Income (−.228) (Neg.) Republican (−.197) Sex (Female) (.156)	(Neg.) Republican (−.309)	(Neg.) Republican (−.254)
Assistance for Blacks (+ support)	None (Neg.) Republican (−.145) (Neg.) Income (−.139)	Education (.188)	Education (.190)

*No measure of warmth toward women in 1992, 96 **No measure of warmth toward Catholics in 1996
Source: American National Election Studies

cues, and recognition that religious values provide a powerful guide for daily life—is highly related to opposition to abortion. A similar relationship appears with the desire to decrease military spending in 1988. Finally, in 1996 this combination is strongly related to opposition to the death penalty. However, it is never a powerful predictor of our measures of social justice or of warmth toward people not like oneself or of lower status than oneself. In 1996, attendance alone of the religiosity variables predicts opposition to abortion. In 1988, religious guidance is strongly related to an *increase* in military spending, the *opposite* of what the bishops' pastoral letter would have encouraged. In seven of nine opportunities, warm feelings toward other Catholics are related to warm feelings toward blacks, Chicanos, the poor, welfare recipients, and women. At least these might suggest a basis for empathy toward the needs of others. Nevertheless, this measure of Catholic communalism is related in significant ways to human life or social justice measures only on the abortion issue in 1988—missing eight other opportunities.

The most frequent predictor variable in the table is Republican Party identification, appearing nineteen times out of thirty-three opportunities. In the politically supercharged environment of the American culture wars, some have claimed that to be a Republican is the only way to be consistent with Christian teachings. For Catholic Republicans, however, it does not appear to work that way. In only one instance—abortion in 1992—is Republican identification consistent with our scoring of church teachings on human life and social justice issues. White Republican Catholics are *less* empathic to people of color or lower status, are *less* willing to respect human life except for that of the unborn, and *less* willing to use government as an engine for increasing opportunity for those of color or lower estate.

Another frequent predictor is level of education. While a higher level of education often predicts greater support for equality of opportunity, empathy for the poor and people of color, decreasing military expenditures, and opposition to the death penalty, it is also implicated in pro-choice sentiment. Being female often predicts this same set of attitudes—supportive on issues of social justice and peace, but pro-choice on abortion. Older Catholics are consistently warmer toward people of color and the poor, but are decidedly cool toward women as a category, perhaps because of their traditionalism on gender roles and opposition to the pro-choice objectives of the women's movement.

The message of table 20.2, in summary, is that deepened religious involvement and commitment among Catholics seems to condition attitudes on some human life issues, but it has little impact at all on social justice issues and even human empathy. The second lesson is that if political parties are indeed "political churches," the church that has increasingly attracted younger Catholics, particularly men, is decidedly stronger in its influence over their social justice and peace attitudes than is the Catholic Church. The same could be said of the younger Catholic women on abortion. A third lesson is that older Catholics, either by values or by life experience, are more warmly inclined toward the poor and the outsider. *Perhaps the most pervasive image from the table is how seldom a central religious variable has political consequences for Catholics.*

INTERPRETATION AND
FURTHER DISCUSSION

The tone of this paper has been "half-empty" rather than "half-full." We think there has been a tendency among Catholic interpreters of religion and civic engagement to compare the present with a Garden of Eden of the past, found in the ethnic parish, Al Smith dinners, Boss Daley's Chicago, and so forth. In this vision, there was always a sense that being a Catholic was different; not only was there unity and solidarity, but it courageously went against the grain of the country. Perhaps our judgments of the present are unduly harsh because we do not have a realistic picture of what was religiously Catholic in the past.

The ethnic Catholic Church, we argue, was the *ethnic* Catholic Church. The church of ethnic enclave was highly successful in activating Catholics who had been for the most part inactive in the homeland. Roger Finke and Rodney Stark document the competitive growth of the Catholic Church in the United States and contrast it with the levels of public religious activity back in the Catholic country or state of origin.[34] The ethnic parish transmitted a sense of commonality. The question is whether it was a Catholic commonality, or an Irish Catholic commonality, a Polish Catholic commonality, a German Catholic commonality, or Italian, or Slovak. The mysteries of the Latin rites may have given a sense of unity to a church headquartered in distant Rome, but the interactions, the friendships, the social support, the economic and political protective associations were with one's own kind. Perhaps the civic and political lessons Catholics in America learned were of a particularistic, not universalistic nature. Perhaps the Church—read the hierarchy, or more recently, the magisterium—never had the universal teaching authority in the minds of parishioners that it attributed to itself. Rite, ritual, catechesis, and piety—yes. But how to live one's political life, other than to be a responsible citizen—no. My Father's house had too many rooms for that. A universal church in faith, private life, and public life may have been outside the scope of many Catholics growing up in America.

Perhaps church watchers did not really notice the cracks in the structure until a decade or so after Vatican II, when a more unified national structure and national voice was to emerge. It did take shape at the level of the bishops and clergy, although vigorous conflicts remain, but it was never very evident at the level of the laity. Were the laity unfaithful or was normatively binding social teaching outside the legitimate scope of the American clergy?

We certainly have evidence that succeeding generations of Catholics are less likely to expose themselves to religious cues about faith and life.[35] First, Mass attendance in all age cohorts of the population in the 1990s is less than it was in the 1960s. Second, younger people are less likely to be regular attendees and more likely never to attend (except for weddings, funerals, or other family events). Third, the index dropped precipitously in the early 1970s—the anti-institutional period—for virtually all age groups, but made a modest recovery in the 1980s for New Deal–generation Catholics. Fourth, the last generation of Catholics to connect or reconnect with the church was in its thirties at the time of the Kennedy election.[36]

Younger Catholics in 1960 or age groups that entered the electorate after that time have successively lower indexes of attendance; from 1968 onward, Catholics entering the electorate not only have lower attendance indexes but they have for the most part never moved in the positive direction. There is far less exposure to the church's teaching at Mass and far less group reinforcement in church settings among the generations that moved so heavily in conservative directions on social issues (males) or became pro-choice on abortion (females especially). Moving into the new millennium, these Catholics now constitute the majority of the Catholic electorate. Ironic indeed that these last two decades of the twentieth century were trumpeted as "the Catholic moment."[37]

It was once believed that infrequent or never-attending Catholics thought politically like other Catholics.[38] No more. Leege contrasted regular-attending and never-attending subsamples across religious traditions—seculars, Jews, mainline Protestants, Catholics, evangelical Protestants, Hispanic Christians, and Black Christians. He assessed evidence across nineteen political measures such as party identification, political ideology, and candidate preference, positions on political issues such as abortion, the economy, affirmative action, underlying attitudes such as moral traditionalism, egalitarianism, authoritarianism, religiosity, and demographic characteristics. The conclusion is that never-attending Catholics, about 30 percent of the sample, are highly distinct from regular attendees and that they are most like seculars in their political thinking. Further of the never-attenders within each religious tradition, the Catholics were least like their regular attendees. As church attendance declines among Catholics, not only is exposure to cues lost, but they are less distinct from secular citizens. Curiously, the younger men who never attend are more conservative on social justice issues, whereas the younger women who more regularly attend are more like the never-attenders in their rejection of church teaching on abortion, but are also more like the older regular-attending women in their support of social justice and peace positions.[39] The mosaic is complicated.

Further, active church-going Catholics are declining as a proportion of the total electorate. Table 20.3, gives several assessments of the size and composition of the "religious vote."[40] The first row for each of the major religious traditions is the proportion of the U.S. adult population in a church body within that tradition. The second row is the proportion of the U.S. adult population within the tradition who claim regular (weekly) attendance. The third row is the one of greatest interest here: the proportion of actual voters (self-report) in the United States who are regular (weekly) attendees within each religious tradition shifted in the 1990s and, among the churched population, evangelical Protestants, not Catholics, have been having their "moment." But there are a lot of votes among the seculars of late.[41]

The final item for discussion is the attitudes of Catholics toward political information and direction by the clergy. Analyzing data from the Notre Dame Study of Catholic Parish Life (2,667 parish-connected Catholics in a multistage mixed probability design), Leege found that most parishioners (83 percent to 56 percent depending on the issue) expected some level of the hierarchy to speak out on aid to poor countries, eliminating poverty in the United States, world disarmament, racial integration, sex and violence on TV, and equal opportunities for women on the job. Still, between 10 and 38 percent felt this was solely a matter of the individual Catholic's conscience.[42] According to data from the 1989 ANES Pilot Study,[43] Catholics are accustomed to hearing their priest or homilist speak out on issues: 83 percent on abortion, 70 percent on homelessness, 67 percent on proper sexual behavior, on down to 39 percent on a just economy, 32 percent on public school prayer, 28 percent on nuclear disarmament. Only 9 percent reported hearing the priest speak out about political candidates. Yet slightly over half (51 per-

Table 20.3. The Size and Composition of the "Religious Vote," 1960–1962: Proportion of Adult Americans Identifying with Various Ethnoreligious Traditions, Proportion of Adult Population Attending Religious Services Regularly within Each Tradition, Proportion of Active Electorate Constituted by Regular Attenders within Each Tradition

	1960	1964	1968	1972	1976	1980	1984	1988	1992	1996
Mainline Protestant White N-H	41	39	37	35	33	30	30	28	22	24
	14	14	12	6	6	5	5	5	4	5
	17	16	14	8	8	6	7	8	4	5
Evangelical Protestant, White N-H	21	21	24	23	22	20	20	21	22	20
	9	8	8	7	7	6	6	8	10	8
	9	8	7	7	8	6	7	9	10	7
Roman Catholic, White N-H	18	21	20	22	23	20	20	17	20	20
	14	14	13	10	9	8	7	6	7	7
	17	16	15	12	10	9	9	8	8	6
Black Christian	8	10	10	10	10	10	10	12	12	13
	3	5	4	2	2	3	3	3	4	4
	2	5	4	2	2	4	3	3	3	3

		(1)	(2)	(3)	(4)	(5)	(6)	(7)	(8)	(9)	(10)
Hispanic Christian	a	*	*	*	*	*	3	6	8	5	8
	b	*	*	*	*	*	1	1	2	2	3
	c	*	*	*	*	*	1	1	2	1	2
Jewish	a	3	3	3	2	2	3	3	2	2	2
	b	*	*	*	*	*	*	*	*	*	*
	c	(4)	(3)	(3)	(2)	(3)	(4)	(3)	(2)	(2)	(2)
Other Wite N-H:											
Mormon, Orthodox, etc.	a	1	2	3	3	2	2	2	1	1	2
	b	*	1	1	1	1	1	1	*	*	1
	c	*	1	1	1	2	2	1	1	*	1
Islam, Buddhist, etc.	a	1	*	1	1	1	1	1	1	1	1
	b	*	*	*	*	*	*	*	*	*	*
	c	*	*	*	*	*	*	*	*	*	*
Secular	a	8	4	4	5	7	10	9	10	15	13
	b	*	*	*	*	*	*	*	*	*	*
	c	(1)	(3)	(3)	(4)	(5)	(9)	(8)	(8)	(12)	(8)

a % of all adults claiming affiliation with the designated ethnoreligious tradition.
b % of all adults claiming regular (weekly) attendance at church, within designated ethnoreligious tradition.
c % of all voters (adults reporting voting) who claim to be regular (weekly) attenders within designated ethnoreligious tradition.
* Designates cell with fewer than five entries, too few for analysis
Source: American National Election Studies, 1960–1996

cent) of Catholics felt it was not legitimate for the clergy to speak out on such issues. This legitimacy figure is slightly lower than evangelicals but higher than mainline Protestants. Further, when a variety of analyses were attempted to determine the actual impact of the messages, among Catholics only abortion cues from clergy seemed to affect political activities. Verba and his colleagues report that the only issue area stimulating increased political activity by Catholics was abortion.[44] For black evangelicals, however, political activity was stimulated by a wide range of social welfare and social justice issues.

Apparently the differential relationship between teaching and political activity has been noticed by leadership elites. Ted Jelen and Clyde Wilcox report that about a quarter of the sample of leadership elites in the academy, business, government, and the mass media think some religious groups have too much influence. Forty-three percent of the media sample felt Catholics had too much influence and 40 percent of the academic sample shared this view; others were well below this level. But the concern was nothing like that expressed over evangelicals; 90 percent of the academic sample, 52 percent of the media sample, and even 52 percent of the business sample and 50 percent of the government sample felt evangelicals/the Religious Right had too much influence.[45] Catholics themselves are split about the degree to which the Church should be involved in politics: 30 percent want a high wall of separation between church and state with no help to churches, 22 percent want the high wall but help for all churches, while 43 percent want protection and help for all churches.[46]

As the agenda has shifted in the contemporary American political system to emphasize private rather than public problem solving, it could very well be that Catholics best manifest their concern for human life, for justice and peace, for the poor through vigorous involvement in eleemosynary institutions. After all, that was the norm in the ethnic parish with its many protective and betterment societies. Unfortunately our political surveys do not ask about that kind of activity. Perhaps the New Deal and Great Society days where Catholics demanded effort out of the government—and got it—were an historical aberration. At least those government programs offered benefits widely throughout the society. Although the ethnic parish model took care of one's own kind, as the late twentieth century unfolded, the great Catholic social service organizations—Catholic Charities, Catholic Relief Services, and inner-city schools—reached out to all kinds of people, with need the only test. Perhaps the research agenda of the future will be to map the ways Catholic charitable acts in this more conservative and self-centered generation lead to *systemic* betterment of society. If indeed they do, the movement away from government as an engine to assure equality of opportunity will not have been as self-centered as it might appear.

NOTES

1. Kenneth D. Wald, Dennis E. Owen, and Samuel S. Hill Jr. 1988, 1990, "Churches as Political Communities," *American Political Science Review* 82, 2: 531–48; Robert Huckfeldt, Eric Plutzer, and John Sprague, "Alternative Contexts of Political Behavior: Churches, Neighborhoods, and Individuals," *Journal of Politics* 55 (1993): 365–81; Christopher P. Gilbert, 1993. *The Impact of Churches on Political Behavior: An Empirical Study* (Westport, Conn.: Greenwood, 1993).

2. Ray Billington, *The Creation of a Democratic Majority, 1928–1936* (Chicago: University of Chicago Press, 1938).

3. William Prendergast, *The Catholic Voter in American Politics*, (Washington, D.C.: Georgetown University Press, 1999), 24.

4. Prendergast, *Catholic Voter in American Politics*, 41–45.

5. Paul Kleppner, "Coalitional and Party Transformations in the 1890s," *Party Coalitions in the 1980s*, ed. S. M. Lipset (San Francisco: Institute for Contemporary Studies, 1981).

6. Both Kleppner and Richard Jensen show how, see Lipset.

7. John R. Petrocik, *Party Coalitions: Realignment and the Decline of the New Deal Party System* (Chicago: University of Chicago Press, 1981).

8. Kristi Andersen, *The Creation of a Democratic Majority, 1928–1936* (Chicago: University of Chicago Press, 1979).

9. Samuel G. Freedman, *The Inheritance: How Three Families and America Moved from Roosevelt to Reagan and Beyond* (New York: Simon & Schuster, 1996).

10. David C. Leege, 1988, "Catholics and the Civic Order: Parish Participation, Politics, and Civic Participation," *Review of Politics* 50 (4): 704–36.

11. Phillip E. Converse, "Religion and Politics: The 1960 Election," *Elections and the Political Order*, eds. A. Campbell, P. E. Converse, W. E. Miller and D. E. Stokes, (New York: Wiley, 1966).

12. Joan Fee, 1976, "Party Identification among American Catholics, 1972." *Ethnicity*, 3 (1): 53–69.

13. David C. Leege and Michael R. Welch, 1989, "Religious Roots of Political Orientations: Variations among American Catholic Parishioners," *Journal of Politics* 51 (1): 137–62.

14. Prendergast, *Catholic Voter in American Politics*.

15. While African Americans, at approximately 2 million people, are a small fraction of the 60 million Catholics in the United States, they would still be larger than any single African-American Protestant denomination. Yet their politics differ little from other African Americans. From 1968 onward they are overwhelmingly and reliably Democratic. They vote even more regularly than black Protestants. They support federal efforts to assure equality of opportunity, welfare economics, an active role for government, and they show compassion for the poor and for criminals. They are more conservative than seculars or mainline Protestants on family, sexuality, and related cultural issues. Even the proportionately few Republicans among them either fail to vote at the federal level or they defect to Democratic candidates. Thus, there is little unique in the story about African-American Catholics.

Latino Catholics are another matter. First, although a variety of reports sets their population over 25 percent of the U.S. Catholic Church, using survey data collected by different houses, we have never been able to find more than 13 to 15 percent of national adult samples who fit a Hispanic or Latino category. Further, of these, as low as 55 percent and as high as 75 percent report their religious identification as Catholic. Even among "Catholics," varying but not inconsequential portions actually worship at evangelical or mainline Protestant facilities but still call themselves Catholic. These findings do not add up to 25 percent of all Catholics in the United States The political side is even more difficult: Mexican Americans are the largest group, are the most Democratic (about two-thirds), but least likely to vote. Puerto Ricans are slightly less Democratic (about 60 percent), and more likely to vote, largely because citizenship is automatic. Current population surveys, however, are showing them eclipsed in size by Dominicans in Eastern cities; we know nothing beyond anecdotal evidence about the politics of Dominicans. Cubans are the smallest of these groups, are overwhelmingly (75 percent) Republican, and have the highest turnout. Yet they are the most concentrated of these population groups and are, thus, a political force only in Florida. Further, a smaller proportion of Cubans are Catholic than of the other large Latino groups. Because the emerging mosaic among Latino Catholics is more recent, we do not have the time series data to follow them with precision. Furthermore, their styles of Catholic religiosity diverge substantially from assimilated Catholics, and most of our measures of religiosity are culturally biased. Therefore, their story—and it is a vitally important one—will have to be told from the Pew-supported project "Hispanic Churches in American Public Life." From this point forward then, all data are for white, non-Latino Catholics or for designated comparison groups.

16. Leege 1993; David Leege, Kenneth D. Wald, Brian S. Krueger, and Paul D. Mueller, *The Politics of Cultural Differences: Social Change and Voter Mobilization Strategies in the Post–New Deal Period* (Princeton, N.J.: Princeton University Press, 2002).

17. Table 20.1 is based on data from the cumulative file of the American National Election Studies. ANES is the "survey of record" for the scholarly community to understand not only each biennial or quadrennial election but also the dynamics of change in the American electorate. They are supported with continuing grants from the National Science Foundation and conducted for the most part through face-to-face interviews of a nationwide probability sample by the Survey Research Center of the University of Michigan. ANES samples are generally accurate within two or three percentage points of the true value on most variables, with higher margins of error for subsample analyses. They yield Catholic samples usually in the 300 to 400 person range.

18. For arguments about the utility of the first three generational cut points, see, Warren E. Miller and J. Merrill Shanks, *The New American Voter* (Cambridge, Mass.: Harvard University Press, 1996); and Paul R. Abramson and John H. Aldrich, "The Decline of Electoral Participation in America," *American Political Science Review,* 76 (3, 1982): 502–521.

19. Jack Germond and Jules Witcover, *Whose Broad Stripes and Bright Stars?: The Trivial Pursuit of the Presidency* (New York: Warner Books, 1989).

20. To get at the reasons for movement we need to examine the special appeals Republicans and Democrats each made to Catholics, and measure which of these appeals were the best predictors of partisan movement. To do this, we tap into data assembled by David Leege, Kenneth Wald, Brian Krueger, and Paul Mueller in *The Politics of Cultural Differences* (Princeton, N.J.: Princeton University Press, 2002). They have conducted a content analysis of Presidential campaign themes in speeches and advertisements from 1960 to 1996. Then, they have used the ANES cumulative file to factor analyze issue positions and feelings toward groups held by the Catholic electorate in each of these campaigns.

Factor analysis allows the scholar to reduce a welter of issue and group feelings into underlying cognitive structures. It sees what kinds of feelings cohere with each other in the minds of American voters. Finally, Leege, et al., have used a procedure called multinomial logit analysis to assess which factors best explain partisan defections and turnout failures. The factors that bundled together feelings and accounted for most of the defections among Catholics during the post–New Deal period are described in appendix 20.1; only statistically significant factors are detailed. The results are shown in appendix 20.2 for the entire Catholic sample. We could not analyze every generational and gender group with these factors because the subsample sizes would have been too small to meet the statistical requirements of this procedure.

21. Wagner, Steven, "The Catholic Voter Project," *Crisis*, November 1998, C2–8.

22. Thomas B. Edsall and Mary D. Edsall, *Chain Reaction: The Impact of Race, Rights, and Taxes on American Politics* (New York: Norton, 1991).

23. Jon Hurwitz and Mark Peffley, "Public Perceptions of Race and Crime." *American Journal of Political Science* 41 (2, 1997): 375–402.

24. Michael Katz, *The Undeserving Poor: From the War on Poverty to the War on Welfare* (New York: Pantheon Books, 1989); Martin Gilens, *Why Americans Hate Welfare* (Chicago: University of Chicago Press, 1999).

25. Leege et. al, 2002.

26. George Gallup Jr. and Jim Castelli, *The American Catholic People: Their Beliefs, Practices, and Values* (Garden City, N.Y.: Doubleday, 1987); Andrew Greeley, *Religious Change in America* (Cambridge, Mass.: Harvard University Press, 1989); and Wagner, 1998.

27. Jonathan Rieder, *Canarsie: The Jews and Italians of Brooklyn against Liberalism* (Cambridge, Mass.: Harvard University Press, 1985).

28. Freedman.

29. Kevin Phillips, *The Emerging Republican Majority* (New York: Doubleday Anchor, 1970).

30. Gerhard Lenski, *The Religious Factor: A Sociological Study of Religion's Impact on Politics, Economics, and Family Life*, rev. ed. (Garden City, N.Y.: Doubleday, 1963); Phillip E. Converse, 1966. "Religion and Politics: The 1960 Election," *Elections and the Political Order*, eds. A. Campbell, P. E. Converse, W. E. Miller, and D. E. Stokes (New York: Wiley, 1966); Andrew M. Greeley, *The Communal Catholic: A Personal Manifesto* (New York: Seabury Press, 1976); and Greeley, 1989.

31. David Leege and Lyman A. Kellstedt, *Rediscovering the Religious Factor in American Politics* (Armonk: M.E. Sharpe, 1993).

32. John C. Green, James L. Guth, Corwin E. Smidt, and Lyman A. Kellstedt. *Religion and the Culture Wars: Dispatches from the Front* (Lanham, Md.: Rowman & Littlefield, 1996).

33. The dependent variables are scored so that a positive coefficient would indicate a position consistent with one that might be inferred from church social teaching and pastoral letters. Ordinary least squares techniques are used for the regression equations. The more the score diverges from zero, the more the demographic, political, or religious factor accounts for the attitude. Only results significant at least at the .05 level are noted on table 20.2.

34. Roger Finke and Rodney Stark, *The Churching of America, 1776–1990: Winners and Losers in Our Religious Economy* (New Brunswick, N.J.: Rutgers University Press, 1992).

35. Leege (1993) mapped the church attendance patterns of all those who called themselves Catholics on ANES surveys from 1960 to 1992. For this paper we have expanded

this mapping to include the 1996 presidential election. The entries for white non-Latino Catholics that appear in Appendix III are divided by eight-year age cohorts. It follows each cohort from the time of adulthood or their age in 1960 until 1996. Each cell in the table subtracts the proportion of that age group who reported regular attendance at Mass from the proportion of Catholics in that age cohort who never attend Mass. The entries in the bottom rows across the table are the average index score for a given election year, and the proportion of the total white Catholic sample that was in the regular/never categories.

36. For example, the thirty-three- to forty-year-olds in 1960 came in with an index of 79 that year; it dropped to 33 in 1976, but recovered to 48 by 1992.

37. Richard John Neuhaus, *The Catholic Moment* (San Francisco: Harper & Row, 1987).

38. Greeley, 1976; Leege and Welch, 1989.

39. Leege, 1996.

40. Updated from Leege, 1993.

41. A colleague in the religion and politics field took the senior author's place at a White House pow-wow in the summer before the 1994 Congressional elections. He reported that, following his presentation about voters driven by faith concerns, both Mrs. Clinton and Samuel Popkin queried, "Shouldn't we make special attempts either to attract or neutralize religious voters?" The legendary James Carville muttered, "Oh, f—— 'em!" and left the room. On election day they learned the consequence of listening to Carville.

42. Leege, 1988.

43. Michael R. Welch, David C. Leege, Kenneth D. Wald, and Lyman A. Kellstedt, "Are the Sheep Hearing the Shepherds? Cue Perceptions, Congregational Responses, and Political Communication Processes." In *Rediscovering the Religious Factor in American Politics*, edited by D. C. Leege and L. A. Kellstedt (Armonk, New York: M. E. Sharp, 1993).

44. Sidney Verba, Kay Lehman Schlozman, and Henry E. Brady, *Voice and Equality: Civic Voluntarism in American Life* (Cambridge, Mass.: Harvard University Press, 1995).

45. Ted G. Jelen and Clyde Wilcox, *Public Attitudes toward Church and State* (Armonk, New York: M. E. Sharp, 1995), 47.

46. Jelen and Wilcox, *Public Attitudes,* 66.

1964

Party Ideology

(I) Govt role/social spending (oppose govt job guarantees, aid to education)

(G) Party (warm toward Republicans, conservatives; cool toward Democrats)

(I) US strength (foreign relations worse, US declining in strength)

(I) Distrust of govt (trust and efficacy battery

Cynical America First/Anti-Communism

(I) Distrust of govt (trust and efficacy battery)

(I) Anti-communism (oppose discussions with communists, foreign aid)

(I) Fear of war (worried about likelihood of war)

1968

Race-based Party Ideology

(I) Govt role/social spending (oppose govt job guarantees, aid to education, FEPC, subsidy of medical care)

(G) Party (warm toward Republicans, conservatives; cool toward Democrats)

(I) Race/civil rights (oppose equal housing access, public accommodations access, mandated school integration, FEPC; pace of civil rights too fast)

Anti-Communism/Law & Order

(I) Vietnam (hawkish toward Vietnam)

(G) Law and Order (warm towards the Military and Police, cool towards Liberals)

(I) Negotiations with communists (oppose interactions with communists)

1972

Conservative Reaction to Change

(G) Social change (cool toward women's liberationists, liberals; warm toward military, police, big business)

(G) Racial change (cool toward civil rights leaders, black militants, blacks in general; warm toward whites, middle class)

(G) Party (cool toward Democrats, labor; warm toward Republicans, conservatives)

(G) Anti-welfare (cool toward poor people, blacks)

(I) Social unrest/crime (support forceful handling of urban unrest, campus unrest; reduce rights of accused; oppose govt help for minorities)

(I) Race/civil rights (see 1968; oppose busing)

(I) Vietnam (agree we should have fought in Vietnam, support slow pace of withdrawal)

ELITE RELIGIOUS LIBERALS

(G) Anti-organized religion (dislike church groups; Prot., Cath., Jews)

(I) Vietnam (see above)

1976

RACE-BASED PARTY IDEOLOGY

(I) Govt role/social spending (oppose govt job guarantees, provision of health insurance, govt solution to unemployment, govt spending)

(I) Social unrest/crime (support harsher treatment of criminals, reduce rights of the accused, support forceful handling of urban unrest)

(G) Party (warm toward Republicans, conservatives, big business; cool toward Democrats)

(I) Race/civil rights (oppose mandated integration, busing, aid to minorities; pace of civil rights too fast)

1980

RACE-BASED PARTY IDEOLOGY

(I) Race/civil rights (oppose busing, aid to minorities, govt job guarantees, preferential hiring of women; pace of civil rights too fast)

(I) Govt role/social spending (oppose govt solution to unemployment, inflation; reduce spending and services)

(G) Racial antagonism (warm toward middle class, whites; cool toward black militants)

(G) Party (warm toward Republicans, conservatives; cool toward Democrats)

(G) Cultural conflict; North-South (warm toward Southerners; cool toward labor, poor people)

RACIAL POPULISM/ISOLATIONSIM
- (G) Minorities (cool toward blacks, Chicanos)
- (G) Cultural conflict: North-South (see above)
- (I) Isolationism (oppose increased defense spending, involvement in world problems; support non-involvement in Afghanistan war)

1984

RACE-BASED PARTY IDEOLOGY
- (I) Govt role/social spending (decrease govt spending on social security, Medicare, food stamps, jobs for unemployed, public schools; oppose govt job guarantees, assurance of equal opportunity)
- (G) Party (cool toward Democrats, liberals, labor, women's movement; warm toward Republicans, conservatives)
- (I) Strength of US (increase defense spending, involvement in Central America, involvement in world problems, US world influence; oppose cooperation with Soviets)
- (G) Welfare (cool toward poor people, people on welfare)
- (G) Race/class convergence (warm toward whites, middle class; cool toward black militants, people on welfare)

1988

RACE-BASED PARTY IDEOLOGY
- (I) Govt role/social spending (decrease federal spending on elderly; social security, homeless, children, services)
- (G) Party (warm toward Republicans, conservatives, military; cool toward Democrats, liberals labor)
- (I) Race/civil rights (oppose FEPC, assurance of equal rights, college admission quotas for blacks, pressure on South Africa; pace of civil rights too fast; blacks must rely on self-help, not govt; favor death penalty)

1992

RACE/CLASS/ORDER-BASED PARTY
- (I) Govt Role/Social Spending (support decrease in federal spending on poor, unemployed, welfare, services)
- (I) Strength of U.S. (support Persian Gulf activities, support US hegemony)

(G) Class (warm toward poor and people on welfare, cool towards big business)

(I) Race/Civil Rights (oppose FEPC, assurance of equal rights, college admission quotas for blacks; pace of civil rights too fast; blacks must rely on self-help, not govt; done too much for blacks already; support decrease in spending for blacks)

(G) Party (warm towards conservatives, Republicans, Police; cool towards Democrats, Labor, Liberals)

Cynicism/Trust in Govt (Efficacy Battery)
Millennial Hopes

(G) Dispossessed (warm towards African Americans, Latinos)

(G) Evangelical Zionism (warm towards whites, Jews, Southerners)

1996

Moral Restorationist Party

(I) Moral traditionalism (oppose legalizing abortion, women's roles outside home, homosexuals in military, job protection for homosexuals)

(G) Party (warm toward conservatives, Republicans, Christian fundamentalists; cool toward liberals, Democrats, women's movement, labor)

(G) Evangelical politics (warm toward Christian fundamentalists; cool toward Supreme Court)

(I) Govt role/social spending (oppose job guarantees, spending on health insurance, services, homeless; not govt duty to reduce rich-poor differences; govt too big)

White Non-Latino Catholic Democrats, 1960–1996

Factors	Stay at home	Defect	Controls	Stay at Home	Defect
1960					
Govt. Role/Social Spending	−.034	.625*	Education	−19.432****	.312
Cynicism/Trust in Govt.	.334	.299	Gender	.881	−1.697**
Strength of U.S.	.701	.372	Income	.074	−.234
Isolationism/Internationalism.	153	.247	Cohort	.364	.041
Race/Civil Rights	.564	−.142	South	.491	1.866*
			Constant	14.677	.129
N	155		LR χ² [20]	24.87	
1964					
Old Social Cleavages	−.177	.642	Education	.430	.096
Party Ideology	.170	1.843****	Gender	−.267	.285
Cynical American First/Anti-Communism	.602***	.831***			
			Income	−.235	−.213
			Cohort	.386	.759
			South	1.413***	1.005
			Constant	−2.006	−3.802
N	213		LR χ² [16]	44.24	
1968					
Race Based Party Ideology	.214	.900****	Education	−.503	−.234
Cynicism/Trust in Govt.	.832****	.436*	Gender	−.779*	−.340
Anti-Communism/Law & Order	.094	.085	Income	−.377*	−.257
Anti-Nativism /Pro-Minorities	.359	.193	Cohort	.967**	.231
			South	.607	.446
			Constant	−.227	.192
N	174		LR χ² [18]	36.38	
1972					
Conservative Reaction to Social Change	.593***	.641****	Education	−.499*	−.286
Cultural Populism	−.118	−.193	Gender	.004	−.096
Elite Religious Liberals	.030	.410****	Income	−.406***	.061
			Cohort	.882****	−.144
			South	.567	.765**
			Constant	−.809	.629
N	304		LR χ² [16]	64.64	
1977					
Opposition to Racial/Social Change	−.296	−.042	Education	−.858***	−.020
Cynical Isolationism/Moral Restorationism	.089	−.216	Gender	.708*	.288
Cultural Populism	.166	−.021	Income	−.423**	.097
Race-Based Party Ideology	.452*	.951****	Cohort	1.056****	.371
			South	.685	−.724
			Constant	−2.227**	−2.430***
N	240		LR χ² [18]	61.14	

1980

Race-Based Party Ideology	.858**	1.491****	Education	−.317	.908**
Retreatist Racial Populism	.196	.299	Gender	.219	.690
Moral Restorationism	−.051	−.023	Income	−.248	−.547***
			Cohort	1.113***	.244
			South	.272	−.011
			Constant	−2.030	−1.653
N	133		*LR χ² [16]*	47.36	

1984

Race-Based Party Ideology	.772*	1.644****	Education	−.357	.789*
Race, Rights, Taxes	.044	−.163	Gender	−.676	−.057
Moral Restorationism	.210	.220	Income	−.320	−.205
			Cohort	.554	.094
			Constant	−.021	.715
			South	.188	−1.436
N	177		*LR χ² [16]*	47.43	

1988

Race-Based Party Ideology	.059	1.883****	Education	−.298	−.296
Cynical Isolationism	−.099	.496	Gender	.111	.971
Moral Restorationism	−.155	.157	Income	−.747***	.275
Racial Interests	.162	−.122	Cohort	.841	1.065*
			South	.795	.404
			Constant	−1.121	−5.481**
N	120		*LR χ² [18]*	44.47	

1992

Race/Class/International Order-Based Party	−.072	.738***	Education	−.685*	ms.038
Cynicism/Trust in Govt	.098	.374*	Gender	−.121	−.326
Black Nationalism	.290	.383*	Income	−.362	.271
Morally Restorationist-Based Party	.515	.421			
			Cohort	1.138**	.652
			South	1.160*	.497
			Constant	−2.141	−2.929
N	189		*LR χ² [18]*	45.84	

1996

Morally Restorationist-Based Party	.291	1.562****	Education	−.454	.786*
Embrace of Internationalism	−.062	.150	Gender	−.196	.480
Outgroup Antagonism	.125	−.303	Income	−.681****	−.746*
			Cohort	2.711****	−.135
			South	.223	.997
			Constant	−5.374****	−.910
N	147		*LR χ² [16]*	52.19	

Note: Multinomial-Logit Regression estimated via maximum likelihood, with voting Democratic as the base category.
* indicates p<.1(two-tail)
** indicates p<.05(two-tail)
*** indicates p<.025(two-tail)
**** indicates p<.01 (two-tail)
The LR χ² [df] statistic is the difference between likelihood ratios of a model estimated simply with a constant and the models reported above. This is similar to the joint F test of OLS regression.
Source: American National Election Studies (1960–1996)

Mass Attendance Index (% Regular Minus % Never) White Non-Latino Catholics by Age Cohort, 1960–1996

Age at Entry	Year of Entry	1960	1964	1968	1972	1976	1980	1984	1988	1992	1996
81+		*									
77+			*								
73–80		20		*							
69–76			86		*						
65–72		92		*		*					
61–68			61		50		*				
57–64		92		44		49		37			
53–60			59		35		*		*		
49–56		77		45		28		25		55	
45–52			61		47		55		8		*
41–48		63		71		63		40		32	
37–44			71		46		41		61		31
33–40		79		64		33		43		48	
29–36			68		41		50		38		42
25–32		78		51		32		29		11	
21–28			63		45		35		41		20
17–24	1960	86		61		15		29		30	
	1964		53		27		27		49		9
	1968			66		19		17		2	
	1972				13		18		25		3
	1976					29		16		1	
	1980						17		4		19
	1984							6		−1	
	1988								−2		−2
	1992									−20	
	1996										−17
Totals: Roman Catholics, White, N-L		75	63	57	34	30	36	23	21	12	13
% of Group in Regular/ Never Categories		77	68	68	54	49	49	47	48	58	49

Source: American National Election Studies, 1960–1996

THERE IS NO CATHOLIC VOTE—
AND IT'S IMPORTANT

E. J. Dionne Jr.

The story is told of Mrs. O'Reilly being taken to the polls by her son. Mrs. O'Reilly had always voted the straight Democratic ticket. Her son, upwardly mobile like so many American Catholics, had arrived in the upper middle class and split his ticket—in fact, he voted for a lot of Republicans.

As had become ritual on election day, the son turned to his mother and asked: "How are you going to vote?"

And she replied, as she always did, "Straight Democratic."

And the frustrated son turned to his mother and said: "You know mom, if Jesus came back to earth and ran as a Republican, you'd vote against him."

She snapped back: "Oh, hush. Why should He change His party after all these years?"

Whatever you believe about Jesus' party affiliation, we can agree that the days when Mrs. O'Reilly's attitudes defined the Catholic community are gone. As David Leege and many other scholars have shown, the Catholic vote was never quite as uniformly Democratic as we remember because of the out-pouring for John F. Kennedy in 1960. Kennedy won roughly four in five Catholic votes, and that would be true even if you excluded a few extra ballots thrown his way in Chicago. Before the Kennedy election, and especially before the New Deal, the Catholic vote was split in part by competition among Catholic ethnic groups. Italians and my own people, the French Canadians, often feuded with the Irish—inside and outside the church—and many of them gravitated toward the Republicans. Nonetheless, Mrs. O'Reilly was representative enough for a long time. Now her son is almost as represen-tative a figure as she. It's fair to say that there is no "Catholic bloc," nonetheless, the Catholic vote is terribly important. Perhaps 35 to 40 percent of Catholics are reliably Republican. A comparable, slightly larger group, is reliably Democratic, and the rest move around.

Just contemplate these names: Ted Kennedy, Mario Cuomo, Bob Casey, Don Nichols, Rick Santorum, Bill Bennett. They are all members of the Catholic Church. They share remarkably little on election day, or in the arguments leading up to it. At our parish, Bill Bennett sometimes sits near Ted Kennedy. This prompted John Carr of the Catholic Conference to say once that our pastor, Monsignor Tom Duffy, must be either very good or very vague. In truth, he's an excellent pastor, but the diversity of his flock is a comment not only on the challenges he faces, but also on the diversity of the political views within the Catholic Church.

Here is another story, probably apocryphal. Al Smith was sitting around with his advisors during the 1928 presidential campaign. As we all know, Smith was attacked viciously in the nativist and anti-Catholic press. They had, among other things, quoted papal encyclicals, arguing that these pronouncements from Rome were quite inconsistent with American ideals. Smith is reported to have stared across the table at his aides and said: "Just tell me one thing? What is an encyclical?"

True or not, the story suggests that there have always been sharp limits to the impact of the church's formal teachings on the laity. My point here is not to be anti-intellectual, but to suggest that in all our discussions, we shouldn't be overly depressed if there is not always a link between what the church says and what many Catholics do or believe. Nor should we think that this is new.

This also means that the differences among us are often rooted in ideas and impulses only marginally connected to the fact that we are Catholic. This does not mean that Catholic teaching is irrelevant to what we think. It simply accepts Peter Berger's sociology that teaches, at least as I read him, that modernity subjects individuals to a variety of forces and ideas and that the modern person assimilates these as best he or she can. A Catholic trade unionist and a Catholic investment banker who disagree on, say, national health insurance or repealing the capital gains tax are not, I suspect, thinking too much about Catholic social thought when they take their respective stands.

For that reason, among many others, one cannot talk about a Catholic vote. One can talk, at most, about a Catholic tendency. Despite a certain convergence of views among Catholics—a concern for social justice, a collective dedication to the value of the family—Catholics haven't voted as a bloc since the days of Kennedy and Lyndon Johnson. Catholics' loyalties are unpredictable and in flux. Polls suggest that Bush and Gore ran essentially even among Catholics in 2000, with Gore having a slight advantage. Bush made gains among Catholics over Bob Dole's 1996 vote—but Bush made gains across many groups in the electorate.

"Catholics may be the most maddening electoral group in American politics," says Steve Wagner, a Republican pollster, "the demographic bloc that drives pollsters, pundits and politicians of all stripes to distraction."

David Leege puts it this way: "Despite a veritable cottage industry of scholars who have studied religion and politics among American Catholics, a single theory that explains the dynamics of Catholic political behavior has eluded their grasp."

Still, politicians and scholars alike keep trying to figure out Catholics because they must. Catholics are the ultimate swing vote. Rooted in the immigrant ethnic urban culture, Catholics have become increasingly upscale and suburban. They embody the classic American progression: from outsider to insider, from striver to achiever, from union hall to country club. On the way, they have become more sympathetic to the GOP. Republicans would not control Congress—and would not have a chance in presidential elections—if they hadn't succeeded in roughly doubling the approximately 20 percent share of the Catholic vote they got in JFK's election.

Upward mobility hasn't had the same effect on Jews and African Americans who defy their class positions. Catholics merely resist theirs. Nearly three decades ago, Milton Himmelfarb, the thoughtful and puckish scholar of American Judaism, wrote that "Jews have the wealth and status of Episcopalians and vote like Puerto Ricans." His point was that no matter how well-off Jews become, most stick with the Democrats and rally to the cause of outcasts. The same is true of well-to-do African Americans.

Picking up on Himmelfarb, you might say that Catholics are situated somewhere between Jews and African Americans on the one side and Episcopalians on the other. (Though in truth, Episcopalians appear to be moving more Democratic). What's discernable among Catholics is not Democratic dominance, but a Democratic tendency, especially when Catholics are compared with white Protestants. Across income, regional and educational groups, white Catholics are consistently 8 to 12 percent more Democratic than comparable white Protestants.

Catholics are also the ultimate "cross-pressured" group—and this, I will argue later, may give Catholics a chance to make a special contribution to American political life. Many blue-collar and lower-middle class Catholics are tugged toward the Democrats on issues of social justice and workers' rights. But when it comes to family and cultural values, including abortion, they lean toward the Republicans. When Ronald Reagan invoked the trinity of "family, work, and neighborhood," he launched a slogan with enormous power in the old Catholic neighborhoods. When Richard Neuhaus and Peter Berger wrote their important volume, *To Empower People,* back in the 1970s—its emphasis was on the very mediating structures Reagan loved to describe—they might well have been writing the manifesto for the Reagan Democrat, especially the Catholic Reagan Democrat.

Young Catholics live, for the most part, in a more complicated social and moral space. Younger Catholics are more traditional than their non-Catholic peers and more modernist than formal church teaching. Leege has found that they're divided by gender in their political allegiances: Younger Catholic women are more Democratic, younger Catholic men more Republican. Here, one sees a gender gap rooted more in contemporary politics than in anything specifically Catholic, since this split mirrors the overall gender gap.

These pressures and ambivalences make Catholics potentially disruptive for both parties. Catholics who are liberal Democrats are more inclined to oppose abortion than other sorts of liberals. Catholics who are conservative Republicans value tradition and community and not just the free market. Catholics who support the death penalty know how strongly their bishops and their pope oppose it. The evidence from a poll conducted by the Pew Forum on Religion and Public Life and the Pew Research Center shows that when you compare those who support the death penalty and those who oppose it, the opponents are far more likely to say their views are primarily motivated by their religious beliefs.

In short, on so many of the issues in American politics, being a Catholic liberal or a Catholic conservative inevitably means having a bad conscience about something.

All this is confounding for lovers of political labels. Consider the difficulty of categorizing two prominent Catholics, the late Robert Casey and Bill Bennett. As governor of Pennsylvania from 1987 to 1995, Casey was as, or more, liberal than any other Democrat on social welfare and union issues. But he was seen by many as "conservative" solely because of his staunch opposition to abortion. Bennett, a solid conservative, has nonetheless said that "unbridled capitalism is a problem . . . for the whole dimension of things we call the realm of values and human relationships."

Bennett was getting at something a senior White House adviser, Sidney

Blumenthal, noticed in 1997: Why had so many Democrats who had been more or less in favor of free trade in the past declined to give the president "fast-track" authority to negotiate new trade agreements. They were insisting that the agreements include social and labor protections, and that the government do more to assist those who lost jobs or income because of free trade. Blumenthal stared at the list of House members who had turned against the president's position and suddenly noticed that most of the defectors were Catholic. "This was not simple protectionism," Blumenthal says now. "It involved a deeply rooted tradition of Catholic social reform and solidarity."

There's debate over what would constitute "the Catholic vote," even if it were agreed that one existed. Many studies focus on white Catholics—the Irish, Italians, Poles, French Canadians, Portuguese, and others who immigrated to America.

The political histories of these groups differ vastly. Because the Irish dominated many urban Democratic machines around the turn of the century, later immigrants—such as Italians and my people, the French Canadians—often received a warmer welcome from the Republicans. FDR's New Deal and Harry Truman's Fair Deal attracted many of these outlying Catholics to the Democratic Party. Ike drew them toward the Republicans in the 1950s. They came home to JFK and LBJ, but turned away again in 1972—partly in opposition to George McGovern's candidacy but also, as Leege says, in reaction to urban racial issues such as school busing. Richard Nixon's campaign targeted what were called, in one of those terrible terms that only political consultants or perhaps we social scientists can invent, "peripheral urban ethnics." The term was more or less a synonym for white Catholics, "the unmeltable ethnics"—or, at least, only partially melted ethnics—that Michael Novak described in the early 1970s.

Since then, Catholics have split their ballots, especially in presidential elections. Along with Southerners, Catholics formed the heart of the bloc known as "Reagan Democrats." Bill Clinton's ability to regain Catholic votes was a building block of his victories. It's worth remembering how Clinton pulled this off. Yes, "The economy, stupid" helped a lot. But Clinton's strategic corrections in Democratic policy were aimed quite clearly at Reagan Democrats, white southerners, to be sure, but also and perhaps especially Catholics.

The Democratic Leadership Council slogan that Clinton helped coin and then adopted, "Community, Opportunity, Responsibility," might have been the headline of a Catholic bishop's statement. Clinton was marrying toughness on crime and pro-work welfare with a general defense of a compassionate state. Even on abortion, Clinton's use of the phrase "safe, legal, and *rare*" to describe his approach gave Catholics a chance to latch onto the last word—to the later frustration of some who thought he lost that word somewhere along the way. Reading Clinton speeches on voluntary national service, on the positive role of churches, on the importance of rebuilding neighborhoods, one could even imagine that he had read Berger and Neuhaus and Michael Novak's early books on white ethnics (if not his later volumes on capitalism). And in 1996, when Clinton was appealing to soccer moms, he talked about school uniforms and school discipline. Haven't we Catholics heard about those things somewhere before?

It's important, increasingly so by the day, to remember that American Catholicism is less and less defined by those white ethnics. The fastest-growing Catholic group today is Latino. And Latinos can't be thought of as a single bloc, either. Cuban Americans are predominantly Republican; Puerto Ricans, Democratic. Mexican Americans in George W.'s Texas are more willing to vote Republican than Mexican Americans in California, who have become a solid Democratic bloc in response to a Republican-backed ballot initiative aimed at illegal immigrants. Florida went from being a Republican state to a nearly Democratic state in part because non-Cuban Hispanic groups, which tend to be Democratic, now substantially outnumber Cubans. And roughly 10 percent of African Americans are Catholic. But since African American Catholics are solidly Democratic, they tend to be treated by both parties as part of the larger African American vote.

Bush, helped along by conservative Catholics like Steve Wagner and Deal Hudson, was well aware of the inroads Clinton had made in the Catholic vote and wanted to reverse the trend. His early rhetoric in the 2000 campaign seemed aimed directly at wavering Catholics—those who were uneasy with what they perceived as congressional Republican indifference to the poor but also socially conservative and disenchanted with the old welfare state. "Compassionate conservatism" was made to order for such voters. It acknowledges an obligation to the poor while asserting that the best way to express concern is through one-on-one, local initiatives. Bush was not shy about using the word "subsidiarity." His approach, as we know, also emphasized church-based charity and social action. The quotations from John Paul II in Bush speeches—such as his call for a "society of free work, of enterprise, of participation"—emphasized the link between individual and social responsibility.

The Bush strategy fit in with Wagner's theories about Catholic voters, probably because Wagner helped create the strategy. Wagner has argued that the old "social justice" orientation of Catholics has giving way to an emphasis on "social renewal." Partisans of social renewal, he says, are "Mass-attending Catholics" who see the country in "moral decline," are suspicious of popular culture, and worry that the federal government is "inflicting harm on the nation's moral character." You can take issue with Wagner—I'd argue many Catholics favor both social justice and social renewal—but it's a useful theory for Republicans.

Things were going swimmingly for Bush until his visit to Bob Jones University in February of 2000. Given the university's embrace of the oldest forms of anti-Catholicism, it was a Democratic tactician's gift from heaven. But memory of the visit faded, and one could argue—I would—that Democrats missed a beat by not focusing on Catholics as much as the Bush campaign did.

Still, Gore did wax Catholic-friendly. His speech on the importance of "faith-based organizations" could have been written by a prelate—or, very nearly, by a Bush speech writer. Gore has spent a good deal of time during the spring of 2000 talking about the importance of family and parental responsibility. His positions on most social justice issues were certainly closer to those of the Catholic bishops than Bush's. But there was also abortion. In the end, the split vote between Bush and Gore might be seen as standing for the split political personality of American Catholicism—a term I use not to describe some sort of mental illness, but a reality. It's a reality, as I'll conclude, that could be quite helpful to American politics.

But before I get to that, I want to stress again something that many people, for good and principled reasons, may want to resist: that political differences within our community have little to do with doctrine, theology or interpretation of the faith. At the risk of seeming a bit determinist, I want to spend a few moments stressing good old-fashioned demographic factors, including class. I do this not to be a Marxist, but to be a realist.

First, while differences between Catholics and Protestants persist at all income levels, the Catholic vote for the Republicans rises quite steadily with income. Andrew Greeley has made the point that over the last one hundred years, American Catholics have become far wealthier. This has been very good news for Republicans.

Second, there are large regional differences in the voting behavior and political allegiances of Catholics, especially white Catholics. Briefly, Catholics who live in the Northeast and Midwest are more Democratic than Catholics who live in the South and the West. One theory here is that white Catholics who remained in the original areas of immigrant settlement are more likely to maintain older loyalties than those who moved away. White Catholics in the South especially vote very much like Southern whites.

Third, you cannot understand political attitudes without understanding who hates whom at a given moment—or, to be more charitable, who is competing with whom for power and position at any given moment.

Just to pick one example of the importance of the who-hates-whom thesis: work by Doug Schoen and Milton Gwirtzman has compared the political attitudes and behavior of Massachusetts Catholics and New York Catholics. Schoen and Gwirtzman found that New York Catholics were consistently roughly 20 points more Republican than Massachusetts Catholics. Why such a difference? Does rooting for the Yankees instead of the Red Sox account for it? No. Both Schoen and Gwitzman theorized that the basic reason was that Catholics in the different states had different rivals.

In Massachusetts, political competition came to be defined for decades as a straightforward contest between Yankees and Catholics—essentially Protestants and Catholics. The Protestants were Republicans so the Catholics were Democrats. In New York, competition was more complex, pitting Catholics, Protestants and Jews—and, later, African Americans and Hispanics—against each other in a complex battle for power. Jews and Catholics were often engaged in a robust competition for influence in the Democratic Party. The result was that one or the other often defected to the Republicans—or, in the case of many Jews in the 1930s and 1940s, to left-of-center third parties. Racial politics further muddied the battle lines. The clearest evidence that this very old cleavage still has an effect is that while many conservative Catholics in New York simply became Republicans, they often did so by way of the New York State Conservative Party founded by two men with the lovely names of O'Doherty and Mahoney who went on to run a man named Buckley for mayor of New York City. Most conservative Catholics in Massachusetts, by contrast, remain Democrats to this day.

When George McGovern carried Massachusetts and—other than the District of Columbia—Massachusetts alone in 1972, I told many friends that it wasn't because of Harvard or MIT. It was because many of my Catholic neighbors were still voting for Al Smith (and, of course, John F. Kennedy). Needless to say, Richard Nixon carried New York in 1972 with a large Catholic vote.

Let us also be frank that reaction around racial issues drove many Catholics toward the Republicans in the 1960s and 1970s. We Catholics have not—to be charitable to us—been in the forefront of the battle for racial equality, even if many progressive church leaders did battle for civil rights in the 1960s. The draft riots, reflecting the opposition to the Civil War among Irish Catholics, in New York, were indicative of Catholic attitudes then. Jonathan Rieder's fine book *Canarsie*, which is subtitled *Catholics and Jews in New York Against Liberalism*, is a brilliant and fair look at racial reaction in the 1960s and 1970s. Yes, there was racism, but some of that racial reaction also grew out of the fact that blue collar Catholics in big cities often found themselves in direct competition with African Americans and Latinos. And Catholic communalism also came into play. Gerald Gamm's work on Boston showing the importance of local community to Catholics is helpful in explaining the complexity of Catholic reaction on race.

I say all this to underscore that we need to face up to the fact that Catholic political attitudes and behavior owe a great deal to social and economic factors and not necessarily to theology. Catholics often take a partisan or ideological position for reasons outside their faith, and then look backward to justify their stance on the basis of faith. This is not unique to Catholics. C. S. Lewis grasped this phenomenon long ago when he argued, "Most of us are not really approaching the subject in order to find out what Christianity says," Lewis wrote. "We are approaching it in the hope of finding support from Christianity for the views of our own party."

But pure skepticism is not sufficient. The fact is that many Catholics reach their political conclusions through reflection upon their faith. To speak for myself, I grew up in a conservative family and became more liberal in large part by reflecting on what Catholicism said about social justice and just war. There are many like me. And there are also many Catholics who began life as New Deal liberals and became more conservative because of their reflections on Catholic teaching about the family and abortion.

Having spoken skeptically of how much attention Catholics pay to church teaching, papal statements, and bishops' letters, it's also worth saying that Catholics hear these arguments even when they do not always agree with them. Oddly, a church that is seen as dogmatic may, in its involvement in the public square, have a moderating effect on politics. Conservative Catholics who cheer the church's stance on abortion are affected by what it says about war and peace and social justice and the death penalty. They are pushed away from a narrowly ideological conservatism. Liberal Catholics who cheer what the church says about social justice and just war are affected by what it says about abortion and family life and assisted suicide. They are pushed away from a narrowly ideological liberalism.

Think of what this means for each of our political parties. Catholic Democrats are, within their party, a moderating force on family issues, abortion and assisted suicide. Catholic Republicans moderate an endorsement of a sink-or-swim free market. Catholic Democrats and Republicans alike call attention to the importance of mediating structures, of solidarity and subsidiarity, of the importance of both social and individual responsibility.

This will not be good enough for those of us who are liberal Catholics and cannot understand why our Republican Catholic friends still endorse huge tax cuts for the rich and are not willing to invest in health care for all or adequate assistance to the poorest in our midst. It will not be good enough for conservative Catholics who cannot understand why their Democratic Catholic friends are not tough enough on abortion, often support gay rights and opposed the impeachment of Bill Clinton.

But this confluence of attitudes may well be useful to our Republic. Catholics may not constitute a powerhouse vote, but we might be an immensely useful ginger group, a kind of leaven in each coalition. On the whole, we are, as William Bole argued in *Commonweal* (September 13, 2002), "soft communitarians." We are likely to find ourselves quite loyally, but not always comfortably, supporting our respective parties. Discomfort is not a bad thing. A bit of discomfort may be exactly what contemporary politics needs.

The days are gone when taking Communion and pulling the Democratic lever are the outward signs of a good Catholic. But all of us might usefully challenge the parties in which we find ourselves. Catholic Democrats might suggest that social justice and a concern for the health of family life go together. Catholic Republicans could argue that acting on behalf of society's least fortunate is part of a consistent ethic of life—and, in the long run, good for the survival of capitalism.

We're supposed be in the world but not of the world. If our faith is actually important to us, we should use it to challenge ourselves, challenge our friends and allies, and challenge our nation.

CATHOLIC REPUBLICANS

Kate O'Beirne

There is no Catholic vote, in the sense that there is a recognizable black vote or Jewish vote. But even though there's not a recognizable Catholic block, there are certainly Catholic—E. J. Dionne calls them tendencies; I call them sensibilities—that do affect how Catholics vote.

Catholics are no longer reliably Democratic. The old Pat and Mike joke had Pat reporting to Mike that he heard Sean O'Connor had voted Republican, to which Mike responds, "That's a dirty lie. I saw him at Mass." It's also certainly true that many former Reagan Democrats, largely ethnic Catholics or southern whites, are now very comfortably Bush Republicans. Over the past twenty years, they have become part of the Republican base. This changing face of the Republican Party is obvious on Capitol Hill: There are more Irish Catholic Republicans in the House than there are Irish Catholic Democrats. These are Reagan babies, who came of age politically during Reagan's presidency.

It's not uncommon to talk to former Irish Catholic Democrats and have them explain to you that the Democratic Party pushed them away. My husband's not a bad example of this—an Irish Catholic Democrat from New York who served in Vietnam in 1968 after graduating from Fordham University. Back in the days of "acid, amnesty, and abortion," the Democrats lost the allegiance of many ethnic Catholics like my husband. They've migrated, over time, over to the Republicans. So, yes, part of this shift occurs as they move up the income scale, but part of it is a range of those cultural issues where many people like Jim O'Beirne felt the Democratic Party no longer represented what it once had.

Having said that, let me also acknowledge that more Catholics call themselves conservative than call themselves Republican. Catholics identify themselves as conservative over liberal on a ratio of two to one, but more identify themselves as conservative than as Republican. This tells me that there's still a Catholic discomfort with the Republican brand name. E. J. Dionne is exactly right: what makes the Catholic vote so important is that such a big piece of it is made up of swing voters—they're up for grabs. That's who the parties compete for. They have to. Those swing voters decide elections. When I was asked, during the course of 2000, who would win the Catholic vote, I said, "Whoever winds up in the White House," because they wouldn't get there without a majority of Catholic votes. As it turns out, of course, Al Gore marginally carried Catholics overall, and won the popular vote.

There is a major oversight in E. J.'s analysis. It's impossible to talk about the Catholic vote and understand it without recognizing that there are two components: one, religious identity; two, religious commitment. E. J. talked about differences among Catholic voters based on class or geography. But the biggest difference is based on whether or not they're practicing Catholics. Across religious groups, according to polls, whether or not you go to church is going to have a bigger impact on your vote than whether you're rich or poor.

The pollsters define active Catholics as attending Mass at least four times a month, which represents, unfortunately, only about 42 percent of those who call themselves Catholic. Overall, 20 percent do not attend Mass in a typical month. In 1980, religiously active Catholics, so defined, voted more Republican than the national average for the first time. I think Reagan's optimism, humor, and deep faith in America appealed to those religiously active Catholics.

By 1996, inactive Catholics voted 55 to 33 in favor of Clinton, while religiously active Catholics voted 47 to 44 for Bob Dole. Overall, Bill Clinton carried 53 percent of the Catholic vote. I always thought Bob Dole, though he carried a plurality of religiously active Catholics, should have had an easier time appealing to Catholics. It's a patriotic vote and he was a veteran. I also thought Catholics would find his sort of worldview appealing. His life's motto is probably something like, "Life is hard, and then you die"—to me, such an appealing Catholic message. But it was not to be. I have to assume many Catholics agreed with others that Bob Dole seemed too old, out of touch, and not quite up to the job. But in any event, religiously active Catholics have been fairly reliably Republican voters over the past twenty years.

Catholics, overall, liked Ike, and voted for Nixon. First time around, they barely gave Ronald Reagan a majority. By 1984, he enjoyed 54 percent—this is the overall Catholic vote. George Bush faired less well among Catholics. In fact, Perot garnered a fair number of Catholic votes. George W. Bush in 2000 made an obvious attempt, as E. J. said, to appeal to Catholics, the first time there was such a serious attempt on the part of Republicans.

I wrote an article early in 1995 pointing out the key role the Catholic vote played in the 1994 elections. For the first time in modern history, Catholics had voted for congressional Republicans, which played a major role in handing the House to Republicans. I don't think there was a Republican on Capitol Hill who appreciated that. But then, Catholic voters very reliably went back to the Democrats down the ticket. Democrats are much more attuned than Republicans to the Catholic vote. That remains the case, although Republicans are making a serious effort. The Democrats appreciate that they've lost a reliable part of their base. If small business owners started abandoning the Republican Party, there would be an awful lot of attention paid to how to win them back. The Republicans passively became the beneficiaries of this disaffection with Democrats; they are unsure how it happened and are still flailing around, but, as I said, are making a serious effort in trying to be more attractive to Catholic voters.

Forty years after a young Catholic candidate traveled to Houston to reassure the local Baptists and Methodists that his faith would be left at the door of the Oval Office, a young Methodist candidate headed out of Texas to make a direct appeal to Catholic voters. As E. J. said, much of George Bush's message rejected the antigovernment rhetoric of the Republicans and the focus on economic issues that frequently characterizes many Republican politicians. The governor talked about touching every willing heart, the need to make sure that no child was left behind. He emphasized the importance of addressing the spiritual needs of the disadvantaged. He said that we shouldn't disdain government. (I was so upset when he said that.) Much of his agenda reflects the Catholic principle of subsidiarity, the emphasis on local control and local options, the need for the government to recruit local faith-based groups in delivering services to the poor; the Bush-Cheney ticket was unambiguously pro-life.

I don't mean to suggest that candidate Bush cynically adopted this message to win Catholic voters. I do think he's a deeply religious man. It reflects his own political philosophy, shaped, in part, by Michael Novak and other Catholic intellectuals. But his Austin operatives were always conscious of the need to appeal to Catholics.

Having said that, what about some of the more well-covered cases during the 2000 campaign—the flap over Bob Jones University in South Carolina? I didn't talk to a single Catholic who much cared about the marginalized views of a school they had never heard of. On the other hand, too little attention has been paid to the ads John McCain ran in Michigan, following South Carolina, and the so-called Catholic voter alert phone calls that Cardinal Maida in Detroit condemned as an improper use of the Catholic religion to try to score political points. Remember, there was a flap over whether or not McCain's campaign was actually paying for them. It turned out that he was. There was a backlash to that: the sensitivity of Catholics seeing their religion used in that way.

Following Michigan, George Bush won the New York State primary and carried Catholic voters in New York. The controversy over those phone calls was still being talked about in New York. But Bob Jones University didn't matter to Catholics. I heard more resistance among Catholic voters who realized that George W. Bush doesn't drink than I did about Bob Jones. The not drinking made them deeply suspicious. I had to explain that he used to have a drinking problem, and that they seemed to think was okay.

Democrats appreciate far more than the Republicans that one matter that unites Catholics of all stripes is anti-Catholicism. A quick example of that would be the flap over the designation of a new chaplain to serve the House. The Democrats were all over that instantaneously, appreciating that if they could make the case that House Republicans had discriminated against a Catholic priest, it would be dynamite. Republicans had no idea that that issue was going to take off, that it was going to be credible, and that it was going to be a problem, for two reasons. First, they were actually quite innocent, dopey, but innocent about the whole incident. Second, talking to Evangelical friends, I found that they don't think there's such a thing as anti-Catholicism. They're surprised that there's a sensitivity on the part of Catholics. All I can figure is that they feel themselves so mocked in the popular culture (you know, the *Washington Post* can actually get away with calling them poor, uneducated, and easily led). They see Catholics as this huge church, with elite universities, who have the respect of intellectuals, whose members are respected, successful people. It's a lack of understanding about the history of anti-Catholicism, about the sensibilities we bring as immigrant ethnics. Having made the case that anti-Catholicism is a potential issue for Catholic voters, I don't think it was in play, even during the primaries, to much extent in 2000.

I want to highlight another potential problem for Republicans—the death penalty. Public opinion is shifting against the death penalty, and both parties, over time, risk being on the wrong side of it. A majority, according to the latest polls I've seen, still support it, but it's down 15 points in the past fifteen years, from about 80 to about 66 percent. Here, Catholics do track with public opinion. Thirty-five percent of Catholics oppose the death penalty, 57 percent favor it. Of those Catholics who oppose the death penalty, 34 percent have come to that decision recently. It clearly reflects John Paul II's recent strong reservations about the death penalty. For the benefit of candidates, *National Review* published a piece last year warning about this shift in opinion. We thought it was potentially far more problematic for George Bush than Al Gore. Both supported the death penalty, but Gore could back it in the abstract, while Governor Bush regularly presided over executions in Texas. Tonally at some parts during the campaign, George Bush was flirting with real problems with the death penalty, making it even harder. As I said, he didn't have the luxury of supporting it in the abstract like Al Gore. I do think that's one of the impacts, as E. J. said, that Catholics, in the base of the Republican Party, can have over time on the Republicans.

One problem in talking about Catholic voters is that, owing to the fact that we have so scrupulously separated religion and politics, politicking in our pews is verboten. Catholics typically don't think of themselves as Catholic voters. They don't self identify as Catholic voters. We are teachers, social workers, business owners, nurses, parents—and we vote as those, which is not to say there aren't Catholic sensibilities. But as I said, we're not self-aware as voters, per se.

Finally the Republican Party couldn't be the majority party if it were not pro-life. The evidence is depressing, for a conservative, but fairly clear that there's probably a national majority for Democratic economic policy. But since the Democratic Party has been in the grip of social leftists, the social issues have made the crucial difference for the Republicans. This is especially true with respect to Catholics, who have migrated to the GOP. Democrats were on the wrong side of ethnic Catholic voters during the cold war. Reagan appealed to Catholics on this ground. He was a strong anticommunist. You can't leave church every Sunday praying for the conversion of Russia and not be impressed with Ronald Reagan's commitment to fighting the cold war, to the need for a strong defense.

We have a new challenge facing us, but it is less ideological than the one that shaped our politics for so many years. With the end of the Soviet Union, the Democrats are less apt to be hurt by the perception that they were sometimes on the wrong side of that fight. A study about Catholic attitudes (carried out by CARA at Georgetown for the Catholics in the Public Square Project) asked Catholic Republicans, what is more important: improving government services in education and health care, even if it means higher spending, or cutting taxes and reducing government spending? Forty-one percent of Catholic Republicans answered higher spending rather than cutting taxes and reducing government spending. These Catholic Republicans are not libertarians drawn to the party because of its small government, lower taxes message. They are there because of a range of social issues. And if the Republican Party were not pro-life, I think many of these Catholic Republicans would go very comfortably back to the Democratic Party and Dick Gephardt's economics. Another blunt polling question asks: who has responsibility for helping poor people? Society or the individual? Catholic Republicans are far friendlier to the proposition that it is society's responsibility as opposed to a caricature of the Republican message: let them pull themselves up by their bootstraps.

So why are Catholics hanging around the Republican Party? A range of social issues—specifically, it seems to me, abortion. Yet, although over time Catholic Republicans have become disaffected with the Democrats, it's also obvious, given party-identification polling data, that they still have not found a comfortable new home in the GOP.

COMMUNITARIAN LITE

William Bole

When President George W. Bush gave the commencement speech at the University of Notre Dame in 2001, he did not hesitate to invoke the legacy of Dorothy Day, the patron saint of American Catholic radicalism, and proclaim "God's special concern for the poor." What stirred these thoughts in a president known for his political conservatism and support for big business? At Notre Dame, Bush was enacting what has been dubbed the "Catholic strategy," the courting of churchgoing Catholics by his administration. After putting that and other political projects on hold after September 11, the Republican National Committee renewed its outreach to Catholics during this midterm election year.

The undertaking is similar to the Republican wooing of evangelical Protestants in past decades, a project that has to be judged a success: churchgoing white evangelicals are now almost wholly appended to the party (having given Bush 84 percent of their vote, according to a post-election survey by political scientist John C. Green and colleagues at the University of Akron). Some strategists believe active Catholics are ready to imitate evangelicals in this regard, moving to the Republican Party because of its political conservatism and promises of moral restoration, including its opposition to abortion. Yet party operatives must also think Catholics are somehow different. Why else would Bush proclaim at Notre Dame a preferential option for the poor?

The Democrats have no parallel scheme to speak of, but there is another Catholic strategy at play among the American bishops, though it has been rather eclipsed recently by their concerns with clergy sex scandals. The bishops have their own ideological approach that can move to the left or the right, depending on the issue. They are often seen shifting in one direction when pressing for government assistance to the needy and in another direction when advocating traditional moral norms regarding birth, death, family, and society. At the core of this approach, however, is a call to Catholics to embrace a communitarian ethic, one that seeks to curb individualistic excess in all quarters of life, from the family to the economy.

Are Catholics in the United States tilting toward either of these strategies? How many are attracted to either the wall-to-wall conservatism of Republicans (with room, at least occasionally, for references to compassion), or to the bishops' more communitarian stance?

From a larger point of view, the pressing question is whether the more than 60 million Americans who call themselves Catholic make a distinct contribution to public life. Are their political values any reflection of Catholic teaching and tradition? Are their views much different from those of other Americans? If so, are they different for religious reasons, because of their faith and exposure to the Catholic ethos?

HALF-FULL OR HALF-EMPTY?

Despite the intermittent buzz about Catholic strategies or, a few years ago, about a "Catholic moment," research about the political sympathies of Catholics, especially the religious factor in those sympathies, is surprisingly sparse or tentative. Some original data and useful measures have been compiled as a result of the three-year-long American Catholics in the Public Square project initiated in 2000 by *Commonweal* and the Faith & Reason Institute in Washington, with support from the Pew Charitable Trusts. The idea was not to see which voting levers Catholics pull or to count their dimpled chads, but to bring to light their underlying values and attitudes toward the connection of their faith to public life. The project commissioned the Center for Applied Research in the Apostolate (CARA) at Georgetown University to conduct focus groups nationwide and two national telephone surveys during election year 2000 (this CARA survey can be found at: www.cara.georgetown.edu/forgeria/Public_Square.pdf).

There will be little astonishment that the opinions of American Catholics are not always in line with Catholic social teaching. Most Catholics are not clones of their bishops, whose rare political blood type reads liberal on economic and international issues and conservative on moral and cultural issues such as abortion. Most Catholics are not card-carrying communitarians, who (if there were such a club) could be counted on to espouse an anti-libertarian attitude or ideology. Nor are they true believers in the consistent ethic of life, which threads through causes such as the rights of the unborn and justice for the poor as well as an end to capital punishment. Many Catholics do, however, nurse sympathies in these directions.

Surveys conducted for the Public Square project signal what could be called a "consistent-ethic lite" or soft communitarianism among Catholics. Other research has revealed Catholics as being somewhat to the left of other Americans on bread-and-butter issues and to the right on lifestyle questions. The research conducted by CARA digs further into these somewhat different political positions, priorities, and self-understandings.

"Somewhat" may begin to look quite different when questions are put to highly religious Catholics, who are—by some measures—alternately liberal and conservative, unlike highly religious Protestants who are more inclined to stay steadily in the conservative corner. The views of these faithful Mass-goers are a leading link to the question of whether religion makes a difference in the political attitudes of Catholics.

An opening question is whether Catholics are at all taken with the idea of folding faith into their political choices. In the telephone survey taken in January and February 2000, 2,635 adult (self-identified) Catholics were asked how much they draw on their faith and values in making political decisions. About one-quarter replied "very much" and 21 percent said "not at all," with the largest portion (38 percent) giving a "somewhat" response, and the smallest (14 percent) saying "not much." One could ruminate on whether this represents a half-full or half-empty glass of Catholic commitment. More revealing, perhaps, is what happens when Catholics talk it over, albeit in the contrived focus group setting.

A review of transcripts of the eighteen sessions, held in fifteen cities, reveals an interesting pattern: though parishioners often started out hazy or contrary on the given subject, faith connections grew as they tossed around the topics. Consistent-ethic language resonated even with some parishioners who seemed ambivalent about one life issue or the other. A police officer in a suburban Phoenix parish, speaking ambiguously about capital punishment, said, "On the other hand, as I get older, I also see the pope's perspective. We cannot take human life lightly and we tend to take [it] lightly."

The focus group participants sounded more Catholic when they had time to consider and shade their first reactions. Some groups warmed to Catholicism's cordial view of political community, with scarcely a nudge from facilitators. Discussions often began with the usual put-downs of politicians and government, before settling into neutral or thankful sentiments. "When you look at it, government's done pretty good. It's fought wars and won them . . . gotten out of depressions. So I think we're a little harsh sometimes," a suburban Atlanta parishioner declared.

Hard numbers, too, tell of a soft communitarianism or "consistent-ethic lite." Consider a pair of findings from the second telephone survey of twelve hundred Catholics in September 2000. Although closely divided between self-identified pro-life and pro-choice people, most opposed access to abortion in most circumstances, the two clear exceptions being a threat to the mother's life and fetal deformity. Arguably, this landed them near the conservative camp on that issue. On social welfare issues and the role of government, however, they cruised toward the liberal side. Sixty-two percent favored "improving government services such as education and health care, even if it means higher spending." Unexpectedly, a fair number of Catholic Republicans—41 percent—held that view. Only 38 percent of all those polled thought "cutting taxes and reducing government spending" were more important.

When it comes to identifying themselves ideologically, Catholics, not surprisingly, are like most Americans more at peace with the conservative label than with the "L" word. More interesting, this identification swings in accord with the category of issues. So Catholics were most likely to think of themselves as conservative on "moral issues like abortion" (42 percent) and least likely to say they are conservative "when it comes to social welfare programs that help the poor and needy" (29 percent). As for self-identified liberals and moderates, both groups outnumbered conservatives on social welfare issues (the Ls just barely), but neither came close to doing so on moral issues. Basically, Catholics split their ideological vote in the January-February 2000 poll.

ARE MASSGOERS DISTINCTIVE?

These leanings can seem weightier among highly religious Catholics. As would be expected, those who said they attend church at least every week or that faith is most important to them are most likely to reject abortion. (Nearly one-third of those surveyed reported attending Mass weekly or more often, and 18 percent saw Catholicism as the most important part of their lives.) They were also more likely than other Catholics to sympathize with the plight of the poor and to support a social assault on poverty. One question asked whether the responsibility for getting poor people out of poverty rests primarily with "poor people themselves" or with society. Among weekly communicants or those who say that faith is most important to them, 70 percent said that society was responsible. That is nearly 20 points higher than among less committed Catholics.

That too might be expected, given the church's social teachings. In any case, the finding suggests these Catholics pursue a distinctive path in American politics. Among Americans generally, greater faith commitment normally equals greater likelihood of political conservatism—across categories of issues—or at least that is the accepted wisdom. "That pattern doesn't hold among Catholics," explains Sister Mary E. Bendyna, a political scientist who supervised the data collection and analysis for CARA with sociologist Paul M. Perl. While religious commitment pulls Catholics in conservative directions on moral and cultural issues, it frequently routes them in liberal directions on social welfare as well as capital punishment and immigration, as Bendyna showed in her illuminating doctoral dissertation at Georgetown two years ago. "Catholics are different," she adds.

Admittedly, the findings about daily-bread liberalism can be open to different interpretations in these and other studies. Still, indications of liberal sympathy on bread-and-butter issues leap out enough to suggest that while Americans may have been more upbeat about the intervening role of government after September 11, practicing Catholics have been well ahead of that political curve. For example, on a cluster of questions related to the scope of government, other data have shown committed Catholics registering as more liberal than liberal Protestants and secular Americans, not to mention evangelicals and other Catholics. (They are, as is to be expected, less liberal than black Protestants and Jews.) They also come across as relatively liberal on race but not on the environment and defense, in research gathered by Andrew Kohut, John C. Green, Scott Keeter, and Robert C. Toth, in *The Diminishing Divide: Religion's Changing Role in American Politics* (Brookings Institution, 2000).

Priest-sociologist-author Andrew Greeley has limned a Catholic imagination or sensibility that sees "grace lurking everywhere," as he styles it in *The Catholic Imagination* (University of California Press, 2000). Could it be that Catholics see grace lurking even in the Social Security Administration? Republican pollster Steve Wagner of QEV Analytics in Washington probably wouldn't put it that way, but even he urges President Bush and others in the Republican Party not to use blanket antigovernment rhetoric "within earshot of Catholic voters" (advice rendered on his Web site, www.qev.com). Coming from a different direction, Notre Dame political scientist David Leege probably wouldn't put it that way either. He allows only that religiously minded Catholics are ever so slightly more likely than less religious ones to sympathize with the poor and favor antipoverty programs, based on data he has analyzed (in "The Catholic Voter," a paper delivered to the joint consultation of *Commonweal* and the Faith & Reason Institute, June 2000; www .catholicsinpublicsquare.org). Leege agrees that Catholics in general look at the world through a more communitarian lens, but he sees pale evidence that this translates into greater zeal for social justice among religiously active Catholics.

The ambiguity of these findings undoubtedly has something to do with the way questions are asked. Perhaps when the questions get too close to the pocketbook, too specific about taxes and spending (and thus removed from general sentiments about helping the poor), middle-class Mass-going Catholics back off. A more interesting possibility has to do with the basic matter of who gets counted as "highly religious." Researchers use standard measures like frequency of church attendance and Bible reading, which supposedly work well enough for Protestants. Specifically Catholic indicators—like whether someone sees the Eucharist as pivotal to one's own Catholic identity—are often lacking, however. Without that sort of empirical lens, we could have too narrow a view of how Catholic identity acts upon Catholics in the public square.

The surveys conducted by CARA took a stab at such measures. The results, although hardly definitive, suggest a high correlation between a communitarian politics (with a social justice outlook) and characteristically Catholic attitudes, including the importance placed on the Eucharist, following church teaching, and learning more about the Catholic faith, as well as helping those in need. Catholics were categorized here as communitarian if they explicitly identified themselves as conservative on moral issues and explicitly admitted to being liberal on social welfare issues. This is a stiffer standard than the measures of opinion on different issues, measures revealing more of a soft communitarianism. Such "hard" communitarians constituted only 10 percent of those questioned, but, all tallied, they scored highest in distinctively Catholic measures.

IS THERE A "CATHOLIC" ETHIC?

So, Catholics may be different, but why they would be is less easy to assess. If they are more likely than other Americans to view the world through a

DRAWING ON THEIR FAITH

As related in this essay, many Catholics evince a "soft communitarianism" that sidles somewhat to the left on social-welfare issues and somewhat right on questions like abortion. Yet there are also "hard" communitarians of the type spotted in one study commissioned by the Public Square Project.

In that CARA survey of Catholic opinion, a little less than two-thirds of the respondents could be placed in clear-cut ideological categories. Respondents were classified as communitarian if they explicitly identified themselves as conservative on "moral issues" and liberal on "welfare" issues having to do with government spending and programs for the poor. That explicit standard was met by 10 percent of the 2,635 Catholics polled. Other ideological types pinpointed in the survey included those who say they are consistently conservative (18 percent of the sample), consistently liberal (16 percent), consistently moderate (16 percent), and libertarian, which is communitarian in reverse—to the right on welfare and left on morality (6 percent).

These "hard" communitarians racked up high scores on the scales of Catholic religiosity (see chart), according to the findings, which came with a two-point margin of error. They are far more likely than any of the other ideological types to say helping the needy is very important to what it means to be a Catholic, and just as likely as conservatives to say the same about the Eucharist. They are somewhat less insistent than conservatives on "following church teaching," but clearly more interested in "learning more about the Catholic faith." Communitarians are also distinctly more likely than conservatives and those of other stripes to say they draw on their faith in making political choices.

communitarian lens, is that because of a distinctive Catholic sensibility? Bendyna, Perl, and other CARA researchers would likely say yes. They seem partial to sociologist John E. Tropman's explanation, in *The Catholic Ethic in American Society* (Jossey-Bass, 1995), that there is a Catholic ethic that values sharing and mutuality above achievement and self-reliance, as well as to Greeley's Catholic-imagination thesis. Some polling (by Greeley and others) has teased this out, but Leege of Notre Dame is among those who demand harder evidence that religiosity tilts Catholics in this direction.

Leege's skepticism has much to do with his reading of religiously active Catholics as not appreciably more sympathetic toward the poor than other Catholics (about which he and others among us will have to agree to disagree, lacking better measures). He is far more impressed by generational factors, including the fact that older Catholics, churchgoing and non-churchgoing alike, tend to be more liberal in these matters than younger Catholics. (This may be a generational difference that transcends religious denominations.) Older Catholics are also more Democratic in party affiliation, though gender is another factor. "And so, it's really a race between the stork and the grim reaper," said Leege in an interview, noting that since the New Deal generation of Catholics, each successive generation has been less communitarian-minded in its politics than the previous one.

There is another precinct to be heard from on this matter. Wagner, the Republican pollster, believes Catholics are making public space for their faith, but that increasingly this space is reserved for moral conservatism or restoration. Pointedly, he argues that committed Catholics are trading in their traditional social-justice orientation, which he derides as "an ideology of victimization," for a "social renewal" orientation that targets declining moral standards. This, he argued at a June 2000 consultation of the American Catholics in the Public Square Project, is propelling them irreversibly into the Republican coalition.

Wagner's latest exhibit A, as presented in the January 2001 issue of *Crisis,* is the 2000 presidential election, in which weekly churchgoing Catholics went for Bush, noticeably though not dramatically, according to several surveys. This, however, isn't hermetic proof that religious faith is shepherding these Catholics into the GOP. Leege points out that in the broad middle class, higher income is usually associated with higher rates of churchgoing, and so strictly on that basis, it is not surprising that weekly communicants might be more likely than other Catholics to vote Republican. In addition, he notes that when it comes to the Catholic vote, the steadiest gains for Republicans have been among younger Catholics, who are less churchgoing than older ones.

Put another way, Wagner argues that religiously active Catholics are ripe for Bush's Catholic strategy, which emphasizes moral restoration. Meanwhile, the CARA findings provide hints that Catholics are open to the other Catholic strategy, the one gleaned from the bishops' communitarian agenda.

LEANING REPUBLICAN?

Are faithful Catholics flocking into the Republican fold? Unquestionably, say the party's proselytizers, though the evidence they offer is in fact questionable.

It is true that Catholics who said they attend Mass once a week went for George W. Bush, by a 53 to 44 margin, according to exit polls, but those who preferred Democrat Al Gore hardly constituted an apostate bloc. Those who reported attending church three times a month opted for Gore by precisely the same ratio that the self-identified weekly worshipers turned out for Bush, according to the exit surveys by Voter News Service (which are not infallible).

Furthermore, while the most frequent Catholic worshipers voted for Bush, they did so far less conspicuously than did other religious Americans. For example, among those who say they attend religious services more than once a week, Protestants gave Bush 74 percent of their vote, compared with 52 percent among the more-than-weekly Catholic communicants, again according to exit surveys.

Lastly, it is far from clear that most religiously active Catholics who went Republican were intending to vote with their faith. As political scientist David Leege points out (see main article), in the broad middle class higher rates of churchgoing usually go hand in hand with higher income. Many of those more-than-average Massgoers may have been voting with their deeper-than-average pockets.

In that spirit, *Washington Post* columnist and Brookings Institution scholar E. J. Dionne believes Catholics can act as a "ginger group, a kind of leaven" in each party, as he said at the Public Square consultation in June 2000. That is to say, Catholics can talk up the limits of free markets among Republicans and the need to temper lifestyle individualism among Democrats. The third possibility, one staked out by Leege, is that neither of these strategies is very appealing to many Catholics.

What, then, of the influence of the bishops, clergy, and Catholic institutions? Are Catholics responding to political cues or social sensibilities deriving from these sources? Catholics are themselves unsure. Among those who draw on their faith "very much" in making political decisions, only about one quarter mentioned the influence of homilies or church leaders, and less than a third pointed to parishes. The largest segment (44 percent) gave a nod to Catholic education, in the data compiled by CARA.

As for homilies, past studies have rated them rickety conveyers of Catholic social attitudes. CARA researchers found that the people they polled thought of social issues as important to the extent that they heard more homilies on such topics, but the association was on the whole a modest one. On this empirical trail we find the usual suspects, those who attend church weekly or more often: these Catholics were the ones most influenced by sermons touching on the poor and social justice. The more frequently they heard such homilies (in their recollection), the more likely they were to see government programs to help the needy as very important. That would certainly pass as a religious influence on social justice thinking.

CREATIVELY AMBIGUOUS

By and large, research for the Public Square project shows that Catholics do have some distinctive ideological traits. Those traits may be strongest in the case of the most active Catholics, who tend to be picky about the conservative causes they support, at least in comparison to committed Protestants, who make fewer distinctions in that regard. Many other, less committed Catholics also like to think of themselves as drawing to some extent on their faith in making political choices. The focus groups indicate further that parishioners are able to see, when given a chance for reflection, that there is a connection between what they believe personally and collectively as Catholics, and the ways in which they live as citizens and voters. They come to recognize a social Catholicism as something that affects their lives in the public square.

The most important caveat to all this might be culled from Leege's research into developments along gender and generational lines. Catholic men and women in their twenties and thirties tend to have weaker ties to the institutional church than other Catholics, and some studies intimate that young men and women are moving politically apart from each other and the church. Leege has found that young adult Catholic men are increasingly attracted to the Republican Party out of devotion to rugged conservative economics, while young adult Catholic women are trending Democratic, lured partly by moral-cultural liberalism ("'choice" in reproductive and lifestyle

Meaning of Faith by Ideological Positions on Issues

Percentage saying each is "very important" to what it means to be Catholic

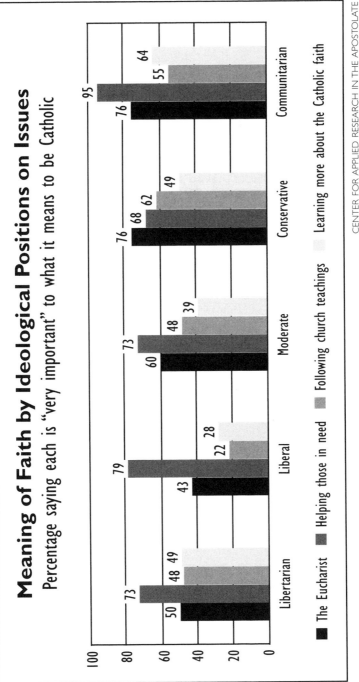

■ The Eucharist ■ Helping those in need ■ Following church teachings ▒ Learning more about the Catholic faith

matters) as well as the old lunch-bucket liberalism. Individualist creeds are fueling these developments, more noticeably among men than women.

One is tempted to say that if this trend sharpens in certain directions, the picture painted here may change radically, as far as a broad engagement of American Catholic identity with public life is concerned. In the aggregate, Catholics, especially males, would come across as less communitarian than libertarian in their sociopolitical priorities. They would come off sounding less like Pope John Paul II and the bishops, and more like Milton Friedman.

This is a tangled "if." For now, the Public Square studies offer evidence that faith is steering many Catholics to a creatively ambiguous place, in but not of the political-ideological worlds. As Democrats or Republicans, Catholics may well be prodding the parties to curb their respective dogmas of exaggerated individualism. If that is the drift, it is a distinct contribution.

INDEX

Index note: page references in *italics* indicate a figure or table.

ABOUT THE CONTRIBUTORS

W. Shepherdson Abell is an attorney, husband, and father living in Chevy Chase, Maryland.

Kirk Adams is on the staff of the Service Employees International Union (SEIU), AFL-CIO.

Mary Jo Bane is Thorton Bradshaw Professor of Public Policy and Management at the John F. Kennedy School of Government at Harvard University.

William Bole is a freelance journalist in Massachusetts and a fellow of the Woodstock Theological Center at Georgetown University, Washington, D.C.

David Carlin, a former *Commonweal* columnist, served in the Rhode Island State Legislature and is a college teacher.

Clarke E. Cochran is Professor of Political Science at Texas Tech University.

John A. Coleman, S.J., is Casassa Professor of Social Values at Loyola Marymount University, Los Angeles.

E. J. Dionne Jr. is a columnist for the *Washington Post* and a Senior Fellow at the Brookings Institution.

Edward E. Dolejsi is Executive Director of the California Catholic Conference.

Thomas J. Donnelly, a retired businessman, lives in Pittsburgh.

William A. Galston is a professor in the School of Public Affairs at the University of Maryland and Director of the Institute for Philosophy and Public Policy.

David Gonzalez is the Caribbean Bureau Chief for the *New York Times*. Prior to that, he wrote the "About New York" column for the *Times*. He lives in Miami with his wife, Elena Cabral and son.

Michael Lacey is a historian and Director Emeritus of the American Program at the Woodrow Wilson International Center for Scholar in Washington, D.C.

David C. Leege is Professor Emeritus of Political Science, and former director, Program for Research on Religion, Church, and Society at the University of Notre Dame.

Dotty Lynch is the Senior Political Editor at CBS News.

Jane Mansbridge is Adams Professor of Political Leadership and Democratic Values at the John F. Kennedy School of Government at Harvard University.

Paul Moses, a former report and editor for *New York Newsday*, teaches journalism at Brooklyn College of the City University of New York.

Paul D. Mueller is a doctoral candidate in political science at the University of Notre Dame.

Monsignor Philip J. Murnion is Director of the National Pastoral Life Center and a priest of the Archdiocese of New York.

Kate O'Beirne is the Washington Editor of the *National Review*.

Stephen J. Pope is Associate Professor and Chair of the Department of Theology at Boston College.

Robert Royal, Director of the Faith and Reason Institute, was a codirector of the project, American Catholics in the Public Square.

William M. Shea is Professor of theology at Saint Louis University.

Margaret O'Brien Steinfels served as *Commonweal*'s editor from 1988 to 2002 and as codirector of American Catholics in the Public Square project.

Peter Steinfels writes the "Beliefs" column for the *New York Times* and is the author of *A People Adrift: The Crisis of Roman Catholicism in America* (Simon & Shuster, 2003).

John J. Sweeney is President of the AFL-CIO.

Don Wycliff is public editor of the *Chicago Tribune*.